CW00545104

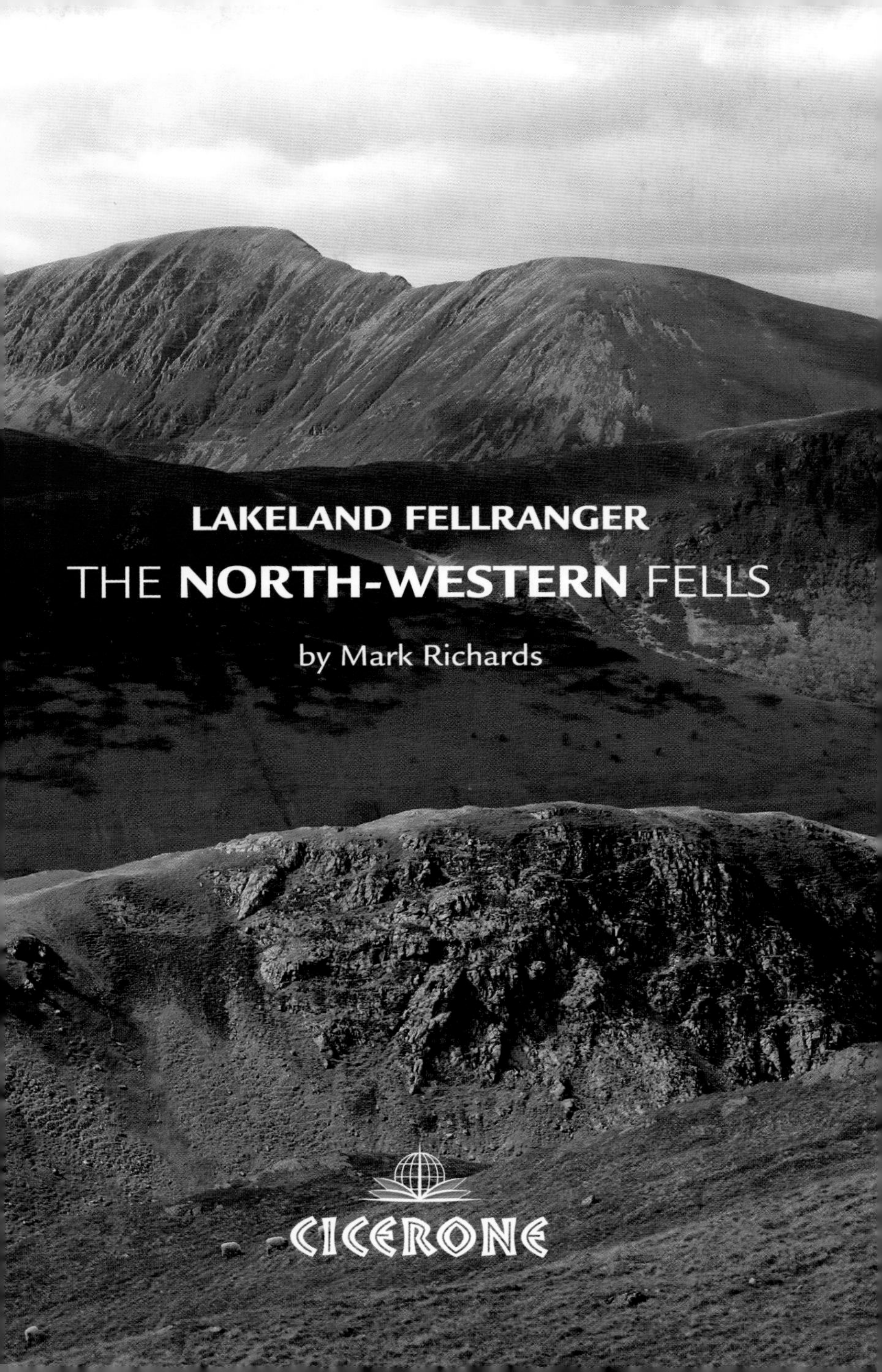

LAKELAND FELLRANGER

THE **NORTH-WESTERN** FELLS

by Mark Richards

CICERONE

First edition by Cicerone Press 2011
ISBN-13: 978 1 85284 545 2

© Mark Richards 2011

Printed by KHL Printing, Singapore.

A catalogue record for this book is available from the British Library.

Artwork and photographs by the author.

 Maps are reproduced with permission from HARVEY Maps,
www.harveymaps.co.uk.

To great mountain days shared with good friends

Front cover: Wandope, Eel Crag, Sail and Scar Crags
rising above Sail Beck from High Stile

Title page: Looking over Little Dale to Eel Crag
and Sail from High Crags on Hindscarth

CONTENTS

ABOUT THE AUTHOR

The Cumbrian fells have held a lifetime's attraction for me. Brought up in the far-flung west Oxfordshire countryside, the romance of the high fells tugged at my emotions from my youth. In 2001 my wife and I were able to up sticks and make a permanent home within sight of the Lakeland mountains. The move was triggered by a commission to research and prepare the Lakeland Fellranger series, which has now found its natural Cumbrian home with Cicerone Press.

My early experience of walking in fell country came in two guises. My mother's cousin was a farm manager on a fell estate near Kirkby Lonsdale. Hence summer holidays were spent gathering sheep and tending cattle. Although busman's holidays from my stockman's life in Oxfordshire, these were great experiences, developing my awareness of the magic of fell country.

By my late teens the lure of mountains for recreation had taken a real hold, and shortly after joining a mountaineering club I met, and became a regular house-guest of, Alfred Wainwright. Just being with such a gifted artist and writer was very special. We shared a delight in drawing and in poring over maps and walking-guide ideas. He quickly saw my own appetite for pen and ink and my passion for the countryside, the fells in particular, and he encouraged me to consider creating my own illustrated guides.

My earliest guides were *The Cotswold Way* (1973), *The Cornwall North Coast Path* (1974) and *The Offa's Dyke Path* (1975). Cicerone then commissioned a trio of hand-drawn walking guides to the Peak District that were published in the early 1980s (and in later editions). Other guides followed, and more recently a fascination with historic landscapes caused me to research and prepare a guide to the Hadrian's Wall Path, with an associated guide exploring the Roman footprint in the Wall's hinterland, with *The Roman Ring*. I am involved in establishing Hadrian's Triumph, a social enterprise company devoted to further diversifying the active visitor's appreciation of the Roman frontier, visit www.hadrianstriumph.org.

Mark Richards 2011

FROM FIRESIDE TO FELLSIDE

Free time spent out on the fell is always the very best of times. You may sit at home poring over maps and consulting guides, letting the imagination run riot, but nothing beats the fun and thrill of actually being out there, walking the dream. To wander by lonely becks and over rough fellsides, to climb to high cairned summits, to sense the freedom, space and sheer beauty of it all is a holistic experience beyond poetic words and pictorial expression. Walkers notice the contrasts of seasons and time of day, the play of light and shadow, the mischievous antics of mist and cloud. They cope with wind and rain, snow and ice in an environment that they come to know by stints and stages. The form and character of each fell become recognisable, like friends from childhood – reliable, and happy in reunion whatever the time span since the last acquaintance. The walker harbours memories of times past with these companions, and relishes new days in their company.

How grateful we are for their existence, these magical fells. Within the small compass of this guide you will find great mountains, deep green dales, wind-whipped lakes, still tarns reflecting the sky, dancing becks, fearsome buttresses, whispering woods, and clouds racing across sweeping pastures inhabited by bleating sheep, the air tingling with the rippling call of skylark and the hoarse rasp of the high, rolling raven – the genius of vintage fellwalking days. And for all our pleasure in solitary wanderings, who has not smiled upon a happy encounter with the best of all fell creatures, fellow fell-wanderers?

↑ Nitting Haws and Blea Crag from Borrowdale

Scots pines on Castle Crag (Chapter 5)

THIS GUIDE

After seven wonderful months devoted to roving research in this group of fells, I feel honoured to know them as good friends, their magic enduringly distilled and instilled. In terms of writing this guide, the present mission is accomplished; in terms of my bond with these mountains, well, that has just begun. No survey of this kind is finite – one can know the fells spatially, but to know them elementally and emotionally is an entirely different journey.

The area covered in this guide is home to 29 fells – each distinct from each other, and each a worthy reward for the energy committed to its climb. Two of its fell-rounds, the Newlands and Coledale Horseshoes, rank with the best in the district.

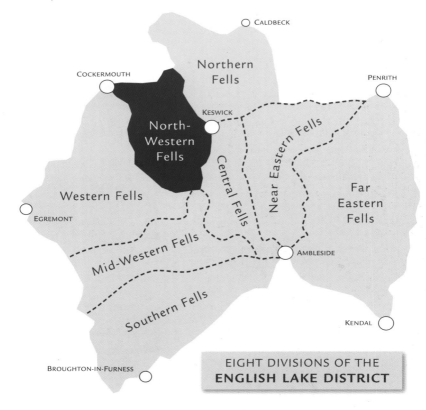

EIGHT DIVISIONS OF THE
ENGLISH LAKE DISTRICT

The region's summits include among their number fells for all the family – such as Catbells and Castle Crag; fells for lovers of mountain stature and structure – notably Hindscarth and Grisedale Pike; great rocky escarpments – like High Spy and Whiteside; great individualists – such as Causey Pike and Barf; impressive situations

Droving in the lane at Armaside (Chapter 11)

– like Dale Head and Grasmoor; and those that sit in picturesque settings – such as neighbouring Rannerdale Knotts and Whiteless Pike.

The group is bounded by four of the most beautiful of Lakeland lakes – Bassenthwaite, Buttermere, Derwent Water and Crummock Water – yet, remarkably, within its bounds there is hardly a sheet of water to be found. There are beautiful dales – some secret, like Wythop and Aiken Beck; some open for all to see, such as Coledale and Newlands; and one, shared with the Central Fells and all the world, Borrowdale, has the finest qualities of any glen, finding its most exquisite expression in the famous 'Jaws'. There are mountain passes to drive over – Honister, Newlands and Whinlatter – and to walk over – Coledale Hause and the Rigg Beck/Sail Beck passage between Newlands and Buttermere. And there are forest tracks to explore in the Whinlatter Park and Wythop sections of Thornthwaite Forest. In fact, this is a mountain range of choice experiences.

Although this guide aims to help readers experience the area from a leisured and recreational perspective, it also takes care to point out that this is a contemporary and historic working landscape, as evidenced in sheepfolds and mine spoil. The hard labour and deprivation associated with both activities is evident for those who choose to see. Now long abandoned, the wreckage of mineral extraction is melding quietly into the fabric of the fells, but the quiet backdrop of pastoral agriculture is the continuing life-blood of this land. A fascination in mining is well rewarded by a visit to the Keswick Mining Museum and its sister site at Threlkeld. As a special treat the Force Crag Mine is occasionally open for guided tours by its owners, the National Trust. Traditional and contemporary farming is much in evidence at such enterprises as the Flock-in tearoom at Rosthwaite and on the Slow Food shelves of Booths supermarket.

Access to the range is good for the motorist, and in addition there are the excellent Stagecoach bus services, all of which have a Keswick focus – the Borrowdale Rambler plies the valley road to Seatoller, and the trans-Cumbria service runs along the A66 (both run all-year round). From Easter to the end of October, the Honister Rambler (77/77A) service runs four times a day clockwise and anti-clockwise from Keswick, making the area particularly accessible. Also written by this author is the bus-stop-to-bus-stop 'StagePath' – a free 36-page full-colour descriptive guide, based on the principles of sustainable transport and green tourism, which is the perfect companion to this volume of Lakeland Fellranger in particular. Copies are available at the Moot Hall Tourist Information Centre, Keswick.

For ease of reference the 29 fell chapters are arranged in alphabetical order. Each chapter begins with a customised Harvey map that illustrates the routes of ascent described in the guide, and shows ridge connections to neighbouring fells to assist in the planning of extended walks. The corresponding text describes routes up the fell from given valley starting points, identified on the map by a number (shown in a blue box). The starting points are listed in the 'Starting Points' table on page 18, and are also given in blue (in brackets) after the ascent route headings in the walks. In many instances there is also a diagram that shows the routes from a given perspective to assist visualisation.

The primary routes to the summit are described, with optional variations given, up to their natural point of connection with the more common route. Where a route follows a defined path this is shown on the map and diagram in red dashes, and where the recommended route follows an intermittent path (or there is no path on the ground at all) this is shown in green dashes. Where a route follows a road it is not picked out by dashed lines. Being aware of the safest lines of descent is important, and advice is given on these for nearly all fells. There are far more paths on the fells than are shown on a conventional Harvey map, and for clarity this guide only shows the paths and routes that are described here.

KEY TO FELL MAPS

⌁	Route as a defined path
⌁	Route as an intermittent or undefined path
▲	Fell summit
2.5	Starting point
4	Route number

For other symbols see HARVEY map key p15.

As a good guide should also be a revelation, a full panorama is provided for each fell summit or better nearby viewpoint. This names the principal fells and picks out key features in their midst, with some more distant features beyond the national park to intrigue. When undertaking the walks in the guide, you are advised to take a map and compass with you (and know how to use them). The map can enhance your day by showing additional landscape features and setting your walk in its wider context, as well as being useful for your own safety. And remember that representation of a route in this guide, in whatever form, does not infer safe passage for all, at any time. The onus is on each individual to weigh up their own capabilities and the prevailing conditions. In fellwalking, as in any mountain travel, knowing when to retreat is often the greater part of valour. The author has taken care to follow time-honoured routes, and kept within bounds of access, yet cannot guarantee rights of way in all cases.

FIX THE FELLS

This series highlights the work of the Fix the Fells project in its restoration of the most seriously damaged fell paths. The process has been a great learning curve and the more recent pitching is superb, ensuring a flat foot-fall where possible, and is easy to use in ascent and descent. The trails are not universally pleasant underfoot, but the process represents a huge step forward for the fell environment. However, invariably these trails are not rights of way, and are therefore beyond the statutory responsibility of the highway authority. Hence Fix the Fells is a partnership of the National Park Authority, National Trust and Natural England, with additional financial support from the Friends of the Lake District, and the whole effort has been made possible by third-party match-funding from the Heritage Lottery Fund. Just as the fells have no rest from walkers, so the need to make good the paths has no end point, most especially pre-emptive repair to stop paths from washing out in the first place.

Necessary path reconstruction snaking down from Coledale Hause

Friendship of the fells – three walkers take a break on Grasmoor

The local business-linked environmental charity Nurture Lakeland also contributes significantly to this work, but with a metre of path costing up to £100 there is every good reason to cultivate the involvement of fellwalkers in a cause that must be dear to their hearts... and soles! Should we not look to raise our game to become fell champions? Make a beeline for **www.fixthefells.co.uk** to mark your commitment to the well-being of the fells by giving a modest donation. Clearly the occasional gift is welcome, but as yet these still represent only a tiny injection. If it were the culture for fellwalkers to make regular donations, so much the better!

ACCESS
May 2005 saw the implementation of the Countryside and Rights of Way (CROW) Act in Cumbria, from which time most rough open country became conditionally accessible to walkers. However, quite the majority of fellwalkers feel at ease only when striding upon a clear path, especially one that has a time-honoured sense of purpose, while the roving instinct, a broad-brush freedom to randomly explore trackless country, appeals to a narrow band of walkers. I love the liberty of exploring open country with a map, but, being wedded to the preparation of practical guides, my liberty is tempered by the need to reflect regular routes properly and, where inventive, to be discerning. Nonetheless, there are a few off-beat walks in this guide to challenge and intrigue those with a similar instinct for wild fell terrain.

SAFETY

Being constantly alive to, and aware of, the potential dangers of walking in high fell country is essential for everyone, and most especially those who come new to this activity. Fell craft, the intuition to know when to proceed and when to retreat, is an important skill to learn. The National Park Authority provides practical, up-to-date advice – from daily weather checks (Weatherline 0844 846 2444, 24-hour fell forecast) to guided walks aimed at absolute beginners. As a first recourse obtain a copy of their leaflet 'Safety on the Fells' and consult their website: www.lake-district.gov.uk.

ADVISORY NOTE

The National Park has prepared a short advisory note for conscientious walkers.
- Place your feet thoughtfully – every single footstep causes wear and tear on the environment. The slow-growing plants that can survive on mountains are particularly vulnerable.
- Keep to the path surface – do not walk along the vegetation at the edge of the path.
- Do not build or add to cairns – paths need stones more than cairns do.
- Do not take shortcuts – water will soon follow your tracks and an erosion scar will develop. Remember, there may be only one of you, but there are another 12 million pairs of feet treading Lake District paths every year.

An important source of advice is the website of the Mountain Rescue organisation for England and Wales, www.mountain.rescue.org.uk. A further pertinent reference is the leaflet sponsored by Cicerone Press in conjunction with the Mountain Rescue service, which covers how to stay safe and enjoy the fells. This gives bullet-point guidance on necessary basic skills, what you need to consider both before you set out and while on the fells, what to take and, critically, what to do if things go wrong. This can be downloaded from the Cicerone Press website – www.cicerone.co.uk.

FELL REVIEW

Visit www.markrichards.info (Lakeland Fellranger section) to study the Fell Review. This contains dedicated galleries that provide a more thorough pictorial record of the author's research, focusing on each individual fell, and a downloadable PDF of the summit panorama.

The Newlands valley from Rigg Beck

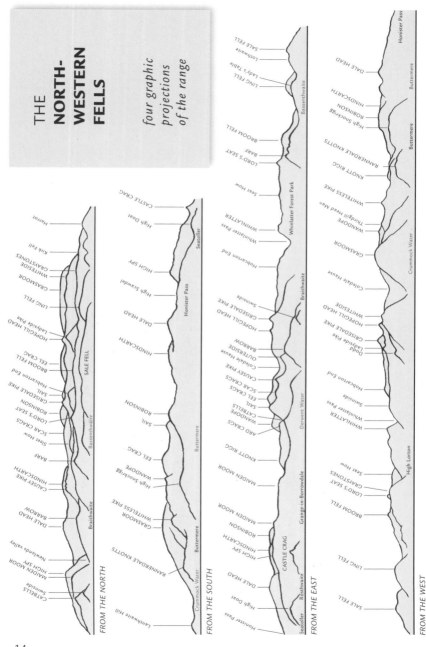

THE
**NORTH-
WESTERN
FELLS**

*four graphic
projections
of the range*

FROM THE NORTH

FROM THE SOUTH

FROM THE EAST

FROM THE WEST

HARVEY MAP KEY

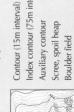

Lake, small tarn, pond
River, footbridge
Wide stream
Narrow stream
Peathags
Marshy ground

Contour (15m interval)
Index contour (75m interval)
Auxiliary contour
Scree, spoil heap
Boulder field
Scattered rock and boulders
Predominantly rocky ground
Major crag, large boulder
O.S. trig pillar, large cairn
Spot height (from air survey)

805

Contours change from brown to grey where the ground is predominantly rocky outcrops, small crags and other bare rock.

Farmland
Fell or moorland
Open forest or woodland
Dense forest or woodland
Felled or new plantation
Forest ride or firebreak
Settlement
Boundary, maintained
Boundary, remains

On moorland, walls, ruined walls and fences are shown. For farmland, only the outer boundary wall or fence is shown.

SCALE 1 : 40,000

Dual carriageway
Main road (fenced)
Minor road (unfenced)
Track or forest road
Footpath or old track
Intermittent path
Powerline, pipeline
Building, ruin or sheepfold, shaft
Fell summits that feature as chapters in this guidebook.

Pike

The representation of a road, track or footpath is no evidence of the existence of a right of way.

0 Kilometres   1

0 Miles

THE NORTH-WESTERN FELLS

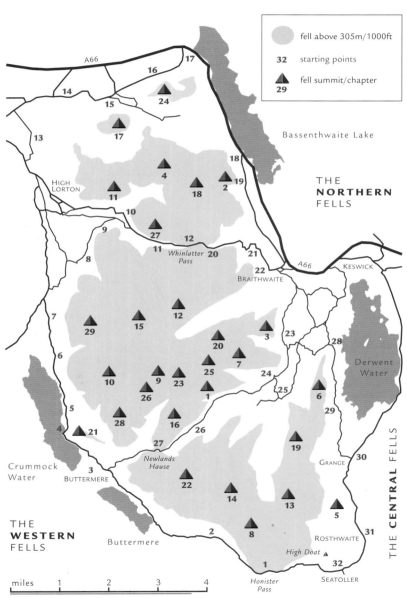

fell above 305m/1000ft

32 starting points

▲ fell summit/chapter
29

A66

17

16

14

24

15

13

High
Lorton

17

4

18

2 19

11

18

THE
NORTHERN
FELLS

Bassenthwaite Lake

10

9

27

11 *Whinlatter
Pass*

12

20

21

22
BRAITHWAITE

A66

KESWICK

8

7

29

15

12

3

23

28

Derwent
Water

6

20

7

24

25

5

10

26

9 23

25

1

16

6

19

28

21

4

5

27

26

29

GRANGE

30

Crummock
Water

3
BUTTERMERE

*Newlands
Hause*

22

14

13

5

THE
CENTRAL FELLS

THE
WESTERN
FELLS

Buttermere

2

8

1

ROSTHWAITE

31

High Doat ▲

32

SEATOLLER

*Honister
Pass*

miles   1   2   3   4

FELL MOSAIC

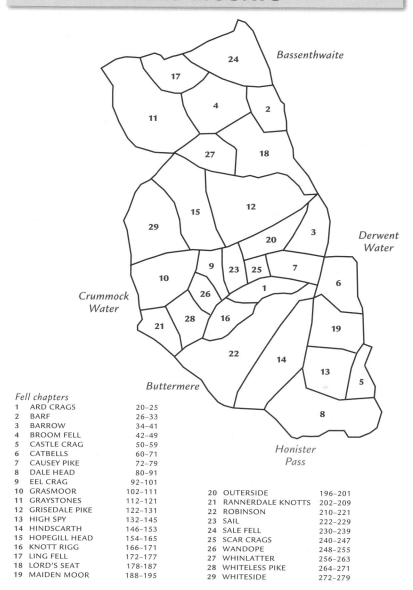

Bassenthwaite

Derwent
Water

Crummock
Water

Buttermere

Honister
Pass

STARTING POINTS

Starting points for ascents are identified on the map for each fell by numbered parking symbols and also in each ascent title by number (in **blue** and in brackets).

	LOCATION	GRID REFERENCE	PARKING	BUS
1	Honister Pass	225 136	P	B
2	Gatesgarthdale	210 148	L	B
3	Buttermere	174 169	P	B
4	Hause Point	163 183	L	B
5	Cinderdale Common	163 194	L	B
6	Lanthwaite Green	159 218	P	B
7	High Liza Bridge	156 224	IN	
8	Hopebeck	169 242	P	
9	Swinside	176 253	IN	
10	Darling How	182 255	P	B
11	Whinlatter Gill	192 245	P	B
12	Whinlatter Pass	205 245	P	B
13	Armaside	151 279	IN	
14	Embleton Church	163 294	L	
15	Wythop Old School	177 294	L	
16	Wythop Church	192 302	IN	
17	Pheasant Hotel	199 307	P	
18	Woodend Brow	218 276	P	B
19	Powter How	221 265	P	B
20	Revelin Moss	209 243	P	B
21	Noble Knott	223 244	P	B
22	Braithwaite	227 236	P	B
23	Uzzicar	233 217	P	
24	Rigg Beck	230 202	P	
25	Chapel Bridge	232 194	P	
26	Keskadale	208 190	L	
27	Newlands Hause	193 176	P	
28	Hawes End	248 213	J	B
29	Brandelhow	249 194	J	B
30	Grange-in-Borrowdale	256 176	L	B
31	Rosthwaite	257 148	P	B
32	Seatoller	245 138	P	B

P – formal, including National Trust and National Park Authority, pay and display car parks
L – lay-by and verge parking
J – Keswick launch jetty
IN – informal parking

B – Borrowdale Rambler or Honister Rambler buses – while these services are regular, seat availability is less reliable and demand can outstrip capacity – particularly frustrating at the end of a day's walk should you want to get back to Keswick.

Scope Beck valley (Chapter 14)

1 ARD CRAGS *(581m/1906ft)*

Travellers wending up the Newlands valley will come upon the impressive little ridge crowned by Ard Crags as they take the sharp bend on Rigg Beck, spying the sudden upthrusting ridge of Aiken Knott and wondering what mighty height they behold. With Knott Rigg it forms a simple sickle-shaped ridge of comparatively modest height well befitting the attention of anyone new to fellwalking. A 'there-and-back' outing from Newlands Hause, keeping to the ridge as far as Aiken Knott, will give you a real sense of the magic of fell country, with no route doubts. The fell-name is unusual, but does not ally with the Scottish for 'headland', however attractive a notion; possibly this was originally Hard Crags.

Ard Crags, southern aspect from High Snab Bank →

↑ Aiken Knott and Ard Crags from Rigg Beck

ASCENT FROM RIGG BECK (24)

Via Rigg Beck   410m/1345ft   2.8km/1¾ miles

The starting point is close to the former site of the Purple House – now the very modern and ingenious New Riggbeck, cleverly concealed in the trees. **1** The more circumspect line. This route takes advantage of a peaceful pedestrian connection with Buttermere leading naturally up the Rigg Beck valley. The path seems to have coped well with the wear and tear of time. The old oak copse set high on the heather slopes of Causey Pike is a fascinating survival, replicated by a similar wood above Ill Gill on the opposite side of Ard Crags. Reaching the natural level pass, curve left off the regular path and find a tangible, if sketchy, path slanting half-left up the grassy slope direct to the summit.

Via Aiken Knott   410m/1345ft   2.4km/1½ miles

2 The head-on climb. Leave the road from the old quarry at the hairpin bend following the regular path up the valley of Rigg Beck. Where the wall enclosure ends bear off left, ford the beck and take the long diagonal line to the gently rising ridge. There is a well-evidenced path through the bracken. The path comes onto the pasture ridge

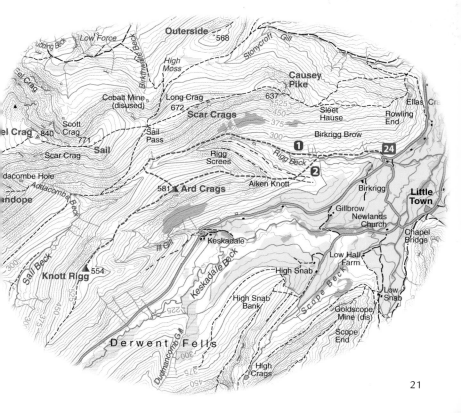

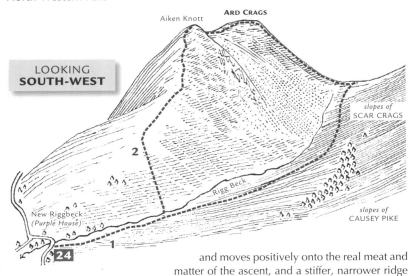

Aiken Knott

ARD CRAGS

LOOKING
SOUTH-WEST

slopes of
SCAR CRAGS

2

Rigg Beck

New Riggbeck
(Purple House)

slopes of
CAUSEY PIKE

24

1

and moves positively onto the real meat and matter of the ascent, and a stiffer, narrower ridge begins winding through the heather onto Aiken Knott. The climb provides handsome views north to Causey Pike and the ancient oakwood clinging to the steep slopes high above Rigg Beck. Mounting through the heather, the full delight of the climb comes to fruition as the path runs along the comparatively narrow ridge top to the summit cairn.

Summit ridge leading to Aiken Knott, with Causey Pike

Keskadale from the summit of Ard Crags

THE SUMMIT

A simple cairn on a continuing ridge immediately east of an obvious notch. The notch gives a lovely bird's-eye view down on Keskadale Farm. The heather spilling off at either hand down the abrupt slopes is a pleasing attribute, as too is the grand panorama – for so modest a fell it provides a real sense of scale. The near bulk of Causey Pike, Scar Crags and Sail contrast with the balanced perspective on Robinson due south.

SAFE DESCENTS

The two ascents are reliable in descent, although the continuing ridge to the north-east via Aiken Knott is steep and uncomfortable should a biting easterly wind prevail.

RIDGE ROUTE

KNOTT RIGG	↓75m/245ft	↑50m/165ft	1.6km/1 mile

Anyone new to ridge walking will find this the perfect introduction. For one thing all neighbouring fells are higher, so you are treated to a grandstand view, and it is grassy all the way, with no deviations to tempt you off course in mist.

PANORAMA

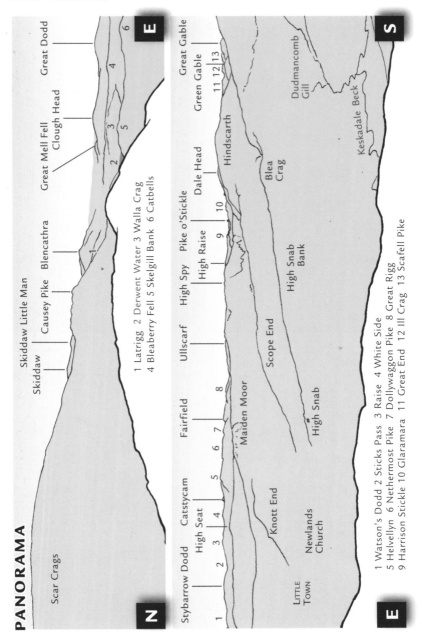

Scar Crags

Skiddaw
Skiddaw Little Man
Causey Pike Blencathra Great Mell Fell Great Dodd
Clough Head

E

N

1 Latrigg 2 Derwent Water 3 Walla Crag
4 Bleaberry Fell 5 Skelgill Bank 6 Catbells

Stybarrow Dodd High Seat Catstycam Fairfield Ullscarf High Spy Pike o'Stickle Dale Head Green Gable Great Gable
Hindscarth

LITTLE TOWN
Newlands Church
Knott End
Maiden Moor
High Snab
Scope End
High Snab Bank
Blea Crag
Dudmancomb Gill
Keskadale Beck

S

E

1 Watson's Dodd 2 Sticks Pass 3 Raise 4 White Side
5 Helvellyn 6 Nethermost Pike 7 Dollywaggon Pike 8 Great Rigg
9 Harrison Stickle 10 Glaramara 11 Great End 12 Ill Crag 13 Scafell Pike

24

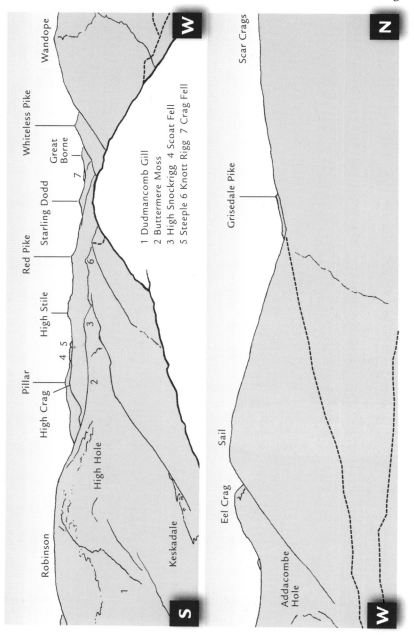

W

Wandope
Whiteless Pike
Great Borne
Starling Dodd
Red Pike
High Stile
Pillar
High Crag
Robinson
High Hole
Keskadale

7
6
5 4
3
2
1

1 Dudmancomb Gill
2 Buttermere Moss
3 High Snockrigg 4 Scoat Fell
5 Steeple 6 Knott Rigg 7 Crag Fell

S

N

Scar Crags
Grisedale Pike
Sail
Eel Crag
Addacombe Hole

W

2 BARF *(468m/1535ft)*

The older name of St Bees Head (Barugh) and Barf have common origins, with *berg* meaning 'the unassailable cliff'. This is certainly true of the former, but not the latter. The white-washed rock on the slopes of Barf known as The Bishop owes its origins to a canny piece of publicity by the proprietor of the original Swan Hotel (now the private Swan House). The hotel later became a private dwelling, and the role of painting The Bishop was taken over by the Keswick Mountain Rescue team, who use this much-loved landmark pinnacle to remind observers of the important service they perform. During an August ascent, with the heather at its best, the author saw a less than common lizard scuttling through the slate debris below Slape Crag and a brace of grouse on the heather moor to the north-west side of the fell.

There are three ways up – via the forest edge of Beckstones Gill (Route 1), the 'no holds barred' head-on climb (Route 2) and by the side door of Wythop Woods (Route 3).

The white-washed Bishop of Barf above Swan House

ASCENT FROM POWTER HOW (19)

Via Beckstones Gill   372m/1220ft   1.6km/1 mile

1 Leave the main road on the byway facing the hamlet of Powter How, with Swan House prominent. A footpath sign on the right directs through a kissing-gate and along a birch woodland way, passing the little white-washed rock known as The Clerk. The path leads over Beckstones Gill to a fence-stile and into the forestry plantation. Join the ascending path, and avoid being drawn too far right as the steeper woodland is reached. The actual path is probably the less obvious path, going more straight up, which comes onto cleared fellside and winds up to meet a forest track. Climb on with this track, watching for the branch right to a fence-stile onto the open fell. Ford the upper feeder gill and slant right, stepping onto the shoulder of Barf, where a clear way leads up onto the headland.

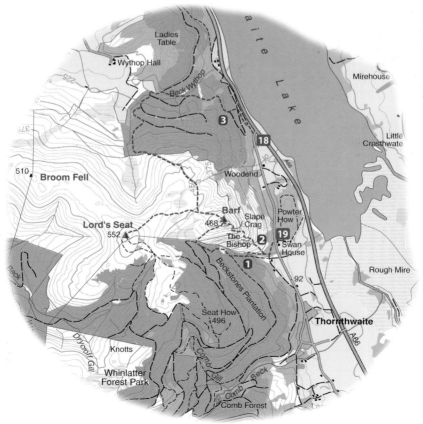

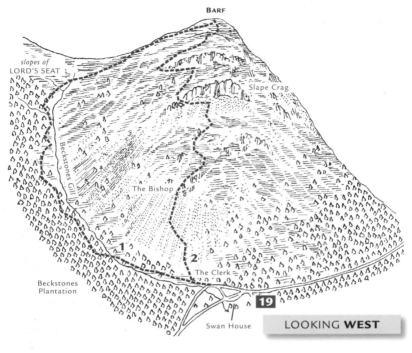

BARF

slopes of
LORD'S SEAT

Slape Crag

Beckstones Gill

The Bishop

Beckstones
Plantation

The Clerk

1

2

19

Swan House

LOOKING **WEST**

Via The Bishop   366m/1200ft   1.2km/¾ mile

2 The path to the top of the fell is very evident, with just one point where specific guidance is needed to overcome Slape Crag. Should you possess walking poles, then this endeavour will be made all the sweeter with their aid.

Begin as with Route 1, but watch for the little white-washed fang of rock, The Clerk. This marks the begin-ning of your labours. Branch right onto the obvious scree run. (Anyone who has climbed Kilimanjaro will recognise the 'three steps up, one slide down' scenario.) Walking poles really make a big difference here. Keep your faith, keep your head down, and duly, with a degree of sweat and toil, you will come alongside the rock pinnacle of The Bishop, in steep circum-stances. At close quarters it is

Oak and rowan below the narrow shelf, left
of Slape Crag, a key point on the direct ascent

Rough Mire and the Keswick vale

every bit a monument worthy of attention – a candlestick set on a pulpit, and a splendid subject to capture in your camera lens.

Continue up the obvious heather-lined path direct from The Bishop, with the going a bit more agreeable. Watch for the walled armchair to the right on a brief level shoulder as you continue climbing through the heather, then bracken, passing up by a mature birch to come onto a patch of scree and slant up the bank to come onto the scree spilling from the base of Slape Crag. The crag-name means 'slippery rock' – a portent of things to come? Well, not if you avoid the direct route that accomplished scramblers have developed, and rather slant left and down to find the key rock-step above a spreading oak tree. You'll bless this specimen, as it directs attention to the one and only means of unlocking this otherwise daunting obstacle.

Gorse, broom and heather immediately impose upon your delicate manoeuvre as you carefully place your boots on the few awkward rock-steps, but the rake is quickly vanquished and the heather trail resumed. It climbs to the base of a ribbed scarp, where the path necessarily traverses left to find the easier ground to overcome it. The upper alps are gained with great elation, as you skip through the last heather clumps to the bare rock top and revel in the marvellous view.

ASCENT FROM WOODEND BROW (18)

Via Wythop Wood   412m/1350ft   3.6km/2¼ miles

3 Your chance to be one in a million by taking this more unusual way up the fell. A practical route exists that is well worth the mild adventure, wending up the forest tracks of Wythop Wood and ultimately onto rough heather moor. Head N with the Beck Wythop road (the former main road), with its C2C71 cycleway sign. After 50m find a footpath sign 'Wythop Hall' on the left, and follow this, initially parallel to the roadway. The path steps up onto a forest track, but goes straight over – see the foot-path waymark opposite, guiding up through the trees, with one minor rock-step, to reach the same forest track at a higher level. Turn right and follow the track, enjoying a handsome view over Bassenthwaite to Skiddaw at the sharp left-hand bend.

Keep to the track for a further 500m, seeking a waymark and short flight of wooden steps down right. Here the track joins the continuing footpath that leads to a foot-bridge over Wythop Beck. After this the path rises, still in woodland, to meet a forest track. Turn left and keep with this main thoroughfare track as it meets the track you left at the steps. Sweep right in felled plantation. Notice right, in the adjacent field, the relics of the silica brickworks that had a faltering life in the 1930s. As the track meets a rougher track on the right, branch up this way, with felled plantation on the right. The track becomes more rutted, angles up into the conifers of Hagg and comes alongside the forest fence. Cross over the tall netting fence at this point onto the open fell and follow the gill left, rising through the shallow ravine to accompany an old broken wall to a wall T-junction. Here bear up right with the wall to find a metal gate on the damp saddle. Barf is in view from here, but is only reached by tramping over the tough moor grass and heather of an intermediate hillock to join the ridge path from Lord's Seat, which leads unfailingly to the top.

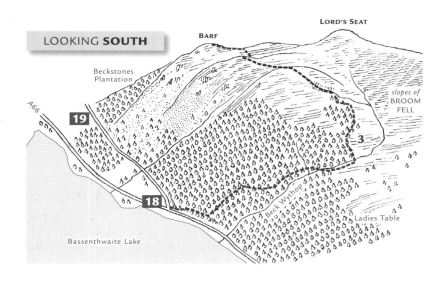

The summit of Barf, looking north-east to Skiddaw

THE SUMMIT

The top is a bare plinth of rock, with a grassy surround. A matter of 7m to the east is the scarp edge. This is a wonderful perch to eat those sandwiches and enjoy a sumptuous view, that has no peers, over the Bassenthwaite vale to Skiddaw.

SAFE DESCENTS

The best way down is via Route 1, Beckstones Gill. Head SW from the summit on the clear path, stepping down to ford the upper course of Beckstones Gill and cross the stile into the forest. Turn left and follow the track, but watch for the path breaking off down the open felled slope. This winds down, becoming steeper upon entry into the conifers and demanding a steadier stride. Lower down find a stile on the left that leads back out of the trees and over the gill again to conclude by passing the white-washed Clerk. Reach the Thornthwaite road opposite Swan House, and Powter How car park is recessed to the left.

RIDGE ROUTE

LORD'S SEAT	↓46m/150ft	↑130m/425ft	1.2km/¾ mile

A well-etched path leads W and descends to skirt to the right of a damp hollow before steadily gaining ground as it drifts SW onto the neighbouring fell-top, with occasional evidence of old metal fence stakes (a fence that began at the gate in the damp saddle, met on Route 3).

PANORAMA

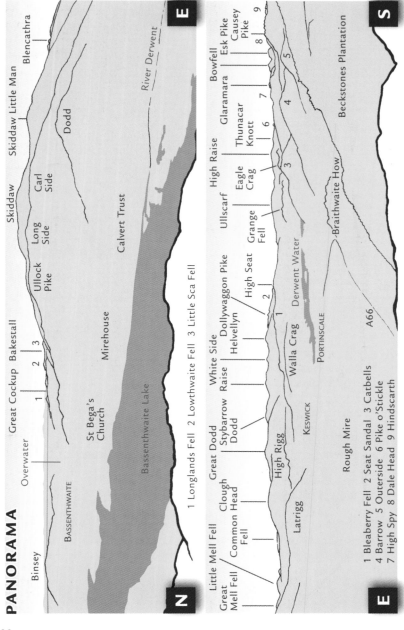

1 Longlands Fell 2 Lowthwaite Fell 3 Little Sca Fell

1 Bleaberry Fell 2 Seat Sandal 3 Catbells
4 Barrow 5 Outside 6 Pike o'Stickle
7 High Spy 8 Dale Head 9 Hindscarth

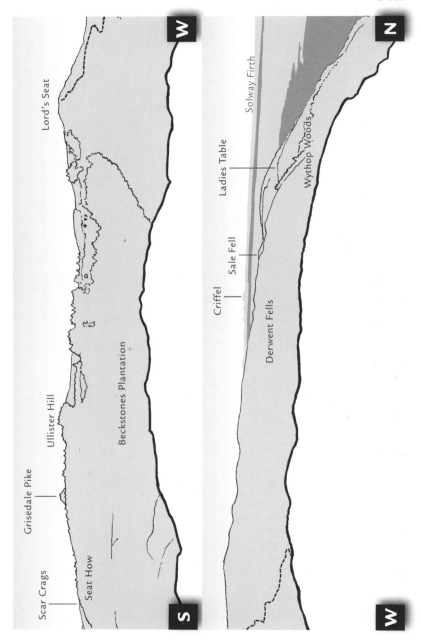

Lord's Seat

Scar Crags

Grisedale Pike

Ullister Hill

Seat How

Beckstones Plantation

W

S

Solway Firth

Ladies Table

Sale Fell

Criffel

Wythop Woods

Derwent Fells

N

W

3 BARROW *(456m/1496ft)*

Travelling west along the A66 beyond Keswick the North-Western Fells jostle for attention, with the bulk of Barrow coming boldly into view dead ahead. Forming a strong division between the Newlands valley and Coledale, Barrow conforms to a simple wedge-shaped ridge, rising purposefully and invitingly from the village of Braithwaite. This climb is the perfect leg-stretcher for your first outing on a fellwalking holiday. Derived from the Saxon word *berg*, meaning 'the hill', the name Barrow shares a common origin with that of Barf – although the latter, being more abrupt, evolved the more abrupt name. Braithwaite, the 'broad clearing', was once a mining community, but is now every inch a tourist haven catering for most pockets, with pubs, hotels, a lively shop and the ever popular Scotgate campsite quite the hub.

Barrow, Stile End and Outerside from Braithwaite

↑ Barrow from Causey Pike

ASCENT FROM BRAITHWAITE (22)

Via the north ridge   366m/1200ft   2.4km/1½ miles

1 The first-thought route to the top. Cross the bridge beside the village shop and follow the Newlands road left until after the final house on the right. Find a bridleway sign directing from the hand-gate/cattle grid along a metalled lane leading up to the Braithwaite Lodge. Pass to the right to the feature yew tree by the barns to a fence-stile/gate, coincident with a crossing footpath. Head on up the field to a hand-gate, keeping company with the ascending path and coming up above the woodland to branch onto the rising ridge. The heavily used grass trod keeps bracken well at bay, and it soars inexorably onto the lovely upper slopes draped in heather. **2** A really pleasing variant breaks right from the hand-gate above Braithwaite Lodge and follows a clear path up through the bracken ultimately to a craggy approach to a ford of Barrow Gill, the lower course of the gill being remarkably deep and repelling to the curious walker. **3** But prior to this, a tiny grassy gill, devoid of bracken, gives an easy route left up onto the ridge at the one obvious dip.

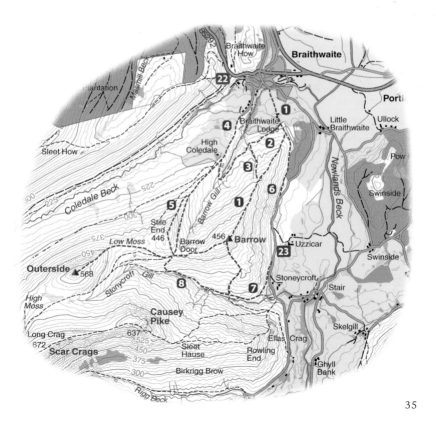

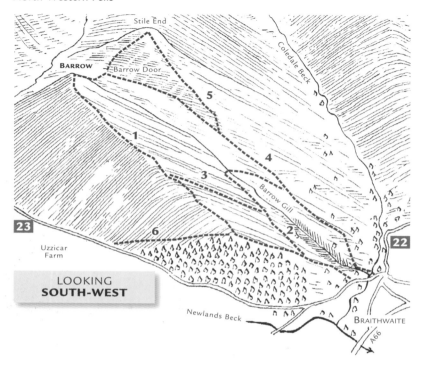

Via Barrow Door and Stile End   400m/1310ft   2.4km/1½ miles

4 A fine way to get the best out of a walk onto Barrow begins again from the village shop and follows the lane S. This leads up to a higher lane by Moss Garth. Veer left short of the Coledale Inn and follow the metalled lane up to a gate. Now an open track, the way leads on uphill passing a reservoir enclosure, and as the copse embowering the ruins of High Coledale is passed, head straight on, with the track as a grassy drove. The path breaking half-left at this point leads attractively to the aforementioned ford of Route 2, which can be followed for a leisurely round-trip to admire the impressive environs of Barrow Gill. However, Route 4 heads towards the rising ridge of Stile End, but opts instead to stay with the drove-way along the eastern flank to reach Barrow Door. **5** The enticing prow ridge can, however, be climbed to crest Stile End – which means 'the steep place'. This little height has no obvious allegiance to either Outerside or Barrow, but makes a entertaining addition on a short fell-round with Barrow. A regular path heads down to Barrow Door and E along the undulating ridge to Barrow.

Stile End from Barrow Gill

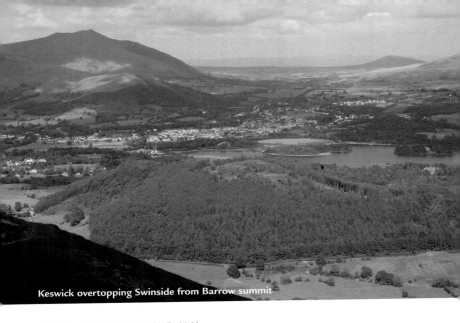

Keswick overtopping Swinside from Barrow summit

ASCENT FROM UZZICAR (23)

Via Stonycroft Gill 366m/1200ft 3.6km/2¼ miles

6 From the lay-by parking follow the road N to where the bridleway drifts off the roadway by gorse, gently rising by the woodland wall to link up with the prime ridge-climb of Route 1.

7 The most direct climbs begin by following the old mine track which leads off the open road immediately south of the lay-by and enters the valley of Stonycroft Gill. The steepest climb takes leave of the track where a tiny gill tumbles from the right. Follow this up by a small dammed pool onto a shoulder, then ever more steeply

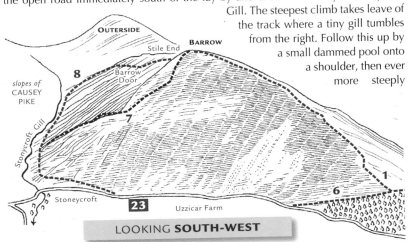

LOOKING **SOUTH-WEST**

up the heather bank, pathless and breathless, to the summit. This energetic ascent is ill-suited to descent! **8** Alternatively, you may simply stay with the rough mine track, seeking a walkers' trail that breaks right, as Causey Pike looms closer overhead, to reach Barrow Door, linking to Routes 4 and 5.

THE SUMMIT

A splendid spot to admire a great view, and worthy of a generous stay, if conditions allow. The Skiddaw massif and Derwent Water take centre stage. The huddle of fells in closest proximity in the western arc are not seen to real advantage. Look over Rowling End to spot Esk Pike and Great End seemingly at the distant head of Newlands.

SAFE DESCENTS

The north ridge is exposed only in terms of being open to the elements – the path is a simple descent for Braithwaite, as is the path heading W to Barrow Door, from where you can continue N to Braithwaite or S into the Stonycroft Gill valley, from where the track brings you to the Uzzicar verge.

RIDGE ROUTE

OUTERSIDE	↓131m/430ft	↑244m/800ft	2km/1¼ miles

Head W to Barrow Door – you may fancy the addition of Stile End, NNW, but the more regular ridge path keeps W, veering over Low Moss to climb the north-east ridge to the summit. The path, rutted in places in the tangle of heather, can be uncomfortable.

Outerside from Barrow

PANORAMA

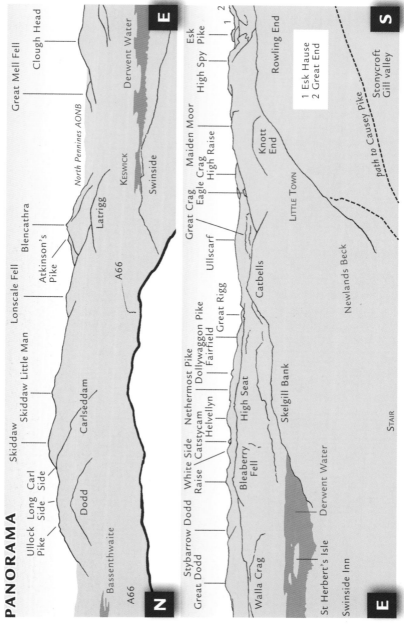

1 Esk Hause
2 Great End

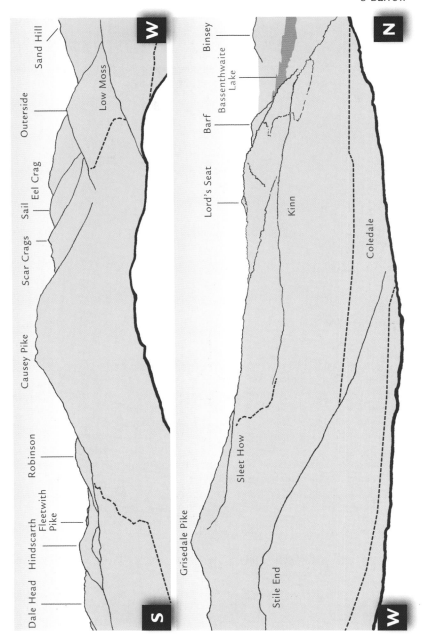

4 BROOM FELL (511m/1676ft)

Gone are the great swathes of broom that gave rise to the fell-name. Except for the handsome summit cairn, the roving rambler might be forgiven for brushing aside the humble merits of this grassy height, the fell being little more than the north-western arm of the Lord's Seat ridge connecting through Widow Hause with Graystones. Yet when taken as part of a round with the senior top this is a grand halting place. To either side of the fell are two contrasting shy valleys, the quiet worlds of Aiken Beck, where conifers are gradually being felled, and Wythop Beck, with pasture farms backed by lovely woodlands and the expansive damp hollow of Wythop Moss at the fell's feet. Keen eyes will spot at Old Scale the remarkable and, for this locality, unusual pattern of cultivation terracing on the great bank directly behind the farm buildings. What agricultural and social history does this betray?

ASCENT FROM DARLING HOW (10)

Via Spout Force and Widow Hause 442m/1450ft 3.6km/2¼ miles

1 A route of two aspects – forested dell and lark-inhabited fell. From the forestry parking off the B5292 Whinlatter Pass road from Lorton there is a choice of route. One option is to follow the footpath signed direct from the car park. This leads down a bank to cross a footbridge over Aiken Beck, then turns right upstream upon the regular path. Embark on the flight of steps and watch for the spur extension leading to a fenced observatory, the only safe view you can get of Spout Force and its rocky ravine. Otherwise, keep left with the protective fencing above the ravine, and pass on and down to the beckside. This point can also be reached from the car park by taking a path that departs the forest track opposite Darling How Farm, near the track barrier. This slips through the short conifer passage to gain a fine view downstream before running quickly down a right-hand bank to ford the beck, immediately upstream of the Spout Force ravine.

The winding path moves upstream, but not close to the beck, weaving through fallen trees and undergrowth to happily emerge onto a forest track in mature conifers. Turn right and keep left at the first track fork, ascending with the main track up the re-entrant valley. At the second junction follow on round the curve of the track to encounter a felled area, skip over the gill and weave

BROOM FELL

LORD'S SEAT

Seat How

Whinlatter
Forest Park

WHINLATTER

Aiken Beck

1

Widow
Hause

2

Darling How

10

slopes of
GRAYSTONES

Spout Force

Scawgill Bridge

LOOKING **EAST**

up the inner edge of the standing mature trees to reach the ridge top in the eastern depression of Widow Hause. Clamber over the fence/broken wall. Join the ridge path ascending E onto the fell, where a level section leads to a final brief climb to the summit cairn.

Forest track to Widow Hause in Darling How Plantation

Broom Fell from Aiken

Via Aiken Beck 427m/1400ft 3.2km/2 miles

2 The quickest way to the top. Follow the forestry track on from the barrier, ignoring the track fork. Keep to the main way until an obvious mature larch tree looms ahead. Here find a footpath waymark inviting you to join the path which runs in harmony with the track but just below and left, beside a wall. This path duly leads down to a ford of Aiken Beck at a waters-meet and follows the succeeding ridge beside young conifers. The path then fords a gill beside the broken wall and follows the wall N, clambering over an awkward fence-stile to accompany the wall direct to the summit.

ASCENT FROM WYTHOP MILL (15)

Via Wythop Moss 442m/1450ft 6.4km/4 miles

3 This route enables you to appreciate the fell's northern aspect and wade Wythop Moss for the fun of it. There is scope for parking at the road junction by the old school and further along the road by the gate below Burthwaite, or indeed at Brunston Bridge in the Wythop Beck valley. Go through the acute right gate at GR183291 close to the track entrance to Burthwaite Cottage. The open track quickly comes to a fork, where you swing left with the more regular passage. This follows the fence above Burthwaite, with new plantings evidenced. Pass on beyond the red wicket-gate, from

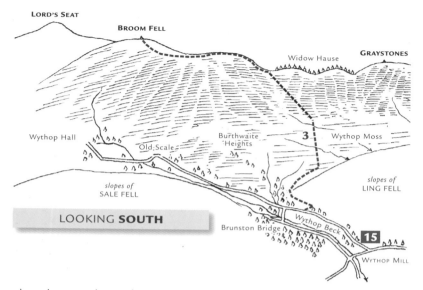

LORD'S SEAT
BROOM FELL
GRAYSTONES
Widow Hause
Wythop Hall
Old Scale
Burthwaite Heights
3
Wythop Moss
slopes of SALE FELL
slopes of LING FELL

LOOKING **SOUTH**

Brunston Bridge
Wythop Beck
15
WYTHOP MILL

where the steep slopes of Ling Fell diminish. Advance to a gate and embark on the long, straight crossing of Wythop Moss. Fear not the perils of an impending bog – it's not that bad – or did the author just strike it lucky? The route is an old sheep drove, with some evidence of walling, and the path slips through a fence-gate close to the mid-point gill ford. At last the dry banks beneath Widow Hause are reached.

Looking back to Ling Fell during the traverse of Wythop Moss

Step over a quad track and ascend half-left to the depression at the eastern end of the plantations in Widow Hause. Join the ridge path and follow this E. After an early rise the winding trail makes easy progress to a final rise to the landmark cairn.

THE SUMMIT
Since Wainwright passed this way a fine currick has been raised adjacent to a more ragged wind-shelter. While it is not known by whom or why it was built, the net effect of this landmark cairn is to make arrival at this spot momentous. The walker feels obliged to consider the view just that bit more carefully, the urge to race on diminished by its presence, and feels happy to be detained. The view is divided between the maritime realm of the greater Solway beyond Maryport and inner Lakeland. There are no wows, just a pleasing prospect to peruse.

Summit cairn, Broom Fell

SAFE DESCENTS
The quickest and surest line to a road is S beside the broken wall. The path leads into the Aiken Beck valley and via an obvious course runs through the young forest via fords, linking to the main valley track down to Darling How.

RIDGE ROUTE

LORD'S SEAT	↓28m/90ft	↑69m/225ft	1.6km/1 mile

Cross the fence-stile and follow the winding grassy trod along the ridge swinging from E to SE on the final climb to the cairnless top.

GRAYSTONES	↓140m/460ft	↑85m/280ft	2.4km/1½ miles

Head W, following the obvious path. This naturally angles with the spine of the ridge SW then W down to the depression, where the wall bounding the forest edge is followed over the intermediate knoll. At the second depression cross the fence-stile and rise S to the small cairn on Graystones.

PANORAMA

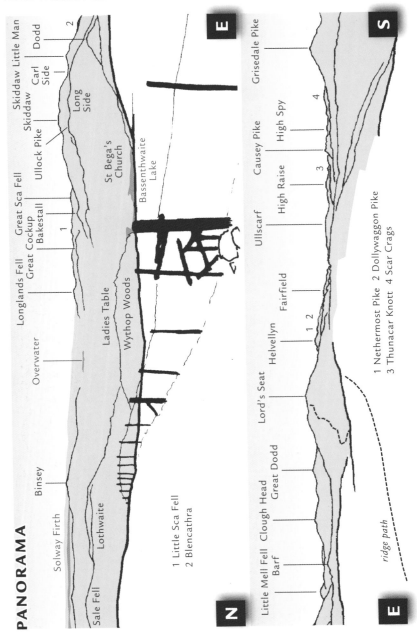

Solway Firth
Sale Fell
Lothwaite
Binsey

Longlands Fell
Great Cockup
Great Sea Fell
Bakestall
Ullock Pike
Skiddaw
Great Sca Fell
Long Side
Skiddaw Little Man
Carl Side
Dodd

Overwater
Ladies Table
Wythop Woods
St Bega's Church
Bassenthwaite Lake

1 Little Sca Fell
2 Blencathra

E

N

Little Mell Fell
Barf
Clough Head
Great Dodd
Lord's Seat
Helvellyn
Fairfield
Ullscarf
High Raise
Causey Pike
High Spy
Grisedale Pike

ridge path

1 Nethermost Pike   2 Dollywaggon Pike
3 Thunacar Knott   4 Scar Crags

S

E

48

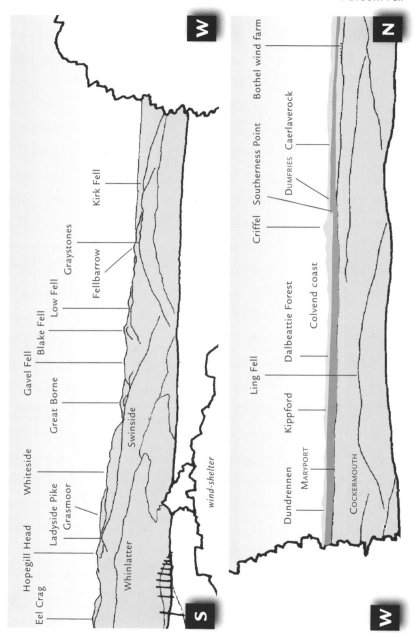

5 CASTLE CRAG *(290m/951ft)*

Buried in the fells, Borrowdale is a magical valley of rock and water, rapturously clothed in a pastoral and sylvan verdancy. In times past the valley was practically land-locked – an inner mountain world, where folk tradition claimed that the cuckoo could not fly… perpetual summer! But the valley is no myth, and its unsullied beauty is most special in its transition towards Derwent Water. Here stands Castle Crag, barbican defender of the Jaws of Borrowdale, rising as a rock-jewel midst a tangle of slate and trees. The hard slate is a handsome building stone once greatly prized. The most palpable quarry on the southern side of the summit has left its mark, colliding the labours of man and nature. Hidden in the lower mantel of foliage on the north-east side of the fell are three cavernous quarries, in themselves architecturally fascinating.

The River Derwent is forced to make its escape at the feet of the twin wooded fortresses of Castle Crag and King's How, long ago taking with it the post-glacial lake that once lay in the sequestered Rosthwaite vale.

Families will love Castle Crag – the exuberant mini-mountain peak requires so little effort and offers so much reward. The short, stiff climb largely beneath a canopy of conifers and native trees culminates upon a neat rock plinth, from where the walker is treated to the most thrilling bonanza of lake and mountain vistas, the sudden drop being a real wow factor. While the fell is commonly climbed from Grange or Rosthwaite, a grand way to experience it is to walk that extra few kilometres from Seatoller and include the diminutive High Doat (Route 6), endowed with its own remarkable outlook into upper Borrowdale and picturesque Stonethwaite.

ASCENT FROM GRANGE-IN-BORROWDALE (30)

Via Broadslack Gill   216m/710ft   2.4km/1½ miles

An enchanting walk, especially when autumn gold tints the leaves. Most of this route is beneath a canopy of trees, quite a rare circumstance for a Lakeland fell walk. Grange, a popular place of refreshment, visited by both the Honister and Borrowdale Rambler bus services, owes its name to the fact that it was a medieval outpost farm of Furness Abbey. Linking across an isle in the Derwent, the oldest structure in the village is Grange Bridge, built in 1675.

1 A lane leaves the main street by the mid-town café, almost opposite the Victorian church, attractively constructed from Castle Crag slate. After passing an ever-open gate the metalled lane forks, and you keep left on the track passing between two camping fields. At the first small footbridge you may opt to bear right on the path leading to Dalt Quarry, with its attractive and reflective pool. However, most walkers will stay put on the more regular way, soaking up the glorious scene of pebbles and trees at the great sweeping bend of the crystal-clear Derwent. After the second footbridge bear right, rising on a track

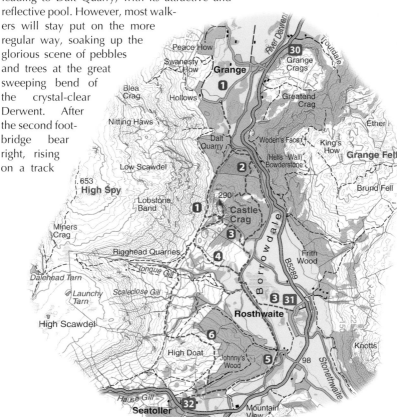

to a gate. The track continues on as a part-pitched way up the secret valley to the east of Castle Crag, drained by Broadslack Gill. After the old sheepfold on the left watch for a path breaking up the slope to a wall-stile. It continues to a fence-stile at the base of the slate tip, with a handsome view towards Goat Crag. Follow the fence to meet and join the main (heavily patronised) path winding up the spoil bank. The upper quarried hollow has so much loose slate that on occasion visitors are tempted to creatively play – currently a multitude of slates stand on edge as open-air art. The summit is reached by keeping right and mounting through the larches.

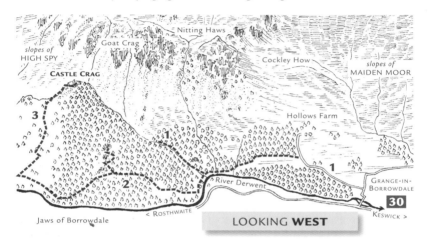

Nitting Haws · Goat Crag · slopes of HIGH SPY · CASTLE CRAG · Cockley How · slopes of MAIDEN MOOR · Hollows Farm · River Derwent · GRANGE-IN-BORROWDALE · Jaws of Borrowdale · < ROSTHWAITE · **30** · KESWICK >

LOOKING WEST

Via the Jaws of Borrowdale   230m/755ft   3.2km/2 miles

2 After the second footbridge at the great bend in the river – where many visitors are understandably lured to pause and gaze – bear left up the short hollow-way to a gate/stile. The path heads on beside the bright waters of the Derwent, here exquisitely living up to its ancient name, 'the oak-fringed river'. The path drifts away from the river, in the process softening some of the unwelcome traffic noise. The path leads through a clearing and comes by steps to a wall-gap where it re-enters woodland.

Coming through a shallow rock-cutting you may reasonably be tempted to bear right on a spur route to visit two notable small caverns. The top cave is the more famous, being associated with the local character Millican Dalton, who died in 1947 at the age of 80 – a remarkable age, considering that it was his habit to use this cave's upper inner portion as living and sleeping accommodation. At the left-hand entrance to The Attic find his etched graffiti 'DON'T'!! WASTE WORRDS Jump To Conclusions' set on the dark downward tilted rock – it is quite hard to decipher. The 'accommodation' has been cleansed of personal effects, although the slate platform he created, as too his little walled 'bedroom', remain. Millican was a real outdoor

Millican Dalton's cave

man who loved the natural world and the adventure of Borrowdale, and who could blame him for acting out his fantasies?

A word of advice: walkers have been tempted to wander on from the upper cavern, as an obvious path does lead right to cross the wooded ridge, and there is even evidence of intrepid scramblers completing the ascent on the north side.

Please treat these apparent paths with disdain. While you can venture onto the wooded ridge for the views, which are indeed good, you should retrace your steps back down to the regular path at the eastern foot of the quarries to continue.

Passing on below the lower cavern – fashioned into an impressive arch – the path wends pleasantly through the much extolled Jaws of Borrowdale woodland to emerge at a kissing-gate into pasture. The continuing track heads for Rosthwaite, but attend to the adjacent fence as the track shapes to curve left, and find here a stile/gate giving access to the bank pasture. A clear path climbs to a proper wall-gap (gate missing) and continues clear through the bracken to a ladder-stile, crossing the wall beside a group of mature pines. This gives access to the foot of the discarded slate, where you join the steep twisting passageway to the top, in part composed of retaining walls, through the spilling shards.

ASCENT FROM ROSTHWAITE (31)

Via the Derwent 230m/750ft 2.4km/1½ miles

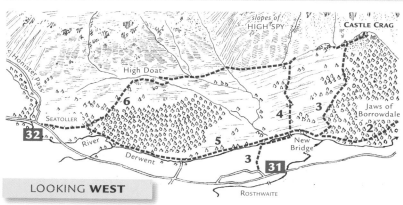
LOOKING **WEST**

The Flock-in tearoom at Yew Tree Farm, Rosthwaite

3 Follow the lane by Yew Tree Farm and its understandably popular Flock-in tearoom. The lane leads to the banks of the Derwent and follows this downstream to cross the cobbled New Bridge. Bear right and, coming to a pair of gates, keep right along the riverside track. The track swings left, and you branch left, crossing the stile/gate to ascend the bank into the trees, with handsome views back into the Stonethwaite valley. Slip through a gateway and complete the initial phase of the climb by crossing a wall via a ladder-stile. Pass the stately pines and embark on the slate trail, winding to the old quarry, then complete the ascent by the path on the right-hand side.

Via the old road — 240m/790ft — 2.8km/1¾ miles

4 An interesting variation, often used as the return on a circular expedition. This takes the left-hand gate after crossing New Bridge. The footpath leads up the open pasture via a fence-stile in an adapted wall-gateway. Apparent on the ground, the path winds up the pasture to a hand-gate in the bounding wall and quickly steps onto the old road, an old miners' track, by the fence sheep-handling pens on the pass. Follow on down for only a matter of 50m before bearing off right, keeping with the wall on the path as it rises below the small crag. Ignore the first fence-stile and continue with the fence close right until confronted by a wall. Here cross the stile, and immediately the ladder-stile over the wall, and ascend the slate trail to the summit.

ASCENT FROM SEATOLLER (32)

Via the Derwent — 226m/740ft — 4km/2½ miles

5 A joyous riverside approach. Leave the National Trust car park via the short lane at the eastern end. Cross the stile and keep the wall to your right, advancing to

River Derwent at Gowder Dub

Chain via ferrata approaching Longthwaite

a kissing-gate where you switch sides, close behind Glaramara outdoor centre. Now in woodland, slip through the left-hand wall at a gap in open ground, and after the next kissing-gate re-enter woodland, with a wall close right, and descend to a hand-gate. The Derwent makes an excited entrance and the path becomes an adventure, with a chain via ferrata aiding progress over the grooved bedrock. Pass through the grounds of Borrowdale Youth Hostel (Longthwaite) and follow the road to pass (not cross) the road bridge. Keep company with the river downstream, by stiles, to join Routes 3 and 4 at New Bridge.

Castle Crag from High Doat

Via High Doat   320m/1050ft   4.4km/2¾ miles

6 The upper gallery route via High Doat. Take leave of the car park as per the previous route, but after the stile fork left. Keep forward on the green path, advancing to a gate, then rise through light woodland with a fence (right) to a gateway giving onto the open slope of High Doat. A clear way exists through the bracken via a second gateway (gate off its hinges) over the top. Make a point of seeking the summit, as few walkers seem to give this grand little summit due regard. The path sweeps over to a wall-stile and winds down and across the pasture to a wall-stile to join the bridleway linking Little Gatesgarthdale with Grange. Turn right to advance along this age-old trade and quarryman's trod, en route crossing two footbridges, to unite with Route 4 just on the saddle before the track descends from a fence-fold.

THE SUMMIT

A knob of bedrock slate forms a conclusive summit. To this is attached a Great War slate roll of honour to the men of Borrowdale. Hence, on Remembrance Sunday, when the weather is too bad for the normal Great Gable service, people gather here to reflect and gives thanks to those who have given their lives in past and, sadly, continuing conflicts. 'Blessed are the peace-makers for they shall inherit the earth' – and from this vantage point the earth is visible as a wonderful gift of air, rock, water and trees in harmonic profusion; the Jaws of Borrowdale is indeed an exquisite place to be and to reflect on life. The situation is at once thrilling and enthralling. This place of beauty was, in ancient times, a temporary last refuge during times of local clan warfare, being the site of an Iron Age encampment – hence the fell-name.

A wind-shelter perched on the top like a bird's nest is useful, but awkward to enter. Larch trees hamper the view east and west, but north and south the walker is treated to sumptuous scenes. Northwards, views extend over the sylvan vale and gracious Grange to Derwent Water and the sleek peaks of the Skiddaw massif, with the wooded bulk of King's How close to hand half-right. To the south lies the land-locked heart of Borrowdale, centred upon the wooded slopes of High Doat and Rosthwaite, backed by Eagle Crag, Rosthwaite Fell, Glaramara and the more remote Great End and Scafell Pike. As a must-visit viewpoint, this is a resounding success.

SAFE DESCENTS

Descend S, taking the utmost care in skirting the east side of the quarry rim through the larches, and keep faithfully to the old quarrymen's paths that zig-zag down to the foot of the slate spoil. A ladder-stile over the wall sets you on course for Rosthwaite or Grange, while the fence-stile to the right leads into the wild pass on the west side of the craggy fellside, joining the old Rigghead track – head N for Grange and S for Seatoller.

Castle Crag summit, with war memorial poppy wreaths

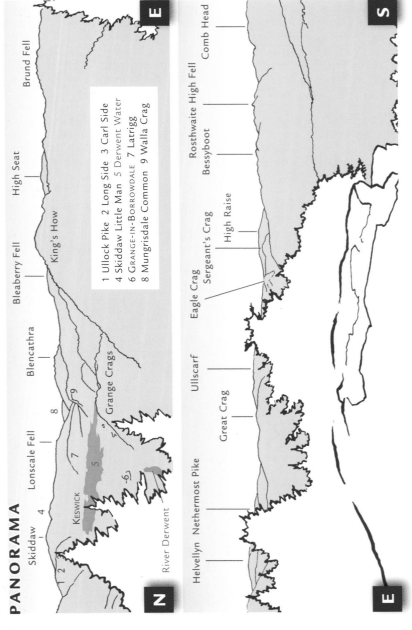

PANORAMA

Skiddaw
Lonscale Fell
Blencathra
Bleaberry Fell
High Seat
Brund Fell

1 Ullock Pike 2 Long Side 3 Carl Side
4 Skiddaw Little Man 5 Derwent Water
6 GRANGE-IN-BORROWDALE 7 Latrigg
8 Mungrisdale Common 9 Walla Crag

KESWICK
King's How
Grange Crags
River Derwent

Helvellyn Nethermost Pike
Great Crag
Ullscarf
Eagle Crag
Sergeant's Crag
High Raise
Rosthwaite High Fell
Bessyboot
Comb Head

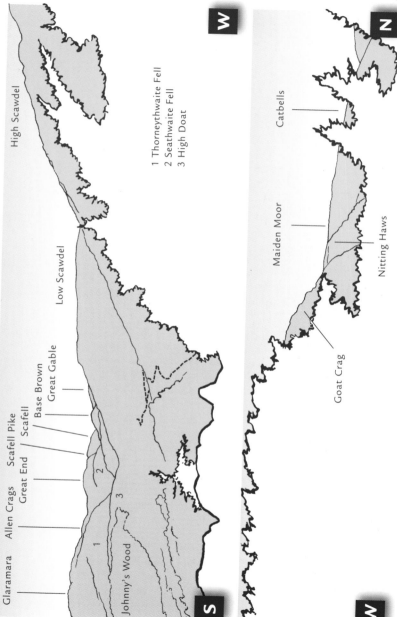

5 Castle Crag

W

N

Catbells

Maiden Moor

Nitting Haws

Goat Crag

W

S

High Scawdel

Low Scawdel

1 Thorneythwaite Fell
2 Seathwaite Fell
3 High Doat

Glaramara

Allen Crags

Great End

Scafell Pike

Scafell

Base Brown

Great Gable

Johnny's Wood

6 CATBELLS (451m/1480ft)

Seekers of solitude must choose carefully when they visit Catbells, as it is rightly popular. If ever there was a fell gifted with Lakeland views, then it is this little gem. Loved by all, for all the right reasons, it's where you bring children to ignite their thrill in mountain scenery. The name itself sounds charming and playful, and it is easy to imagine our little feline friends dancing for joy on its slopes with their merry bells a'jingling... shades of Beatrix Potter! In truth the name alludes to the former haunt of wild cats, long gone from the scene, also evidenced across the lake in Cat Gill, beside Walla Crag. The bell-shaped summit explains the fell-name, hence the 'bells' – in the plural as it includes the first rise from Hause Gate, which is known as Mart Bield, 'the shelter of pine marten'.

The fell was exploited for lead from the late 18th century. Large spoil debris is seen in Yewthwaite Comb, as too are the part-obscured spoil banks running down to the shores of Derwent Water. These were linked to the Brandelhow Mine, which was worked in shafts and levels, while the Old Brandley Mine, evidenced from the ridge top of Skelgill Bank, down the eastern flank, was open-cast. The area saw greatest activity during the 19th century, with mining ending in the 1890s.

The fell terminates the northward arm of the great ridge stemming from High Spy via Maiden Moor, which divides Borrowdale from the Newlands valley. This simple ridge permits several options for ascent and proximity to Derwent Water, which is serviced by the most delightful round-lake Keswick launch that allows you to indulge in the lovely combination of lake cruise and fell-climb.

Car parking has sensibly been moderated along the narrow road beyond Brandelhow Wood, but there are a few lay-bys still available north from Manesty Wood for occasional use, and even a small road-side quarry. An enterprising landowner has also eased matters by opening a portion of pasture opposite Gutherscale Lodge for a day-parking fee (currently £3), but this is not available. A further sustainable transport asset is the Honister Rambler bus service (from Easter to end of October only). This service plies the minor road at the fell's eastern feet, from which walkers may happily begin an ascent.

ASCENT FROM HAWSE END JETTY (28)

The name Hawse End refers to the old road from upper Borrowdale, coming by Grange, that arrived in the lower valley in this vicinity ('hawse' refers to a passage through the hills). Many walkers will content themselves with parking at a price in the field opposite Gutherscale Lodge (when available) or stride from Portinscale with the Cumbria Way, but the Keswick launch is the more exhilarating option.

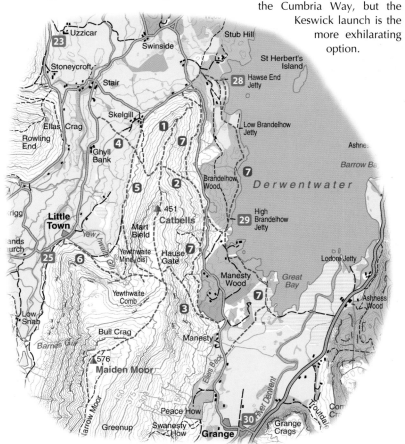

Keswick launch en route south by Brandelhow Park

Via Skelgill Bank 380m/1250ft 2.4km/1½ miles

1 A path leads directly up from the jetty, through the woodland fringe, to the double hairpin bend with a cattle grid in its midst. At the top hairpin bear right, and almost at once step onto the rising part-pitched path from the National Trust collecting box. This switches left by the rails and leads up onto the first nose of the bracken-clad ridge, where a further path is met coming from the opposite side. Set to work

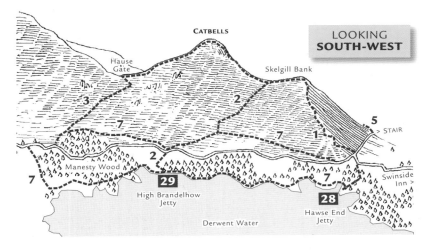

climbing the ridge, with some pitching and inevitable loose gravelly debris on the over-subscribed path. Near the top of Skelgill Bank, find a small plaque to Thomas Arthur Leonard who died in Conway in 1943, a prime mover in the open-air movement to create opportunities for working people to gain access to these wonderful places. Coming onto the crest of Skelgill Bank is a moment of quite some elation. The parade along its undulating grassy 'roof-top' gives wonderful views on either hand, although fell-lovers will get most thrill from the Newlands fell array, with Causey Pike impressively on show. The final bare rock path to the summit is most comfortably handled in ascent.

ASCENT FROM HIGH BRANDELHOW JETTY (29)

Via Brandelhow Mine   380m/1250ft   2km/1¼ miles

2 Head up, half-left, in the woodland to exit via a hand-gate. Bear uphill amid evidence of mining spoil on a path that is shielded by fencing from the old Brandelhow Mine workings, en route to the open road. Step onto and straight over this road to the quarry, bearing up the right-hand path. Follow this on its steady rise until, at its highest point, a clear path steps purposefully up left, through the bracken, heading steeply to the saddle on Skelgill Bank. Join the ridge path and turn left to engage in the final pull to the top.

Catbells from Skelgill Bank

ASCENT FROM GRANGE-IN-BORROWDALE (30)

Via Hause Gate   380m/1250ft   3.2km/2 miles

3 Follow the road from Grange until, just after Manesty House and before woodland, you find a path ushered off the road left around a large stone. This leads to a gate and up an area of spot-pitching, which remedies a patch of sorely worn path. Keep up left at the path-fork, zig-zagging to Hause Gate (where 'gate' referred to a natural gap rather than an actual gate). Here turn right to complete the ascent.

ASCENT FROM UZZICAR (23)

Via Stair and the Conservation Walk   366m/1200ft   3.2km/2 miles

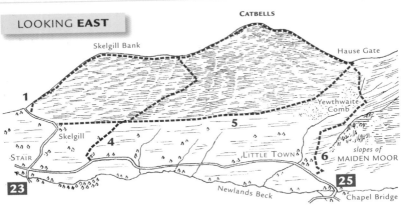

4 A stair-way to a heavenly height. Stair has little capacity for casual parking – walkers may opt to use the generous verge parking above Uzzicar Farm and wander down with the field-path by the remnants of the old Barrow lead mine to Stair Bridge. Cross, and after passing the Newlands Adventure Centre (remarkably first opening its doors in 1905) turn right by the community hall and the RA's Gordon Walker Hut to follow the minor road S. After some 450m seek a gate on the left at a bend, with a permissive path notice. This Conservation Walk is one of the wider benefits of an agricultural land management scheme. Entering rushy fields follow the open track to a new field-gate/stile in a fence/hedge. Ascend the next field to cross a fence-stile, continue up the ensuing pasture and cross an open ditch to reach the top right-hand corner of the field. Ignore the first stile/gate on the right, head up through the recessed gate/stile and ascend the field to a hand-gate in the intake wall. Now at the foot of the open fell-slope, step over the lateral drove-way and follow the inviting ascending path through the bracken as it hairpins en route to the skyline saddle. Join the ridge path to complete the climb up the steepening ridge of Catbells, with some awkward bedrock to negotiate.

Via Yewthwaite Comb   380m/1250ft   4km/2½ miles

The pinnacle of Catbells, east of the summit and little more than a metre high

5 You can start at Stair, following the byroad up to Skelgill Farm. Turn immediately right, after the road-gate, to the gate giving access to the lateral drove-way running S above the intake wall. Alternatively, you can reach this gate via the minor road leading SW from Gutherscale Lodge. Both routes then follow the drove-way for about 1km (just over ½ mile), passing beyond the summit. Then seek a track forking half-left that climbs steadily across some scree above the untidy legacy of the Yewthwaite Mine, with a moment's rock-step hampering speedy progress. On reaching the open saddle of Hause Gate, join the ridge path leading left (N) to the summit.

ASCENT FROM LITTLE TOWN (25)

Via Yewthwaite Comb   335m/1100ft   2km/1¼ miles

This is Mrs Tiggywinkle country, a prickly little character hatched up in Beatrix Potter's mind from her time staying at nearby Lingholm. Little Town was a hamlet of eight landholdings in 1578, and had been known as 'Litleton' prior to this time, suggesting a community long rooted in this spot.

6 Follow the road up from Chapel Bridge to go through the gate immediately prior to the first house. This leads onto a track which hairpins, keeping up left as it comes alongside the wall. As the wall shapes to curve left, bear right at the path-fork. The clear path duly rises to a double ford of Yewthwaite Gill (nice waterfall here) and ascends by a fold and the remains of mine structures up a loose trail. It comes eventually onto grass as it climbs to the broad Hause Gate saddle. Bear left following the simple ridge path to the summit.

LOWER-LEVEL WALK FROM HAWSE END JETTY (28)

Circular walk from the Keswick launch   120m/395ft   5.2km/3¼ miles

Many visitors love the Lakeland waters for their shoreline trails and never set foot on the high fells. As a half-way house they may consider this little excursion via the Keswick launch. It shares the low-level pleasures of the lapping lake with a slightly elevated made-way (suitable for wheelchairs) along the eastern lower slopes

The bare summit of Catbells looking to Derwent Water

Walkers boarding the Keswick launch at Hawse End Jetty

Castle Crag from the wheelchair-accessible path by Great Bay

of Catbells, and offers marvellous views over the fringing trees to Derwent Water's grand surround of fells.

7 Step off the launch and follow the nearshore path S, a walk full of charm and many scenic moments. En route to High Brandelhow Jetty pass the cupped-hand carving, an amazing feature installed by the National Trust to mark their centenary, set amid the first property they acquired in the Lake District in 1902, Brandelhow Park. Pass on by the jetty, keeping to the shore and skirting round a bay recovering from the debris deposits from the old Brandelhow lead mine, although the boathouse and dwelling on Brandelhow Point will attract most admiration. After a hand-gate pass by a timber garage to another gate following the roadway. Ignore the leftward access to the Abbot's Bay and come by The Warren. Turn left off the metalled roadway following the footpath beside the fence – this leads by a lovely view across Abbot's Bay.

The newly engineered trail leads on by a wall-gate onto a winding passage across low marsh, with serpentine boardwalks constructed from recycled plastic. Shortly after the 's'-shaped boardwalk, close to Great Bay, take the slightly less than obvious path half-right that leads by a gate at a woodland corner and on across pasture by further gates to the road. Turn right, passing Manesty House, to leave the road on the bridleway. After gaining height by a gate, take the first fork right to come above the woodland tight by a wall. Above Brackenburn, pass a scenic seat and tablet on the small outcrop to the memory of Sir Hugh Walpole. The path, an easily graded grand parade, comes down to meet the road at a small quarry, only to take off again immediately beyond. The path, which is deemed suitable for wheelchair users, rises and then drifts gently down again to rejoin the road. At the road bend, keep right with the path down to a kissing-gate, where it regains the road briefly on its second hairpin before heading right, down by the wall, to cross a metalled road and regain Hawse End Jetty… and your journey back to Keswick. How good was that?

Walkers descending Skelgill Bank

Catbells backed by Skiddaw from Maiden Moor

THE SUMMIT

Bare rock with no scope for a cairn to survive a zillion kicking feet. The view is everything. Come prepared to idle and be amazed. There are two main types of visitor – those who admire Derwent Water and those who dream of the fells and survey the North-Western Fells beyond, with the ridges of Knott End, Scope End and Robinson a brilliant composition.

SAFE DESCENTS

The easiest footing on the ridge is to be found to the south. Head back to Hause Gate and choose to descend left down to the Manesty road, or right via Yewthwaite to Little Town or even the drove-way north to Skelgill and Gutherscale.

RIDGE ROUTE

MAIDEN MOOR	↓92m/300ft	↑217m/710ft	2.4km/1½ miles

Follow the ridge path S, with just the one minor rock obstacle on Mart Bield, leading down to Hause Gate. Pass on through on the worn trail which leaves no scope for doubt on the rise onto Maiden Moor – that is, unless you fail to take the slightly less prominent path half-right as the scarp edge is reached. This leads attractively round the brink to crest Bull Crag and reach the modest summit cairn.

PANORAMA

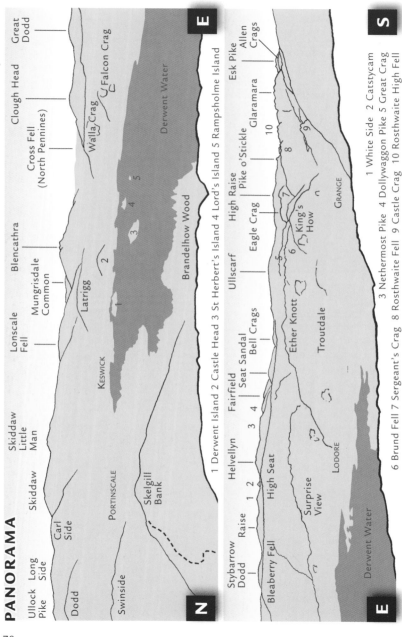

Ullock Pike — Long Side — Dodd — Swinside — Skiddaw — Carl Side — Skiddaw Little Man — PORTINSCALE — Skelgill Bank — Lonscale Fell — Mungrisdale Common — Latrigg — KESWICK — Blencathra — Cross Fell (North Pennines) — Clough Head — Great Dodd — Walla Crag — Falcon Crag — Brandelhow Wood — Derwent Water

N **E**

1 Derwent Island 2 Castle Head 3 St Herbert's Island 4 Lord's Island 5 Rampsholme Island

Stybarrow Dodd — Helvellyn — Raise — Bleaberry Fell — High Seat — Surprise View — LODORE — Derwent Water — Fairfield — Seat Sandal — Bell Crags — Ether Knott — Troutdale — Ullscarf — Eagle Crag — King's How — GRANGE — High Raise — Pike o'Stickle — Glaramara — Esk Pike — Allen Crags

E **S**

1 White Side 2 Catstycam 3 Nethermost Pike 4 Dollywaggon Pike 5 Great Crag 6 Brund Fell 7 Sergeant's Crag 8 Rosthwaite Fell 9 Castle Crag 10 Rosthwaite High Fell

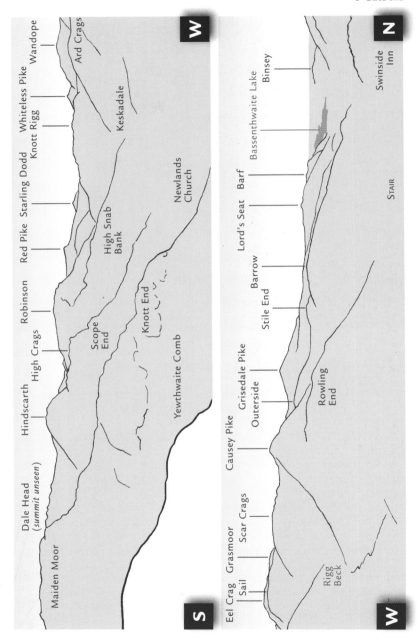

7 CAUSEY PIKE *(637m/2090ft)*

W hat makes the Lakeland Fells so popular? Well, it is probably their distinctive forms, their compact arrangement, inviting ridges and deeply incised valleys. In their midst Causey Pike is a stand-out character – the sort of chap who talks loudly at parties, you know the one! The situation is eye-catching, the climb hugely reward-ing and the view from the top lip-smackingly good.

Not only this, but the fell marks the beginning of a wonderful ridge upon which the walker may claim three fine summits, culminating upon Eel Crag, from where there are further choices for a full fell-round, including Wandope, Grasmoor, Hopegill Head and Grisedale Pike. The fell could be seen as part of the Coledale Horseshoe cohort, but it manages to stay aloof and therefore belong every bit as much to Newlands – but only visually, for it is a peninsular pike.

The fell is commonly climbed from either Uzzicar or Braithwaite, although the odd fellwalker slips up Rigg Beck to clamber onto Sail Hause, 'backtracking' over Scar Crags to the fell-top before heading down via Rowling End. The abiding memory of Causey is the heather, particularly on Rowling End, and, almost hidden up the Rigg Beck valley, a copse of ancient oakwood – is this a reminder of what the fells may have looked like several centuries ago before the intense grazing of sheep?

ASCENT FROM UZZICAR (23)

Via Sleet Hause 534m/1750ft 2.4km/1½ miles

1 Step off the road on the south side of Stoneycroft Bridge. The path takes a positive line climbing across the fellside with intimate views across the valley to the heather-clad Barrow. Where the path turns more sternly to the task of climbing to the skyline, a new series of zig-zags has been bulldozed, securing the trail for many years to come. Sleet Hause is a fine spot to stop and enjoy the startling contrasts of fellscape either side of the ridge.

Via Rowling End 536m/1760ft 2.8km/1¾ miles

2 Sleet Hause can be reached by a more scenically exciting option along the Rowling End ridge itself, beautifully clothed in heather. This initially follows Route 1, but after crossing a lateral path keeps a close harmony with the rising edge above Ellas Crag. The hard pull is rewarded by a sumptuous outlook deserving of a long contemplative rest on the turf couch.

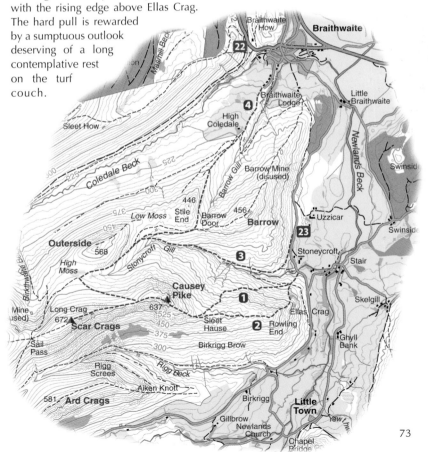

73

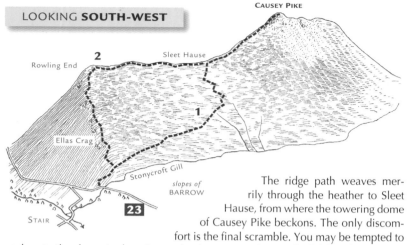

LOOKING **SOUTH-WEST**

CAUSEY PIKE

Rowling End

2

Sleet Hause

Ellas Crag

1

Stonycroft Gill

slopes of
BARROW

23

STAIR

The ridge path weaves merrily through the heather to Sleet Hause, from where the towering dome of Causey Pike beckons. The only discomfort is the final scramble. You may be tempted to explore to the sheep trod cutting under the outcropping on the left-hand side – this avoids the rocks and provides a novel way to circumvent the crag and claim your mountain – and ewe may find this fun!

If the head-on approach seems a bit daunting, or you want a good return route after gaining the summit, then Routes 3 and 4 will appeal.

Via Stonycroft Gill

534m/1750ft   4km/2½ miles

3 Follow the old miners' track, leading off from the parking verge above Uzzicar, which heads up the Stonycroft Gill valley. Keep with the track all the way to High

Causey Pike and Rowling End from Skelgill Bank

Causey Pike summit dome as seen during the latter stages of the ascent from Rowling End

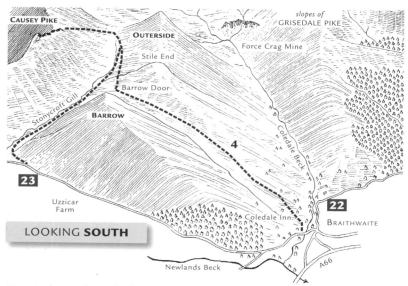

CAUSEY PIKE

slopes of
GRISEDALE PIKE

OUTERSIDE

Force Crag Mine

Stile End

Barrow Door

Stonycroft Gill

BARROW

4

Coledale Beck

23

Uzzicar
Farm

LOOKING **SOUTH**

Coledale Inn

22

BRAITHWAITE

Newlands Beck

A66

Moss in the southern shadow of Outerside. Seek a path that makes E up the grassy fellside, not exactly obvious until you are underway. However, a path has materialised – created, it would seem, by walkers leaving the ridge in order to avoid the steeper eastern side of the fell.

ASCENT FROM BRAITHWAITE (22)

Via Barrow Door   564m/1850ft   5.2km/3¼ miles

The High Moss path (see Route 3) onto the fell can also be attained direct from Braithwaite. There is scope for parking in the village street, although the route as described starts from the popular parking spot at the start of the Coledale miners' track, situated up the Whinlatter road.

4 Follow the lane beyond the Coledale Inn. After a gate it becomes an open track, and after the embowered ruins of High Coledale runs on as a green drove, casting aside the bracken, with Causey Pike in view dead ahead through Barrow Door. Continue naturally S, coming up into the gap of Barrow Door, between Barrow and Stile End. Here veer right on a clear path that joins the old miners' track from Stonycroft and leads confidently on to High Moss.

THE SUMMIT

It would seem that the bold knob attained at the top of the climb from Sleet Hause is the summit, but there might be some doubt about that. There are up to seven vying tops to the west, and each has some trace or more of a cairn, but it has to be conceded that this probably is the summit by a few millimetres. As a primary ridge-end,

76

Summit of Causey Pike

Causey Pike from Scar Crags

Causey Pike has a character all its own. The concept of a causeway is most apt from whatever level it is surveyed.

SAFE DESCENTS

The 'invented' path from the saddle at the west end of the Causey tops provides a sure line of descent W to High Moss, where the free-running old miners' track, originally constructed as a mineral line, gives a confidence-booster route E, straight down the Stonycroft Gill valley.

RIDGE ROUTE

SCAR CRAGS	↓54m/180ft	↑89m/290ft	1.2km/¾ mile

You would be hard pressed to get lost on this ridge route – although in misty conditions you could slip past the modest summit cairn and arrive at Sail Pass, bemused! The ridge runs slightly S of E, passing some peat hags and cotton grass tufts, onto the edge that climbs to the summit. The views down the south declivity into Rigg Beck are quite special.

PANORAMA

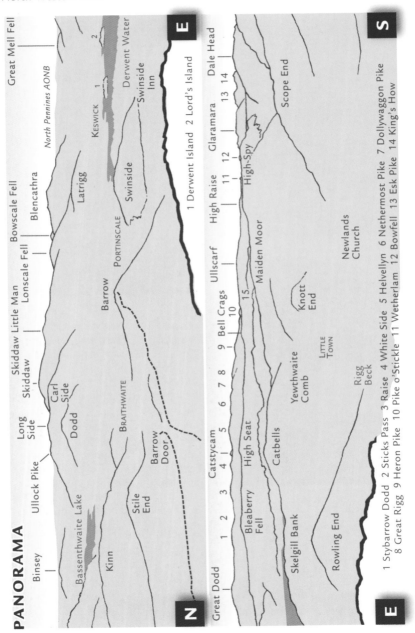

E

Great Mell Fell

North Pennines AONB

Derwent Water

Swinside Inn

KESWICK

1

2

Latrigg

Bowscale Fell

Lonscale Fell

Blencathra

Swinside

PORTINSCALE

Skiddaw Little Man

Skiddaw

Barrow

Long Side

Carl Side

Skiddaw

Dodd

BRAITHWAITE

Ullock Pike

Binsey

Bassenthwaite Lake

Kinn

Stile End

Barrow Door

N

1 Derwent Island 2 Lord's Island

S

Dale Head

Scope End

13 14

Glaramara

High-Spy

12

High Raise

11

Ullscarf

Maiden Moor

Newlands Church

Bell Crags

Knott End

10

15

9

LITTLE TOWN

8

7

Yewthwaite Comb

6

5

Catstycam

4

High Seat

3

Catbells

2

Bleaberry Fell

Rigg Beck

1

Skelgill Bank

Rowling End

Great Dodd

E

1 Stybarrow Dodd 2 Sticks Pass 3 Raise 4 White Side 5 Helvellyn 6 Nethermost Pike 7 Dollywaggon Pike
8 Great Rigg 9 Heron Pike 10 Pike o'Stickle 11 Wetherlam 12 Bowfell 13 Esk Pike 14 King's How

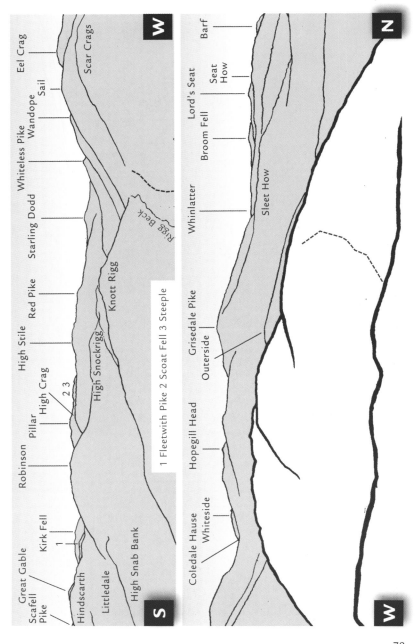

W

Eel Crag
Scar Crags

Sail
Wandope
Whiteless Pike
Starling Dodd
Red Pike
High Stile
High Crag
2 3
Pillar
Robinson
Kirk Fell
Great Gable
Scafell Pike
Hindscarth
Littledale
High Snab Bank
High Snockrigg
Knott Rigg
Rigg Beck
1

S

1 Fleetwith Pike 2 Scoat Fell 3 Steeple

N

Barf
Lord's Seat
Seat How
Broom Fell
Whinlatter
Sleet How
Grisedale Pike
Outerside
Hopegill Head
Coledale Hause
Whiteside

W

8 DALE HEAD *(753m/2470ft)*

Looking down, as might a presiding judge, upon the wild upper reaches of the Newlands valley, the fell lends both dignity and grandeur to the dale head. It might be said to portray certain feminine traits – in performing several tasks at once! The fell sends out its motherly embrace to the great ridges of High Spy with Hindscarth, and down its southern slopes forms a bridge-head with the western fells on Honister Pass, while below the sub-plateau of High Scawdel it has an elegant presence in Borrowdale in the form of High Doat, a lowly ridge with an attractive petticoat of native oakwood.

Dale Head has masculine aspects, too, not least in the well-named Great Gable Crag, spilling down upon the head of Gatesgarthdale in a series of riven ridges and the remnants of slate-quarrying caverns, far too dangerous to casually explore. In its northern shadowed lap is evidence of copper mining, which with the Rigghead slate quarries in Tongue Gill provide added interest for the fell-wanderer. In Dalehead Tarn the fell possesses the largest sheet of water in the North-Western Fells – and with several lesser sparkling jewels close by on High Scawdel, this is a lovely interlude upon your fell journey.

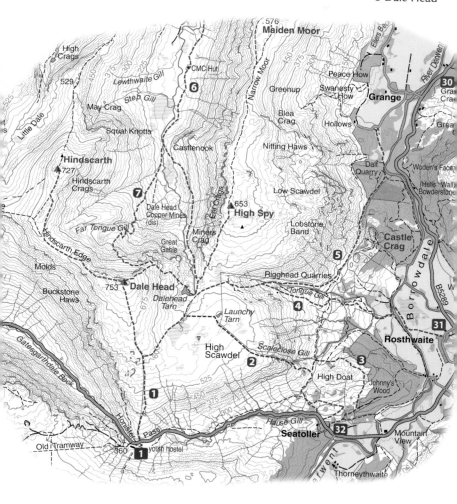

ASCENT FROM HONISTER PASS (1)

Direct   396m/1300ft   2km/1¼ miles

1 Perhaps the easiest navigation in the book! Step off the road on the right-hand side of the fence and follow it N. The path is not exactly faithful, drifting away from the fence at an early stage as it passes an old fold before coming back into line. Suddenly the fence ends, having served its purpose in defending the dangerous quarried hollows – although a former metal fence did continue to the top. Propelled thus far by

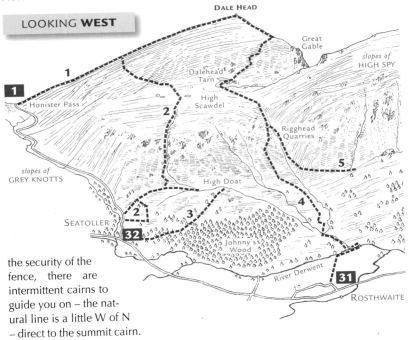

LOOKING WEST

DALE HEAD

Great Gable

slopes of HIGH SPY

1

1

Honister Pass

Dalehead Tarn

High Scawdel

2

Righead Quarries

5

slopes of GREY KNOTTS

High Doat

2

3

4

SEATOLLER

32

Johnny's Wood

River Derwent

31

ROSTHWAITE

the security of the fence, there are intermittent cairns to guide you on – the natural line is a little W of N – direct to the summit cairn.

ASCENT FROM SEATOLLER (32)

Via High Scawdel   655m/2150ft   4.8km/3 miles

As an alternative start, it is possible to wander up above Seatoller and take the old road, criss-crossing the modern highway, to reach Honister Pass at the youth hostel and modern slate mine enterprise and thus join Route 1 at its birth.

2 Yet the fell-wanderers' route deserves first consideration. At the head of the hamlet there is a choice. You can bear right at the first gate, facing the track-bridge on the left, which leads to a row of cottages, and follow the old road by two further gates. Alternatively, rise up the modern road to the first bend and step up through the hand-gate and climb more directly. As the two routes come together, veer up the grass bank path to a hand-gate to follow on N beside the wall. After three walls come together, set back to the right, march on a further 60m to find a small boulder beside the path on the left.

3 This interim point can also be reached taking a route via High Doat. Exit the National Trust car park at its eastern end, cross the stile and follow the green-way straight ahead, climbing via a gate into light woodland. Continue with a fence, right, to go through a gateway and climb onto the bracken slopes of High Doat, then continue on a clear path via a further gateway. The path runs handsomely over the

Slate mine incline from Honister Mine

fell-top, curving W down by a wall-stile, and after crossing the bracken-free hollow clambers over a wall-stile onto the bridleway. Turn left beside the wall and quickly come to a boulder beside the path.

At this point, Routes 2 and 3 meet. Leave the regular path and climb the steep pathless bank, thus avoiding bracken and outcropping, and as the slope eases find traces of a path leading to a hand-gate in a stout wall. From here there is little evidence of a path, but the route simply follows the upper course of Scaleclose Gill and the subsequent fence to the sharp fence-corner, and bears right to reach Launchy Tarn. The name possibly means 'long stride', which is not an invitation to test! Head due W to join the path running S, to the south of Dalehead Tarn. Follow this as it gently rises and curves right to meet the fence above the highest re-entrant quarry. Turn right and follow the fence and subsequent cairns N to the summit, with Route 1.

ASCENT FROM ROSTHWAITE (31)

Via Rigghead 685m/2250ft 5.6km/3½ miles

High Spy from the top of Great Gable Crag

4 Follow the walled lane from the Flock-in café. This leads to and over New Bridge, where you bear immediately left to the double footbridge. Cross the stile after the first footbridge, now following the new flood-bank W beside Tongue Gill. Cross a plank-bridge to a stile, from where you ascend the winding track up the bank (ignore the inviting ladder-stile), rising to go through a gate. Bear up half-left onto the lateral track and, in effect, step straight over it to find a green corridor path that leads up the ridge, avoiding bracken, to reach a wall-stile. The continuing path mounts the slate spoil, passing to the right of the old quarry dwelling (now a locked mountain hut) and running on level over slate shards to join the ascending path from Tongue Gill. Keep up with this fascinating trail by steps, passing intriguing mine cavities and ruined sheds to reach the fence-stile at the top of the valley. Follow on with the palpable path to ford the outflow of Dalehead Tarn, skirting to the left of the large outcrop to wander by the north side of the large rushy pool. Embark on the now well-pitched trail climbing steeply onto the shoulder comfortably (if exposed in climatic terms!) above Great Gable Crag, and continue naturally up the ridge to the summit.

ASCENT FROM GRANGE-IN-BORROWDALE (30)

Via Rigghead   716m/2350ft   6.8km/4¼ miles

5 A side-door approach, full of scenic surprises. Follow the Hollow Farm access lane leading S from the midst of the hamlet. Keep left off the metalled roadway at the fork, and pass between camping fields to come by the river. After the second footbridge bear right up the track by a gate onto the part-pitched track leading through the impressive defile of Broadslack Gill on the west side of Castle Crag. After coming over the brow, follow on, choosing the right-hand track where it forks. This old mine approach leads up into the Tongue Gill valley and climbs by a stile to join forces with Route 4 at the lovely flight of slate steps.

ASCENT FROM LITTLE TOWN (25 – off map N)

A springboard for two routes – both are the common resort of walkers in descent, effectively shortening the Newlands Round, but in ascent these are fabulous climbs of great scenic merit.

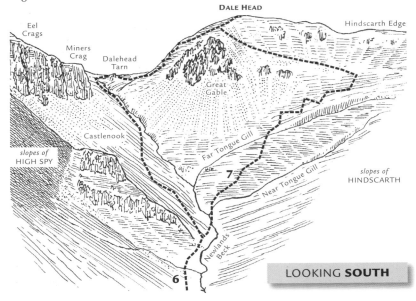

Mallard on Dalehead Tarn

Via Dalehead Tarn
610m/2000ft   6.4km/4 miles

6 Follow the valley track S from Little Town – this is used by climbers lodging in the Carlisle Mountaineering Club Hut, situated 1.6km (1 mile) up the valley. Pass on beyond this adapted miners' dwelling and pass under the Castlenook spur, by mine spoil banks. The track fades as it approaches a fork. Here bear uphill, climbing steadily over rough ground – you may keep beside the beck and inspect the impressive sequence of cascades, but the higher path is the preferred way. This leads up beneath the line of cliffs marshalling High Spy to come above the upper ravine and ford the beck, the outflow of Dalehead Tarn, in harmony with Routes 4 and 5.

Via Dale Head Copper Mines
610m/2000ft   5.6km/3½ miles

7 After passing beneath Castlenook headland, ford Newlands Beck as Near Tongue Gill feeds into the valley beck. Follow the green-way, an old miners' track climbing steadily S to ford the more impressive Far Tongue Gill, with its slabby walls. The green-way now follows a sequence of hairpins as it climbs to the site of the upper copper mine. Pass the remnant shed on a clear path that works SE up to the highest adit on the steep slope directly below the fell's head-wall. A narrow trod ventures onto the shoulder where Routes 4 and 5 converge. You may be tempted to descend to view the dramatic dale scenes from the top of Great Gable Crag, with gullies falling on either hand, but you must backtrack to continue, as there are no safe ways down.

THE SUMMIT
Here stands a cairn that does real justice to the situation, a worthy rival to High Spy's handsome standard. It has been modified of recent years from the fat-bellied

Copper-mine ruin backed by Great Gable Crag

edifice Wainwright reported, although the top is a bit chaotic. That the highest ground is a few strides to its west is no cause to quibble. The cairn has been set purposefully on the brink. Given a half-decent day, the temptation to sit and soak up the long view down the Newlands 'glen' to the distant Skiddaw will be taken up with alacrity. On several occasions the author has

Dale Head summit cairn

perched here and watched the movement of cloud shadows across the scarp of High Spy and chatted to a succession of walkers who, for some unknown reason, seem intent on racing on, when for the sake of 20mins they could create an enduring memory of the wider fell-world from this stunning location.

SAFE DESCENTS

The one sure recourse in foul weather is the path S to Honister Pass, where you might just encounter the hostel warden's fowl (cock and laying hens)! A chain of cairns and then a fence make this a reliable way in mist. But if your destination is lower Newlands, then you need to follow the ridge path NE, watching for the right-hand turn leading onto the pitched path tilting down to Dalehead Tarn. Ford the outflow and follow the path, above the beck's right bank, into the valley.

RIDGE ROUTE

HIGH SPY	↓268m/880ft	↑168m/550ft	2.4km/1½ miles

Follow the ridge path down NE, watch intently as this path breaks right – modern pitching has made this a more pleasant trail, en route to the northern shores of Dalehead Tarn. Pass to the right of the large outcropping and ford the outflow beck, following the rising path N, with a handsome craggy views, notably of Great Gable Crag on Dale Head across the gulf of the upper Newlands Beck ravine. The path weaves steadily on to the tall cairn.

HINDSCARTH	↓96m/315ft	↑70m/230ft	2km/1¼ miles

The ridge path has little to hamper its progress W, and the modest outcropping prior to the descent to the wide saddle is passed on the S side – although watch for the low metal stumps of the old fence that once ran along the ridge. Along Hindscarth Edge, a natural lateral path has evolved that shortcuts the way N to the summit.

Path to Honister Hause from near the Dale Head summit

PANORAMA

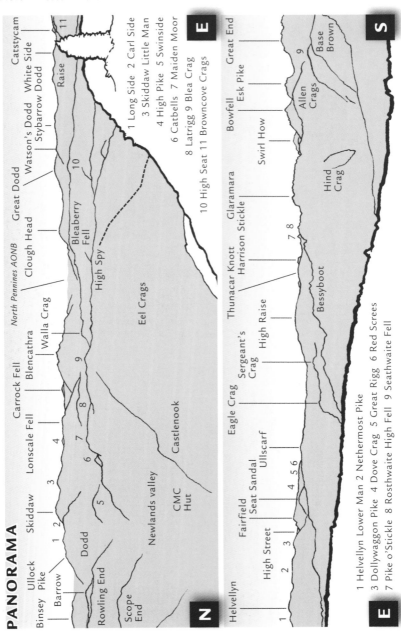

N

Binsey · Ullock Pike · Skiddaw · Lonscale Fell · Carrock Fell · Blencathra · Walla Crag · North Pennines AONB · Clough Head · Great Dodd · Watson's Dodd · Stybarrow Dodd · White Side · Catstycam

Barrow · Dodd · Rowling End · Scope End · Newlands valley · CMC Hut · Castlenook · Eel Crags · High Spy · Bleaberry Fell · Raise

1 Long Side 2 Carl Side
3 Skiddaw Little Man
4 High Pike 5 Swinside
6 Catbells 7 Maiden Moor
8 Latrigg 9 Blea Crag
10 High Seat 11 Browncove Crags

E

E

Helvellyn · High Street · Fairfield · Seat Sandal · Ullscarf · Eagle Crag · Sergeant's Crag · High Raise · Thunacar Knott · Harrison Stickle · Glaramara · Swirl How · Bowfell · Esk Pike · Great End

Bessyboot · Hind Crag · Allen Crags · Base Brown

S

1 Helvellyn Lower Man 2 Nethermost Pike
3 Dollywaggon Pike 4 Dove Crag 5 Great Rigg 6 Red Screes
7 Pike o'Stickle 8 Rosthwaite High Fell 9 Seathwaite Fell

88

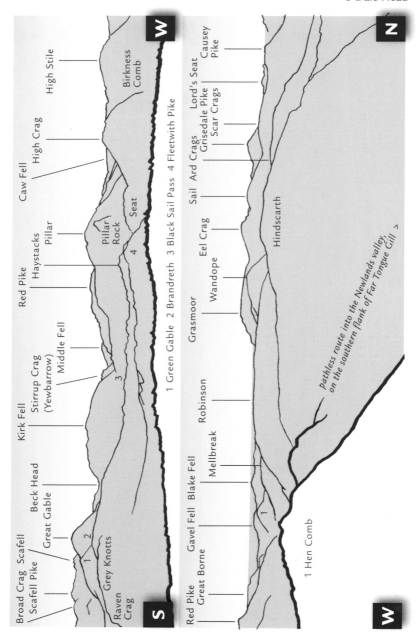

W

High Stile
High Crag
Caw Fell
Red Pike
Haystacks
Pillar
Kirk Fell
Stirrup Crag (Yewbarrow)
Middle Fell
Beck Head
Great Gable
Scafell
Broad Crag Scafell
Scafell Pike
Grey Knotts
Raven Crag

Birkness Comb
Pillar Rock
Seat

1 Green Gable 2 Brandreth 3 Black Sail Pass 4 Fleetwith Pike

S

N

Lord's Seat
Causey Pike
Grisedale Pike
Scar Crags
Sail Ard Crags
Eel Crag
Grasmoor
Wandope
Robinson
Mellbreak
Blake Fell
Gavel Fell
Red Pike
Great Borne

Hindscarth

pathless route into the Newlands valley, on the southern flank of Far Tongue Gill

1 Hen Comb

W

89

PANORAMA from High Doat

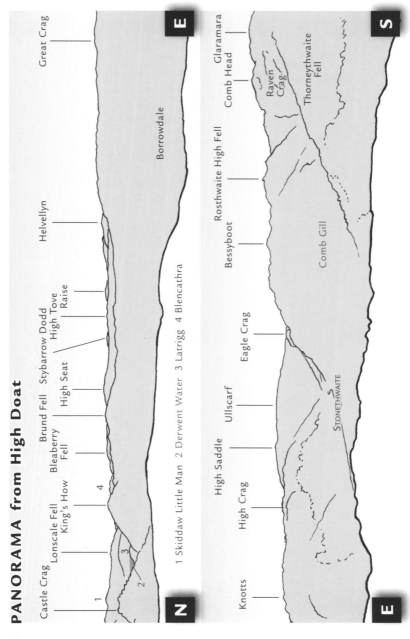

E

Great Crag

Borrowdale

Helvellyn

Stybarrow Dodd
High Tove
Raise

Brund Fell
High Seat

Bleaberry
Fell

Lonscale Fell
King's How

Castle Crag

N

1 Skiddaw Little Man 2 Derwent Water 3 Latrigg 4 Blencathra

S

Glaramara
Comb Head

Raven
Crag

Thorneythwaite
Fell

Rosthwaite High Fell

Bessyboot

Comb Gill

Eagle Crag

Ullscarf

STONETHWAITE

High Saddle

High Crag

Knotts

E

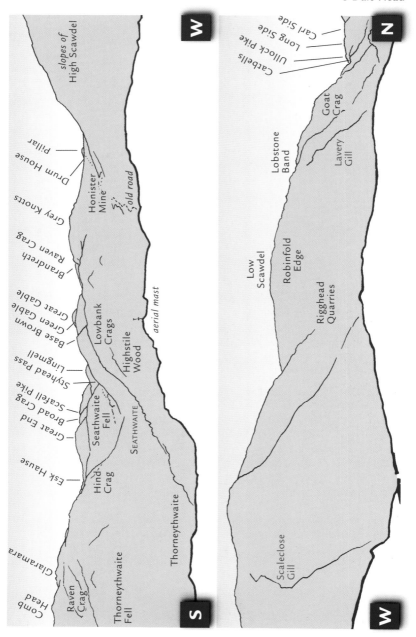

Top panel (W / S):

slopes of High Scawdel

Drum House pillar
Honister Mine
old road
Grey Knotts
Brandreth / Raven Crag
Great Gable
Green Gable
Base Brown
Lowbank Crags
Highstile Wood
Styhead pass
Lingmell
Scafell Pike
Broad Crag
Great End
Seathwaite Fell
Esk Hause
Hind Crag
aerial mast
SEATHWAITE
Claramara
Comb Head
Raven Crag
Thorneythwaite Fell
Thorneythwaite
Thorneythwaite

Bottom panel (N / W):

Catbells
Ullock Pike
Long Side
Carl Side
Goat Crag
Lobstone Band
Lavery Gill
Low Scawdel
Robinfold Edge
Rigghead Quarries
Scaleclose Gill

9 EEL CRAG *(840m/2756ft)*

The fell-name, which means 'the dangerous or evil cliff', is an odd borrow. The actual Eel Crag lies some way down the fell to the north, frowning upon the latter stages of the ascent from Coledale. As so often, a lower feature has been adopted for the whole fell, although the OS persist in calling this Crag Fell. By whatever name, this is a fine mountain – the culmination of handsome ridges and, as travellers over Newlands Hause will attest, no shrinking violet, a focal subject that simply must be climbed! In long perspective it is the craggy dale-head attraction in Coledale, while towering above Sail Beck it has a gullied character, spilling into the corrie of Addacomb Hole.

The fell most frequently comes under walkers' feet as part of the Coledale Horseshoe from Braithwaite, one of the best circuits in Lakeland. Being right at the heart of things, there is the opportunity to include it in an matching round from Lanthwaite Green or Buttermere – either is an equal triumph of fellwalking pleasure.

ASCENT FROM BRAITHWAITE (22)

Via Coledale Hause

762m/2500ft   6.8km/4¼ miles

1 Not every walker needs to tackle the Coledale Horseshoe in skyline fashion. You can use the old mine track up Coledale to good effect to claim your mountain direct. Where the track forks, short of the derelict buildings associated with the old Force Crag Mine, veer down left to ford Coledale Beck. Stick firmly to the main rough trail leading W that climbs above the side-ravine with a fine view of the impressive Low Force.

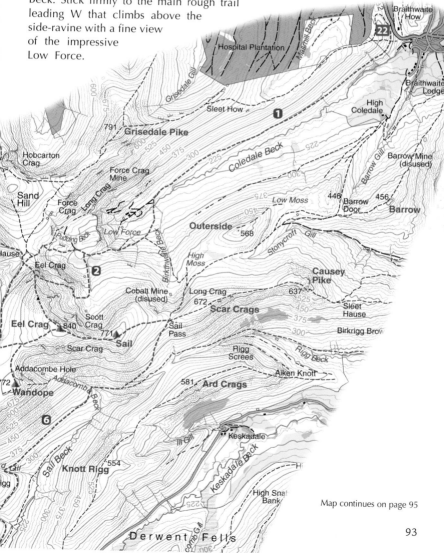

Map continues on page 95

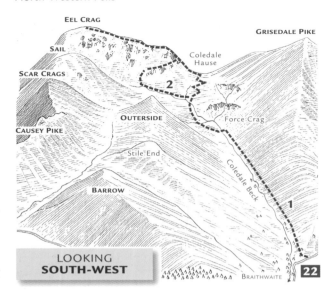

EEL CRAG

GRISEDALE PIKE

SAIL

Coledale
Hause

SCAR CRAGS

2

OUTERSIDE

Force Crag

CAUSEY PIKE

Coledale Beck

Stile End

Lanthwa
Wood

BARROW

1

LOOKING
SOUTH-WEST

BRAITHWAITE

22

Crummock

Higher up, the Fix the Fells team have secured the path with a tidy serpentine section up the steeper slope that comes under Eel Crag to reach Coledale Hause. There are two options at this point – the tougher being to clamber up the loose scree trail direct to the right of the outcropping and join the shelf route heading straight to the summit, while the regular way keeps beside the head-stream of Gasgale Gill (Route 3).

Via the shelf route

762m/2500ft   6.4km/4 miles

2 The off-beat patrol will relish the shelf route. This leaves the merry trod of the multitude immediately after the gill that drains the comb between Sail and Eel Crag joins the ravine above Low Force Crag at GR195212. Step over the remnants of a stone dam in a marsh and clam-ber up the right-hand side of the gill, with no path to encourage you. Arrive at the rimmed hol-low, which presumably once held a tarn.

Strike up right from this breached bank, climbing towards the higher comb, but keep right over the shoulder. Higher Tower Ridge may attract confident scramblers, but the

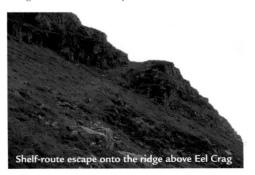

Shelf-route escape onto the ridge above Eel Crag

Map continued from page 93

sure course lies along the gallery shelf, with evidence of a path quickly materialising from the odd little cairn (created by walkers, it must be deduced from the advice AW gave in his guide). Pass a small alcove bield as you aim for the obvious green shelf on the headland due west above Eel Crag (the actual cliff of that name). During this

95

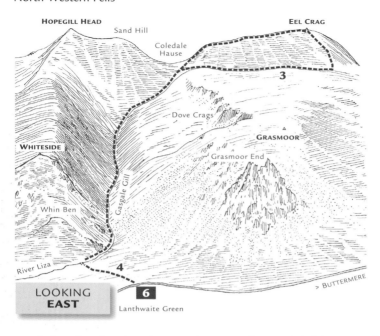

LOOKING **EAST**

stretch there is a fine view down on the new trail up to Coledale Hause, down on Low Force and across the wide upper dale to Grisedale Pike. Come up the step onto the ridge precisely where the steep direct path from Coledale Hause (Route 4) joins the ridge top. Bear naturally left, climbing easily to the summit.

Via upper Gasgale Gill	762m/2500ft	6.8km/4¼ miles

3 From Coledale Hause the made-path continues SW beside the headstream of Gasgale Gill (until it was radically repaired this path had been a gully, in certain places 2m deep) to the nameless saddle between Eel Crag and Grasmoor, with its peaty pool. Turn left up the strong path, climbing easily over grass NE to the summit.

ASCENT FROM LANTHWAITE GREEN (6)

Via Gasgale Gill	790m/2590ft	5.2km/3¼ miles

4 Cross the open common to the footbridge and either follow the beck upstream, coping with an entertaining rock-step beside a handsome waterfall, or clamber up the fell, taking the right-hand branch off the ascending path to Whin Benn. This goes via a stepped rock-step to meet up with the beckside path running on up the wild valley. The beck-name, Gasgale, seems to be a corruption of 'the goat's ravine', the streaming gullies spilling from the Whiteside ridge being a likely environment for these little creatures in the past. There is no doubting the path, although heavy rain

Eel Crag from Sand Hill overlooking Coledale Hause

has caused notable landslipping. The beck has some lovely cascades near the top. Come onto the level grassy saddle of Coledale Hause. While the easy recourse is to keep company with the headstream (Route 3), the more thrilling option is to head up the facing scree slope to join the shelf route (Route 2). The going is not a problem in fair weather, but the stones are loose, so take care and minimise the wear, tear and disturbance for those that follow you.

ASCENT FROM BUTTERMERE (3)

Via Whiteless Pike   747m/2450ft   5.2km/3¼ miles

5 The fell highway. Follow WHITELESS PIKE Route 1 (page 265) and the continuing ridge via Saddle Gate, then take the lovely ridge by Thirdgill Head Man onto the broad expanse of grass leading to the saddle cross-path, where you veer right (NE) to the top.

Via Sail Beck   836m/2740ft   7.6m/4¾ miles

6 Possibly the return route of choice after following Route 5, but a grand way in its own right. Follow SAIL Route 3 (page 225), which leads up the west side of the Sail Beck valley on a strong path traversing Whiteless Breast. After fording Addacomb Beck, and as the heather begins, encounter a cairn and fork up left to reach Sail

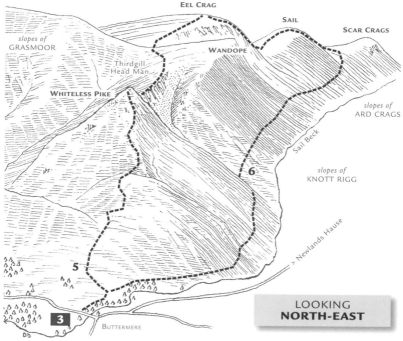

EEL CRAG

SAIL

SCAR CRAGS

slopes of
GRASMOOR

WANDOPE

Thirdgill
Head Man

WHITELESS PIKE

slopes of
ARD CRAGS

Sail Beck

6

slopes of
KNOTT RIGG

> Newlands Hause

5

3

BUTTERMERE

LOOKING
NORTH-EAST

Pass. Cut back onto the ridge on the unsightly path from Sail Pass, and continue over the intervening summit and down the narrow connecting ridge that climbs the exhilarating east ridge onto the summit plateau.

THE SUMMIT

A stone-built OS column stands back from the edge on a domed summit bereft of rock features. The commanding situation is a pedestrian meeting place and a well-loved viewpoint right in the heart of the group. The panorama is generous, rivalling Grasmoor in all but depth, unless you stand on the edge and look north.

OS column on the summit of Eel Crag

SAFE DESCENTS

For all the remote situation, there are reliable routes at hand to get you to safety in hostile weather. For Braithwaite descend SW to the saddle and follow the engineered path N to Coledale Hause, bearing NE (right) into Coledale itself entirely on good footing.

RIDGE ROUTES

GRASMOOR	↓122m/400ft	↑135m/445ft	2km/1¼ miles

Descend SW to the saddle and continue up the corresponding steep trail to pass a prominent cairn. The path keeps a bias to the southern edge to revel in the spacious views and reach the large compartmentalised summit shelter-cairn.

SAIL	↓99m/325ft	↑30m/100ft	0.8km/½ mile

Descend ESE, curving to the E as the ridge narrows through the dip and rises over slabs to the plateau. The summit cairn lies a little to the left, off the strict line of the regular ridge path, beside peaty pools.

WANDOPE	↓102m/335ft	↑35m/115ft	1.2km/¾ mile

Descend SW, but well short of the saddle veer S, coming along the edge above the hanging valley of Addacomb Hole to reach the little cairn on the grass at the tip.

Eel Crag from Sail

PANORAMA

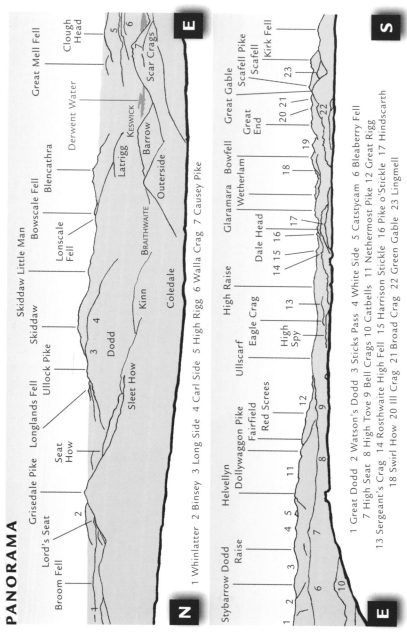

N

Broom Fell · Lord's Seat · Grisedale Pike · Longlands Fell · Ullock Pike · Skiddaw · Skiddaw Little Man · Bowscale Fell · Great Mell Fell · Clough Head

Seat How · Sleet How · Dodd · Lonscale Fell · Blencathra · Latrigg · Derwent Water · KESWICK · BRAITHWAITE · Kinn · Coledale · Barrow · Outside · Scar Crags

E

1 Whinlatter 2 Binsey 3 Long Side 4 Carl Side 5 High Rigg 6 Walla Crag 7 Causey Pike

Stybarrow Dodd · Raise · Helvellyn · Dollywaggon Pike · Fairfield · Red Screes · Ullscarf · Eagle Crag · High Spy · High Raise · Dale Head · Wetherlam · Glaramara · Bowfell · Great End · Great Gable · Scafell Pike · Scafell · Kirk Fell

S

E

1 Great Dodd 2 Watson's Dodd 3 Sticks Pass 4 White Side 5 Catstycam 6 Bleaberry Fell
7 High Seat 8 High Tove 9 Bell Crags 10 Catbells 11 Nethermost Pike 12 Great Rigg
13 Sergeant's Crag 14 Rosthwaite High Fell 15 Harrison Stickle 16 Pike o'Stickle 17 Hindscarth
18 Swirl How 20 Ill Crag 21 Broad Crag 22 Green Gable 23 Lingmell

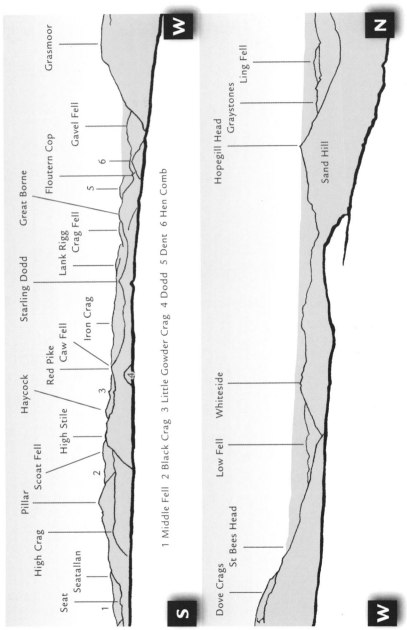

Grasmoor

Gavel Fell

Floutern Cop

Great Borne

6

5

Lank Rigg

Crag Fell

Starling Dodd

Iron Crag

Caw Fell

Red Pike

Haycock

High Stile

Scoat Fell

Pillar

High Crag

Seat

Seatallan

1

W

S

1 Middle Fell 2 Black Crag 3 Little Gowder Crag 4 Dodd 5 Dent 6 Hen Comb

3

2

Ling Fell

Graystones

Hopegill Head

Sand Hill

Whiteside

Low Fell

St Bees Head

Dove Crags

N

W

101

10 GRASMOOR *(852m/2795ft)*

The paternal elephant of the range stands with his back proud of all else, and with his mighty wrinkled head – all seeing, all knowing – frowning benignly down upon Crummock Water. He stands solidly forward of his hilly herd, which are deeply incised by wild valleys, notably Rannerdale Beck and Gasgale Gill (which seems to generate its own forceful gusts buffeting walkers en route to Coledale Hause). Evidently shepherds knew it as the high pasture, the 'grass moor'. Much of the fell's western flanks are draped in heather and not a little scree, and only the eastern aspects offer scope for the said grass.

A high proportion of walkers choose to reach the summit by the proverbial back-door via Wandope Moss, rejecting the more obvious, energy-sapping direct assaults. But this is a fell to bring out the best in you, and demanding climbs – including routes described here via Grasmoor End (Route 1), Dove Crags (Route 2) and, for the more cautious, Lad Hows (Route 5) – are rewarded.

The fell also fits well into a grand circuit that may include Whiteside, Hopegill Head, Eel Crag, Wandope, Whiteless Pike and even the puppy of the range, Rannerdale Knotts, all in one mighty fell-gather.

ASCENT FROM LANTHWAITE GREEN (6)

Gasgale Gill provides four prime routes to the top – the first being the most thrilling of all!

Via Grasmoor End   700m/2300ft   2.4km/1½ miles

1 Traverse the open common and take the inviting bracken-free path up the gentle slope SE, prior to the footbridge. Ahead looms Grasmoor End. It looks like a daunting climb, on the angle between the north and west faces, but once underway you should have every cause to be chuffed that you overcame any doubts. Choose a fair-weather day to get the best out of the craggy environs and impressive outlook. A stream of light scree gives a clue as to the line to be taken, and this is not as bad as first impressions may suggest. The path makes its way up into the heather, gaining an open grass gully that climbs to a heather- and bilberry-draped shelf. Move round to the right and up a rock-step – although now on rockier ground, the whereabouts of the path is never in question. A further rock-step and the rocky terrain invites you on.

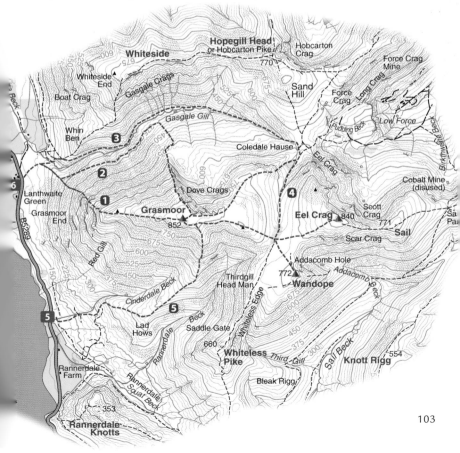

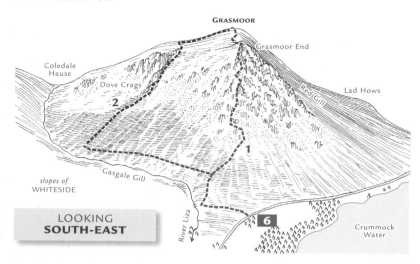

GRASMOOR

Grasmoor End

Coledale
Hause

Dove Crags

Red Gill

Lad Hows

2

1

slopes of
WHITESIDE

Gasgale Gill

River Liza

LOOKING
SOUTH-EAST

6

Crummock
Water

Continue into a longer, tighter gully, this time a bit more demanding on your energies. This brings you onto a rock headland, an inviting place to pause, and thereafter
the easy arête brings further visual excitements across the bilberry-tiered and gullied
face of Grasmoor End. The ridge continues like a step ladder, with sprigs of prostrate juniper clinging to the rocks. The whole experience is enhanced by the view
down on Crummock Water, backed by the dark escarpment of Mellbreak. Driving

Rock headland on the direct ascent from Lanthwaite Green

Sunny aspect on Dove Crags

ever upwards the ridge eases, delivering you onto a tame grassy top adorned with a small cairn – you might divert momentarily right to enjoy the crest-top view down Grasmoor End. The ridge from here is broad, open and interspersed with gravelly scree at an easy angle, and leads up by a second excuse for a cairn to the summit wind-shelter.

Via Dove Crags

700m/2300ft   3.2km/2 miles

Rock-step beside
Dove Crags on Route 2

2 A route for walkers who confront Grasmoor End as they begin Route 1 and buckle. Short of the pale scree, veer left along the narrow trod in the bilberry, passing above a solitary larch tree and contouring into the Gasgale Gill valley on the northern slopes of Grasmoor. The narrow path undulates as it comes across scree and, by a little alcove structure, moves along the heather slopes below the high scree-streaked slopes. As these are passed, watch for the first grass slack up the heather bank. This leads steeply, but surely, to the corrie lip, where you bear right up onto the rising edge of Dove Crags – taken to mean 'the crag frequented by rock doves'. There is one slab section, but nothing to hinder steady progress as all the time walkers revel in hand-some views down the cliffs into the comb. The climb eases, with some marvellous arêtes and gullies to gaze down upon, and duly gains the plateau at the corrie corner. At this point bear SW to reach the summit.

Via Coledale Hause   700m/2300ft   5.6km/3½ miles

3 Cross the open common to the footbridge spanning Liza Beck (the watercourse draining the Gasgale Gill valley) and then you have a choice. Either follow the beck upstream, coping with an entertaining rock-step beside a handsome waterfall, or clamber up the fell, taking the right-hand branch off the ascending path to Whin Benn to avoid the outcrop above the gorge. Continue and meet up with the beckside path running on up the wild valley. There is no doubting the path, although heavy rain has caused some notable landslips. The beck has some lovely cascades near the top. Come onto the level grassy saddle of Coledale Hause. Turn up with the beck and step off the engineered path. After some 200m angling SW onto the rising slope, pick up a path that brings you onto the north-east ridge, and be watchful of the re-entrant edge of the Dove Crags corrie. Head direct to the summit, with little surface evidence of a path in the later stages.

Via the headstream of Gasgale Gill   700m/2300ft   6km/3¾ miles

4 The engineered path up the higher valley (Route 3) leads to a saddle cross-paths with attendant pool. Bear up right after the initial bank, pass a prominent cairn and follow on along the edge parade, revelling in the southerly prospects.

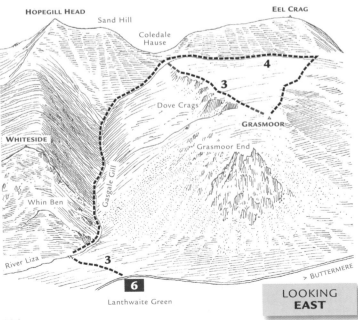

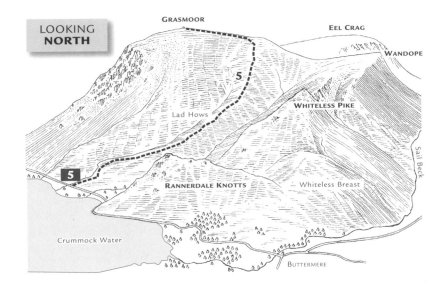

LOOKING **NORTH**

GRASMOOR

EEL CRAG

WANDOPE

WHITELESS PIKE

Lad Hows

Sail Beck

5

RANNERDALE KNOTTS — Whiteless Breast

Crummock Water

BUTTERMERE

ASCENT FROM CINDERDALE COMMON (5)

Via Lad Hows 760m/2495ft 2.8km/1¾ miles

5 A really grand climb, with a good path all the way, eminently better than the purgatory of nearby Red Gill. The path effectively starts by following Cinderdale Beck, but breaks up the bracken bank among rocks as the cascades come close. The path bears onto the ridge SE, climbing onto Lad Hows to weave through the heather. It keeps to the high ground as it moves NE, climbing inexorably northwards and sustaining the steep ascent until the scarp top is reached, where the route follows the edge path left to the summit.

THE SUMMIT

To fellwalkers the summit is an exaltation, a high-ranking viewpoint, and a place to idle after the rigours of the climb and to survey a magical mountain scene. Most attention is drawn to the crowd of fells to the south-east, backed by the Scafells.

Cairn on southern brink of Grasmoor summit

Grasmoor End from near the top of the direct ascent

Heather moor on Lad Hows

SAFE DESCENTS

The Lad Hows ridge leading S and SW from the plateau edge, some 200m east of the summit, may seem steep, but it has few pitfalls in reaching the road by Crummock Water. In a similar league is the path that heads E to the cross-path saddle, from where you head N for Coledale Hause and then either W down the Gasgale Gill valley or E down Coledale for Braithwaite.

RIDGE ROUTES

EEL CRAG	↓135m/445ft	↑122m/400ft	2km/1¼ miles

Head E, descending from the prominent cairn down a bank to the cross-paths. Keep your easterly course on a palpable path that rises and curves NE to the summit OS column.

WANDOPE	↓112m/370ft	↑30m/100ft	1.6km/1 mile

From the cross-paths veer SE through the grass to the summit cairn poised on the tip above Addacomb Hole.

PANORAMA

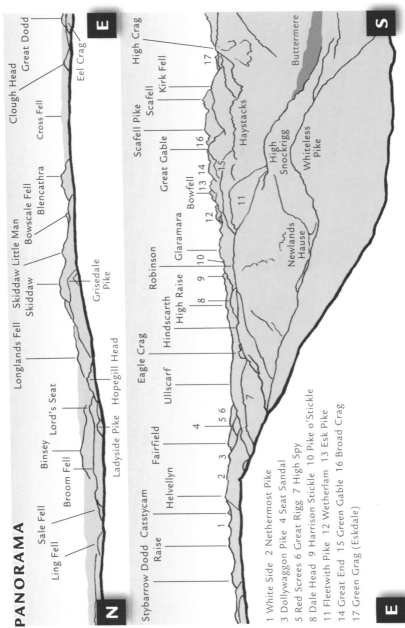

1 White Side 2 Nethermost Pike
3 Dollywaggon Pike 4 Seat Sandal
5 Red Screes 6 Great Rigg 7 High Spy
8 Dale Head 9 Harrison Stickle 10 Pike o'Stickle
11 Fleetwith Pike 12 Wetherlam 13 Esk Pike
14 Great End 15 Green Gable 16 Broad Crag
17 Green Gable (Eskdale)

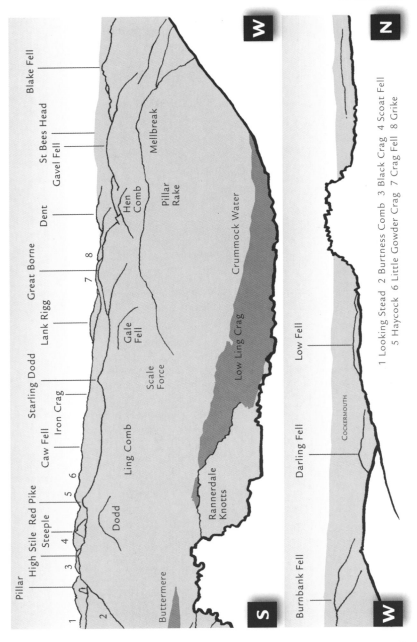

W

N

S

W

Pillar
High Stile Red Pike
Steeple
Caw Fell
Starling Dodd
Iron Crag
Lank Rigg
Great Borne
Dent
Gavel Fell
St Bees Head
Blake Fell

Buttermere
Dodd
Ling Comb
Scale Force
Gale Fell
Rannerdale Knotts
Low Ling Crag
Crummock Water
Pillar Rake
Hen Comb
Mellbreak

Burnbank Fell
Darling Fell
Low Fell
COCKERMOUTH

1 Looking Stead 2 Burtness Comb 3 Black Crag 4 Scoat Fell
5 Haycock 6 Little Gowder Crag 7 Crag Fell 8 Grike

111

11 GRAYSTONES *(456m/1496ft)*

Rising directly east from High Lorton this grassy height offers relaxed walking and charming views. Fellow walkers are at a premium as you trip from top to top, alone – but not lonely. The skylark sings from these pastures and so will you.

The fell forms the eastern extremity of the Lord's Seat ridge, sheltering the lower reaches of Lorton vale. The higher part of the fell has three distinct elements – Kirk Fell, with its wonderful viewpoint cairn, a most rewarding spot from which to survey the Vale of Lorton and the Loweswater Fells, as well as, beyond the head of Sware Gill, two tops on the main mass of the fell, of equal merit as viewpoints, although perhaps not rivals to Kirk Fell.

Routes to the top can be long and engrossing or, like Route 4 from Scawgill Bridge, sweaty and quick! There is no recognised route direct from the village of High Lorton.

Graystones from Swinside

ASCENT FROM HARROT HILL FARM (13)

Via Kirk Fell 366m/1200ft 4.4km/2¾ miles

1 In terms of gradient, probably the easiest ascent in the book. The enchanting back lane linking Hundith Hill Road with Armaside Farm carries little more than farm traffic, the green strip in the middle indicative of the light use, so the rare visitor driving through will sense that they are entering a real Lakeland backwater. Park thoughtfully along the verge, avoiding farm entrances. At Harrot Hill Farm, home of Joyce's Limousin herd, a footpath sign directs off the road through the gated barns. The track leads by further gates. Ignore the branch right to the mast, and instead keep ahead via a gate by young hedges on the rise of Harrot. The open track veers across an open field to become a green-way inclining up beside the line of beech trees to reach a stile.

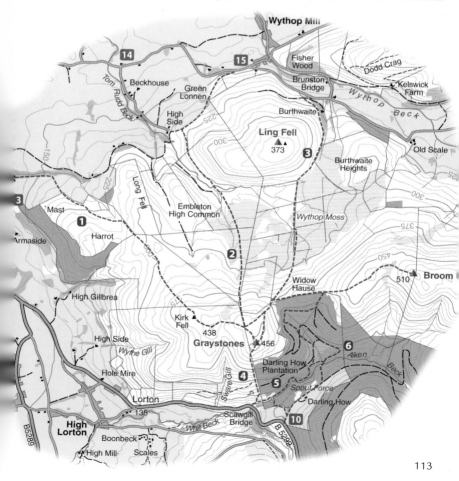

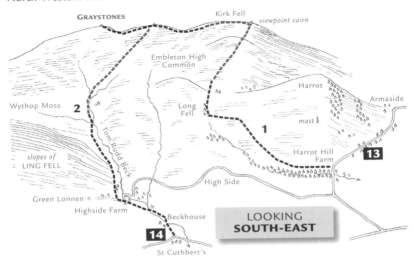

A clear path leads on, and where the gorse ends with a old boundary bank visible, veer half-right, with only sheep paths in the open pasture, aiming to the right of the skyline hill top, where you find a fence-stile. The direct route keeps to the high ground SE, but the viewpoint cairn on the western brink of Kirk Fell (SSE) thoroughly deserves a visit, although there is no path. Walling-stone hollows lie adjacent to this handsome outlook over Lorton Vale. Cross the grassy top of Kirk Fell, marked by two stones. Keep NE to join up with the direct route, which becomes a more evident path as it crosses a depression before climbing onto a subsidiary top, with outcropping. Go through the wall-gap and veer half-right on the path that dips and rises to the summit cairn.

Viewpoint cairn on Kirk Fell

ASCENT FROM EMBLETON CHURCH (14)

Via Tom Rudd Beck   366m/1200ft   4km/2½ miles

Sheep find shade on Embleton High Common

2 St Cuthbert's Church has a generous lay-by parking space, intended for parishioners first and foremost. Follow the private road directly opposite, with the footpath sign 'High Side'. The gated lane leads up by several lovely beckside dwellings to arrive at the barns of Highside Farm, with the white-washed farmhouse up to the left. Pass on through the gate and bear uphill with the green lane, descriptively called Green Lonnen.

This attractive green-way can be considered as an alternative line of approach, starting from the old school at Wythop Mill. There has been some recent scrub clearing done, and the lane is a pleasing interlude as it straddles the north-western slopes of Ling Fell.

Find a footpath signed right at a gate 'Embleton High Common'. The path follows a hedge beneath a bank of gorse to join an open track. Follow this through a gate, and where the track forks keep right to a fording point in Tom Rudd Beck. When the tracks splits in two, take the left-hand option rising directly ahead (SSE). The track quickly dwindles and is lost, but this line avoids the bracken and gives a view of three old larch trees on the far bank, and you advance to a metal gate in an intervening fence. The going is potentially damp through the rushes, with several old drainage trenches to cross, and then you pass the foundations of a wall by the merest trace of an old reservoir before the slope steepens. Ascend the mossy slope to come beside the rising fence/old wall and arrive at a hurdle-gate, which has to be crossed carefully. Keep up the rushy bank alongside the old wall and pass above a massive stone, where two field boundaries converge on the far side, to cross an old wall/fence and complete the climb. The grassy ridge path is met and followed left through a shallow hollow to the summit.

ASCENT FROM WYTHOP MILL (15)

Via Wythop Moss   350m/1150ft   4km/2½ miles

3 Adjacent to the old primary school is a suitable verge on which to park and begin your walk. Follow the road, with its lovely views into the Wythop valley, to a gate

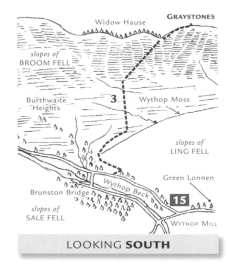

Widow Hause • GRAYSTONES
slopes of BROOM FELL
Burthwaite Heights **3** Wythop Moss
slopes of LING FELL
Green Lonnen
Brunston Bridge • Wythop Beck **15**
slopes of SALE FELL
WYTHOP MILL

LOOKING SOUTH

acutely set to the right before the access drive to Burthwaite Cottage. The open track quickly comes to a fork, where you swing left with the more regular passage. This follows the fence above Burthwaite, with new plantings evidenced. Pass on beyond the red wicket-gate, from where the steep slopes of Ling Fell diminish. Advance to a gate and embark on the long, straight crossing of Wythop Moss. The route is an old sheep drove, with some evidence of walling, and the path slips through a fence-gate close to the mid-point gill ford. At last (and very welcome) the dry banks beneath Widow Hause are reached. Step over a quad track and ascend half-right to the dip in the ridge to the right of the Widow Hause plantation. Clamber over the fence-stile and follow the path up the bank in a SW direction to reach the summit cairn.

ASCENT FROM DARLING HOW (10)

Via Scawgill Bridge   296m/970ft   1.6km/1 mile

4 Descend directly from the first parking area on a path that slips down the bank and over the Aiken Beck footbridge. Turn left, passing through a hand-gate, short of Scawgill Bridge (you can also park at the bridge and connect with the route via the adjacent hand-gate). After some 30m find a path that switches acutely right up through the gorse and loose slate debris to accompany the forest-bounding wall steeply (hence the pigeon-hole steps created by walkers over the course of time). The slope eases, thankfully, above the brief rock-step, and the path slips through the broken wall to reach the summit. How quick was that?

Rock-step in wall met on ascent from Scawgill Bridge

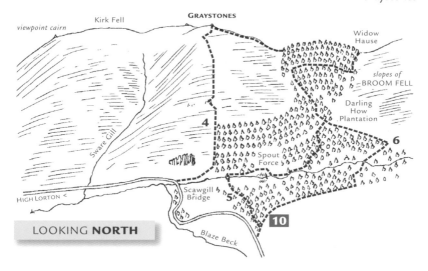

viewpoint cairn
Kirk Fell
GRAYSTONES
Widow
Hause
slopes of
BROOM FELL
Darling
How
Plantation
Sware Gill
4
Spout
Force
6
HIGH LORTON <
Scawgill
Bridge
5
10
Blaze Beck

LOOKING **NORTH**

Via Widow Hause   305m/1000ft   2km/1¼ miles

5 The fell's eastern slopes are planted in conifers, and their forest tracks provide this interesting alternative approach that includes an intimate view over the Spout Force ravine. As with Route 4, descend direct to cross the Aiken Beck footbridge, but this time turn upstream. The embowered path includes steps, and a spur brings the questing walker to a little viewing platform where the picturesque Spout Force is seen to

Spout Force

Broken wall traversing the Graystones summit

advantage. Step back and then continue in confined circumstances tight beside a defending fence above the ravine. The path dips down to the beckside, but does not cross it. Instead keep up through the scrubby stumps and young conifers entwined with the odd bramble and fallen limb to come up into the mature forest and duly join the forest track. Turn right and at the track junction bear left. Ascend with the main track up the re-entrant valley and at the second junction follow on round the curve of the track to encounter a felled area. Skip over the gill and weave up the inner edge of the standing mature trees to reach the ridge top in the eastern depression of Widow Hause. Clamber over the fence/broken wall. Join the ridge path, turn left and follow the forest edge in the pasture over the rise and down to the second depression. Here cross the fence-stile and ascend the bank SW to reach the summit cairn.

6 A simpler start to Route 5. Follow the forest track, passing the barrier below Darling How Farm. Where the track forks, descend left. The track crosses Aiken Beck and rises into the plantation to unite with Route 5 at the second junction.

THE SUMMIT

Two high points vie for top billing, dissected by the broken ridge-crossing wall. The cairn to the east seems to make sense as the summit, although the top on the west side is a better stance. The view from either spot is not stunning, but there is plenty to study on the maritime front, and both the Aiken Beck and Hobcarton valleys are easily visible.

Hopegill Head from Scawgill Bridge ascent

SAFE DESCENTS

The path beside the broken wall leading due S brings you to Scawgill Bridge... in a hurry! A steep grassy path such as this can be troublesome when wet or icy. In other directions the ground is less steep, but the journey much longer. Route 1 to the NW via Kirk Fell is entirely on firm ground, whereas Routes 2 and 3 encounter Wythop Moss.

RIDGE ROUTE

BROOM FELL	↓85m/280ft	↑140m/460ft	2.4km/1½ miles

A simple matter. Descend NNE to a fence-stile and follow the edge of the Darling How Plantation over the Widow Hause ridge. At the end of the forest edge ascend the open bank onto the fell and follow a clear path all the way, curving SW to reach the handsome summit cairn.

PANORAMA

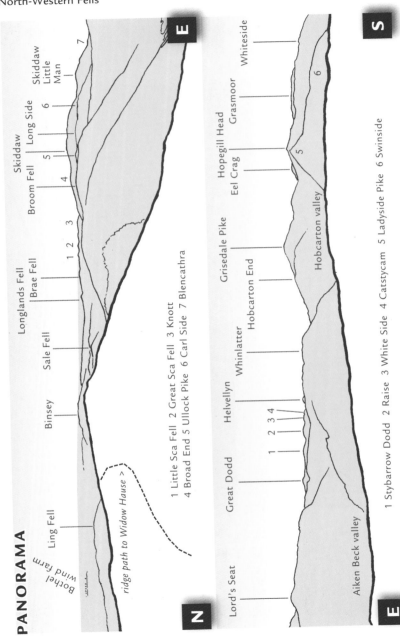

Bothel wind farm

Ling Fell

Binsey

Sale Fell

Longlands Fell
Brae Fell

Broom Fell

Skiddaw

Long Side

Skiddaw Little Man

1 2 3   4   5   6   7

ridge path to Widow House >

1 Little Sca Fell 2 Great Sca Fell 3 Knott
4 Broad End 5 Ullock Pike 6 Carl Side 7 Blencathra

N   E

Lord's Seat

Great Dodd

Helvellyn

Whinlatter
Hobcarton End

Grisedale Pike

Hopegill Head
Eel Crag

Grasmoor

Whiteside

1 2 3 4

1   5   6

Aiken Beck valley

Hobcarton valley

1 Stybarrow Dodd 2 Raise 3 White Side 4 Catstycam 5 Ladyside Pike 6 Swinside

E   S

120

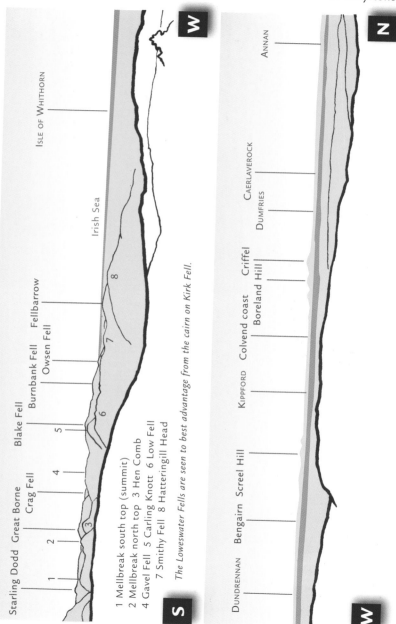

S

Starling Dodd · Great Borne · Blake Fell · Burnbank Fell · Fellbarrow
Crag Fell · Owsen Fell
Isle of Whithorn
Irish Sea

W

1 Mellbreak south top (summit)
2 Mellbreak north top 3 Hen Comb
4 Gavel Fell 5 Carling Knott 6 Low Fell
7 Smithy Fell 8 Hatteringill Head

The Loweswater Fells are seen to best advantage from the cairn on Kirk Fell.

N

Dundrennan · Bengairn · Screel Hill · Kippford · Colvend coast · Criffel · Caerlaverock · Annan
Boreland Hill · Dumfries

W

12 GRISEDALE PIKE *(791m/2595ft)*

A bold individuality marks out this peak. It holds attention from afar, notably the eastern approaches to Keswick, and many resolve to climb it without even knowing its name – its fame does not go before it, you have to find it for yourself. Grisedale itself, 'the valley where swine forage', lies between the culminating north-east and east ridges, its lower depths consumed by conifers. Indeed, Grisedale Pike has a commanding presence over Whinlatter Forest Park, from where many ascents begin. The fell is also the first prominent summit on the perennially popular Coledale Horseshoe. Once this stirring objective is gained, the remainder of the horseshoe somehow falls away to be taken in your stride.

The steepness of the fellsides, especially on the 5km (3 mile) Coledale flank, keeps walkers resolutely on the ridges. However, as a novel exception, independent foot travellers may relish the wander up the Hobcarton valley (Route 7), finding the grassy finish onto the ridge quite painless. In fact the close-up view from the route of Hobcarton Crag, beneath Hopegill Head, ensures consistent entertainment.

The wanderer will also enjoy seeing the Force Crag Mine (Route 1) in a thrilling setting backed by Low Force. Above this, the hanging valley of Pudding Beck gives further encouragement for cautious exploration in this mined landscape, where deposits of copper, zinc, lead and barytes were extracted from the 16th century until final closure in 1991. The only access to the mines is through the present owners, the National Trust, which organises formal mine tours led by experienced guides.

122 ↑ Grisedale Pike from Lord's Seat

ASCENT FROM BRAITHWAITE (22)

Via Coledale Hause   700m/2295ft   7.6km/4¾ miles

1 This route may be a contender for a return route should you wish to limit your walk to this one peak. Pass the barrier and follow the old mine track along the lower slopes of Kinn. As the secured mine buildings of the former Force Crag Mine draw near, Grisedale Pike's southern slopes soar above your head. Veer left at the track fork and, after fording Coledale Beck, set to work on the rough trail leading initially S, which curves W as the higher comb is entered. Excellent repair work has been done on the trail, especially higher up on the new serpentine way to the saddle of Coledale Hause. Turn right (N), taking the right-hand path at the fork and heading NE well above the High Force cliff. The path connects with the ridge path from Hopegill Head and continues up the well-defined ridge to the summit.

Via Kinn   732m/2400ft   4.8km/3 miles

2 The most common starting point, so parking can be an issue. The path quickly steps up the bank on the right, climbing to a fence-stile. From here the grass path eases

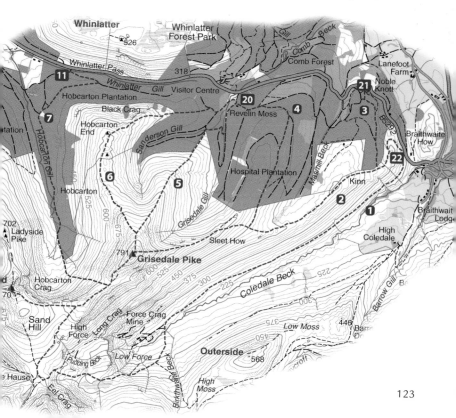

Walking party visit the Force Crag Mine

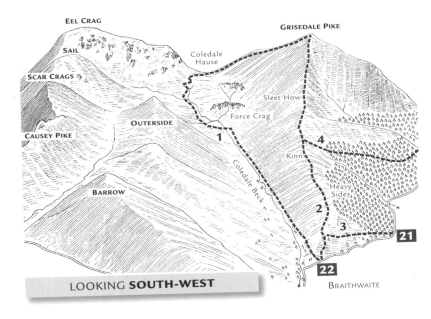

LOOKING **SOUTH-WEST**

through the bracken onto the ridge top of Kinn, a name thought to derive from the Old Norse for 'cheek'. There ensues the most marvellous promenade above the deep trench of Coledale Beck, with Causey Pike and Eel Crag probably the most appealing subjects in the spacious view. As the Masmill Beck valley terminates on the right, the path swings right, naturally pitching up onto the heathery skyline of Sleet How. This narrowing ridge steepens and becomes rougher underfoot on the abrupt climb up the east ridge to the summit.

ASCENT FROM NOBLE KNOTT (21)

Via Kinn   630m/2070ft   5.2km/3¼ miles

The modest car park above Braithwaite, serving the popular path onto the Kinn, quickly fills in fair weather, so it is good to know that there is this alternative start point less than 800m up the Whinlatter road at Noble Knott. **3** Step up from the car park, passing the forestry post with the vertical legend 'Heavy Sides Trail'. The path levels and then declines to meet a path coming up from the left. Now on a gentle rise, meet up with a level forest track. Go left and follow this to the turning bay. A footpath sign 'Grisedale Pike' directs you on through to a stile in the forest-bounding fence. Go forward only a matter of 40m to link with the path rising through the bracken from the Braithwaite car park. From here follow Route 2 to the summit.

ASCENT FROM REVELIN MOSS (20)

Via Hospital Plantation   700m/2295ft   3.2km/2 miles

4 From the car park situated above Comb Bridge strike out by following the forest track leading SE. As this ascends, keep left at the first junction and then right at the fork (forest post 45), rising into cleared space with open views to Skiddaw and the Bassenthwaite valley. At the next junction keep right, as the route continues its gentle rise before levelling out and exiting the forest at a fence-stile after the seat and turning bay. Traverse the fell-slope ahead on a thin sheep trod, avoiding the bracken as best you can, and link up with Route 2 part-way up its climb onto the skyline ridge of Sleet How.

Via the north-east ridge   700m/2295ft   2.8km/1¾ miles

5 Start from the free car park. This is popular with bikers and family walkers who arrive in numbers to explore the tracks and trails of this forest adventure world, so expect a certain jostling for parking space. Pass the barrier and follow the track to find and cross the footbridge spanning Grisedale Gill – the one point at which you have contact with the watercourse from which the fell is named. The path curves round to join a forest track at a wide bend. Here go right, and at the next junction keep left to find a prominent sign directing left off the track for 'Grisedale Pike'. Cross a fence-stile and ascend beside the old wall (evidence of a subsequent metal fence is almost lost). A steady plod ensues up the north-east ridge, which gives a good excuse

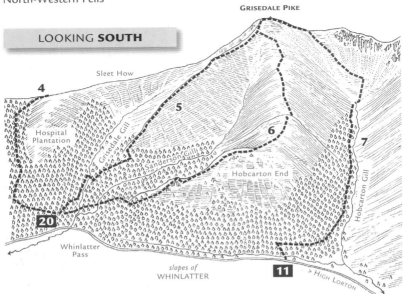

LOOKING **SOUTH**

GRISEDALE PIKE

Sleet How

4

5

6

7

Hospital
Plantation

Grisedale Gill

Sanderson Gills

Hobcarton End

Hobcarton Gill

20

Whinlatter
Pass

slopes of
WHINLATTER

11

> HIGH LORTON

to pause periodically and glance back at an increasingly wonderful view towards Skiddaw. As height is gained and the ridge becomes more pronounced, the view gradually extends over a series of intervening ridges towards the distant Helvellyn range. A 'bench' outcrop might tempt a pause before the final steady rise to the bare rock summit.

Via Hobcarton End   700m/2295ft   3.2km/2 miles

6 Step back down from the car park and follow the open forest track left to cross Comb Beck (the combined waters of Sanderson and Grisedale Gills). The track passes down by their confluence and rises, all beneath a mantle of mature conifers. Where the track makes an exaggerated bend at a junction go round right with the track, and at the next fork bear left into a dark tunnel. A second fork left, with orienteering post, brings you into a unmarked, and ever more forbidding tunnel path, which includes a curious four strides of path pitching. Thankfully, the path ultimately emerges from dense labyrinth onto heather moor. What joy! The path winds handsomely onto the ridge, from where you can revel in the view down into Whinlatter Pass (right) and of Grisedale Pike (left) as it rises gracefully above Sanderson Gill. The path tends to veer left, avoiding the ridge-end cairn, but this should be visited for the lovely view it provides of the Lord's Seat group.

Follow the heather ridge, crossing a fence-stile by cairned knolls – the impressive Hobcarton valley lies to the right, focused upon Ladyside Pike and the craggy peak of Hopegill Head above Hobcarton Crag. The ridge path leads to the next, more considerable step and then dissolves on the final rise to the summit, where you may

Hobcarton End from the fold on Whinlatter

either go straight on, with some scree to cross, or veer half-left to join the old wall on the final section of north-east ridge.

ASCENT FROM HOBCARTON (11)

Via the Hobcarton valley   488m/1600ft   3.6km/2¼ miles

Hobcarton End from the fold on Whinlatter

Grisedale Pike summit looking to Skiddaw

7 This dale-head route deserves to be more commonly appreciated. It is a fabulous experience, the climb on soft mossy grass coming late on, and is remarkably easily accomplished. The star attraction, Hobcarton Crag, is in a wild and lonely setting. From the car park head E past the barrier on the forest track, turning right at the first track junction – this is the main forest track leading into the Hobcarton valley. Where the track ends, at a lightly fenced turning circle, slip down the continuing gravel bank into rushy ground leading to a fence-stile. Cross the stile and follow the fence, keeping it close left, to its termination – in its latter stages it takes the form of a gathering fence for a triangular sheep-gather fence-fold. From the top post angle half-left, climbing across the grassy slope. The scree is easily avoided as a broad mossy grass strip leads on up to the skyline. On meeting the old wall and ridge path go left naturally to the summit.

THE SUMMIT

The bare slate summit, ornamented with the stubby remnants of an old metal fence waiting to trip the unwary, has a modest cairn. A block of tilted slate provides a convenient eastern shelf to rest and take refreshment while shielded from prevailing westerlies. Older OS maps carry mention of a mythical 'shelter', although the only lee is natural and partial. The view holds the gaze on the eastern fell parade across upper Coledale and, more distantly, towards the Helvellyn range. You will notice that Scafell Pike directly overtops Great Gable to the south.

SAFE DESCENTS

If Braithwaite is your destination, and comfort underfoot more important than issues of time, then follow the ridge SW. This crosses the nameless intermediate height, and on the subsequent descent fork left down to Coledale Hause, from where a clear winding trail leads E to ultimately ford Coledale Beck and join the mine track. The east ridge is steep and stony at the top, and a far better choice is the north-east ridge, which brings you easily down to the forest tracks of Whinlatter Forest Park and Comb Bridge.

RIDGE ROUTE

HOPEGILL HEAD	↓116m/380ft	↑95m/310ft	2km/1¼ miles

A broken ridge wall is a sure guide in mist – it descends then climbs over the intermediate nameless hill above the deep wild dalehead of the Hobcarton Gill valley. The path splits at a cairn at the beginning of the descent, so be on the lookout for it and keep right. Hold to the clear ridge path, watching to avoid the perilous edge on the right in foul weather, and climb naturally to the summit, which has all the same bare rock characteristics of Grisedale Pike.

Ridge wall, pummelled by walkers, leading towards Hobcarton Head

PANORAMA

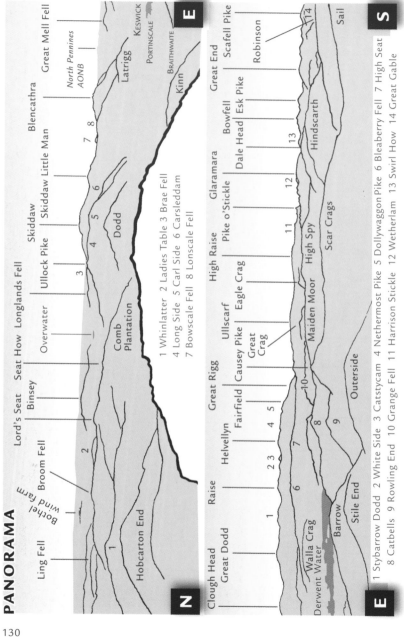

E

Great Mell Fell

Blencathra

Skiddaw

Skiddaw Little Man

Ullock Pike

Longlands Fell

Seat How

Lord's Seat

Binsey

Broom Fell

Ling Fell

KESWICK

PORTINSCALE

BRAITHWAITE

Latrigg

Kinn

North Pennines
AONB

Overwater

Dodd

Comb
Plantation

Hobcarton End

Bothel
Wind Farm

N

1 Whinlatter 2 Ladies Table 3 Brae Fell
4 Long Side 5 Carl Side 6 Carsleddam
7 Bowscale Fell 8 Lonscale Fell

S

Great End

Scafell Pike

Robinson

Bowfell

Dale Head Esk Pike

Glaramara

High Raise

Pike o'Stickle

Ullscarf

Eagle Crag

Great Rigg

Fairfield

Helvellyn

Raise

Great Dodd

Clough Head

Great
Crag

Causey Pike

Maiden Moor

High Spy

Scar Crags

Hindscarth

Sail

Outerside

Stile End

Barrow

Walla Crag

Derwent Water

E

1 Stybarrow Dodd 2 White Side 3 Catstycam 4 Nethermost Pike 5 Dollywaggon Pike 6 Bleaberry Fell 7 High Seat
8 Catbells 9 Rowling End 10 Grange Fell 11 Harrison Stickle 12 Wetherlam 13 Swirl How 14 Great Gable

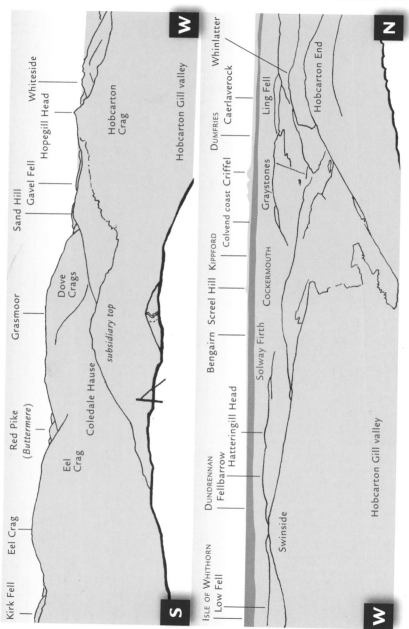

W

Whiteside
Hopegill Head
Sand Hill
Gavel Fell
Grasmoor
Dove Crags
Red Pike (*Buttermere*)
Eel Crag
Coledale Hause
Eel Crag
Kirk Fell
subsidiary top
Hobcarton Crag
Hobcarton Gill valley

S

N

Whinlatter
Caerlaverock
DUMFRIES
Colvend coast Criffel
KIPPFORD
Ling Fell
Graystones
Hobcarton End
Screel Hill
Bengairn
COCKERMOUTH
Solway Firth
Hatteringill Head
Fellbarrow
DUNDRENNAN
ISLE OF WHITHORN
Low Fell
Swinside
Hobcarton Gill valley

W

13 HIGH SPY *(653m/2142ft)*

The attractive fell-name suggests a place of keen-eyed observation, perhaps from a time when Borrowdale folk had to be wary of marauding Border Reivers. Travellers coming into Borrowdale by Lodore will get a solid view of the fell, with Blea Crag a pronounced peak, although the summit is unseen. As a whole the fell forms the craggy, somewhat confused backdrop to the west side of the famous Jaws of Borrowdale (although Castle Crag is, in fact, a dependency of High Spy, it is treated as a separate fell in this guide). This eastern declivity, centred upon Goat Crag, suggests scope for adventurous ascent, and such routes are described here. Only two conventional routes exist – one created by shepherds (White Rake, Route 7) and the other by quarrymen (Rigghead, Route 4) – while the steep scarp sections of Routes 5 and 6 are straight out of the locker of fell adventure, being secure but pathless.

Crags are not restricted to High Spy's eastern face for, with equal impact, the western escarpment is buttressed by Eel Crags, a popular venue for climbers. Generally there is little hint of an easy ascent along the steep ground forming a wall to the upper Newlands valley, although one route has been researched and is described below (Route 2).

The passage of walkers on High Spy is a natural one, as the ridge forms part of the Newlands Horseshoe, an entertaining day that can also include Catbells, Maiden Moor and Hindscarth – a circuit best undertaken clockwise.

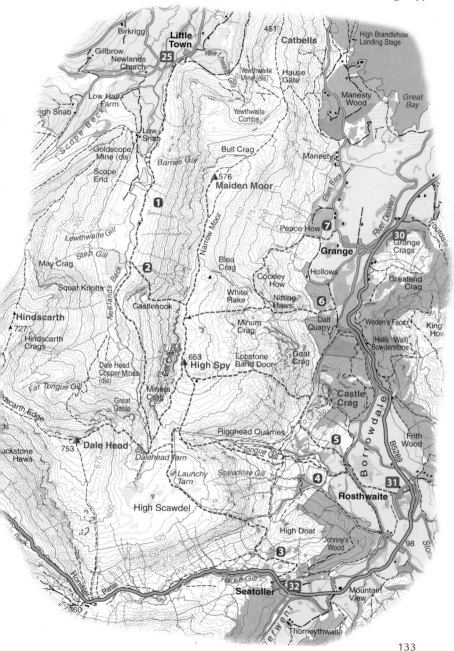

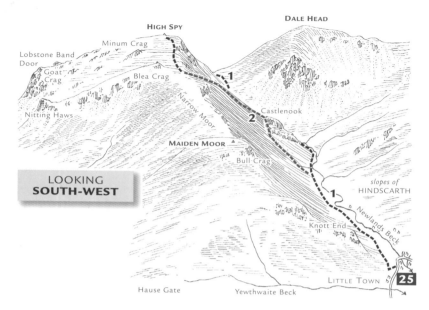

LOOKING
SOUTH-WEST

ASCENT FROM LITTLE TOWN (25 – off map N)

Via Dalehead Tarn   610m/2000ft   6.4km/4 miles

Carlisle Mountaineering Club hut and Castlenook

Squat Knotts on Hindscarth from Castlenook

For all the verdant riches of Borrowdale, the absence of cars makes the upper Newlands valley prime fellwalkers' territory. It is from this aspect that the fell comes into its own, and the valley floor provides a grand environment from which to study the fell's rugged qualities. **1** From the parking spot at Chapel Bridge walk back up the road towards Little Town, stepping over the stile on the right to come onto the open green track, which otherwise starts at the farming community from a gate. This old miners' way leads on along the dale floor. After 1.6km (1 mile) the track passes the Carlisle Mountaineering Club hut and enters the wild upper quarter, passing beneath the stubby spur of Castlenook. The track forks at the approach to a ford. Here bear uphill, climbing steadily over rough ground (you may keep beside the beck and inspect the impressive sequence of cascades, but the higher path is the preferred way). The route leads up beneath Eel Crags to come above the upper ravine, the outflow of Dalehead Tarn. As the fell opens, cut back left up the well-worn ridge path, with its stirring cliff views, and climb, unhurried, to the summit.

Via Castlenook   610m/2000ft   4.8km/3 miles

2 If you are not deterred by rank heather, and fancy an unorthodox climb, the Castlenook ridge presents a unique challenge. Leave the valley track shortly after passing the climbers' club hut and before the wall ends, angling up the wide gill debris, bracken-free, and working your way up the slope to the obvious broad tilted rake at the top of the craggy Castlenook spur. At the base of the rake find a mine adit, a stooped entrance that invites a cautious entry – you cannot but be amazed at the situations in which the miners worked. Continue up the rake. This is pathless terrain, but there are no obstacles to reaching the high shoulder, a fine viewpoint with traces of a bield (shelter), showing that shepherds have been this way too.

Take a break to collect your energies, as from hereon the climb, straight up, is pure heather for some 300m (1000ft). The occasional lateral sheep trod provides brief respites, but generally you are making headway on a spring mattress! You'll be hard pressed to do it without a few breathers, and the outward views never fail to reward the essential pauses. Arrival on the level ridge seems surreal – ridge-strollers cruise by as if along a seafront promenade, while you find a stone seat to restore your sense of equilibrium! The handsome summit cairn lies 400m due south (right).

ASCENT FROM SEATOLLER (32)

Via Scaleclose Gill   616m/2020ft   3.6km/2¼ miles

3 At the head of the hamlet bear right at the first gate opposite the bridge and track approach to a row of cottages on the left. Follow the rough cobbled former toll road by two further gates, or rise up the modern road a further 50m to the first bend and step up through the hand-gate to climb more directly. As the two routes come together, veer up the grass-bank path to a hand-gate and follow on N beside the wall. Watch where three walls come together, set back to the right, and march on a further 60m to find a small boulder on the left of the path. At this point leave the

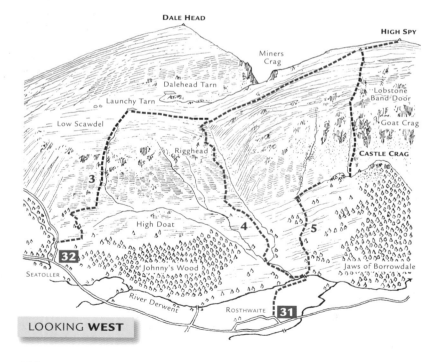

path and climb the steep pathless bank, thus avoiding bracken and outcropping. As the slope eases, find traces of a path leading to a hand-gate in a stout wall. From this point there is little evidence of a path, but the route simply follows the upper course of Scaleclose Gill and subsequent fence. The heather growth on the far side contrasts markedly with the grassy wet waste underfoot. Curve round the sharp fence-corner, bearing right to quickly pass Launchy Tarn – the name possibly means 'long stride'. Head downhill (N), effectively beside the fence, passing the stile from Rigghead Quarries to skirt round the right-hand turn of the fence. Here join company with the path rising from a stile in this fence and climb the open grassy fell. Come over a cairned brow to reach the summit through a hollow.

ASCENT FROM ROSTHWAITE (31)
These two choices, the regular and the rare, both begin by following the lane from Yew Tree Farm to cross New Bridge.

| *Via Rigghead Quarry* | 580m/1900ft | 4km/2½ miles |

4 The regular route switches left to encounter the two-part footbridge beside the stony Derwent, and slips over the stile in the midst to follow the flood-bank beside Scaleclose Beck. The path crosses a plank-bridge, then a stile, and winds up the pasture to a field-gate. It then veers up left, crossing the lateral track to ascend the grassy rigg. Brushing through the bracken, climb to a wall-stile to reach the old quarry building, now a climbing club hut. Pass on beyond it to naturally join the pitched path ascending Tongue Gill. The stepped path climbs through the lower spoil and adits of Rigghead Quarry, above which bear purposefully right to cross the fence-stile at the fence-corner. The fell-path leads on up the open slope, passing over a cairned intermediate top to reach the ultimate cairn.

| *Via Lobstone Band Door* | 620m/2035ft | 3.2km/2 miles |

5 The instinctive fell-explorer will relish this crafty route. From New Bridge turn right, taking the first left-hand gate to enter a pasture. Head up the bank to reach a wall-gate,

Pillow lava at Lobstone Band Door

bear right and step onto the lateral bridle track linking Seatoller with Grange. Pass the fence-fold on the hause and start down the cobbled track – but only so far, as the aim is to gain the old slate cave up to the left. Get to the point approximately level with the right-hand regular path onto Castle Crag. A faint quarryman's way winds up the left-hand

Hindscarth from Miners Crag

ridge to the spoil and ruins in front of the walled slate cave. Having peered tentatively into the walled entrance, embark on the fell-climb proper on the right-hand side, ford the gill and maintain a right-hand bias following the broken slabby edge to reach the rank heather, where the slope eases. The heather continues, but sheep trods give comfort underfoot. A cairn top will attract attention, but the greater interest is Lobstone Band Door up to the right – a narrow gap in the rocky ridge. The fascination comes in the form of the coarse volcanic rock exposures – diverse concentrations of lava that have formed medallion-shaped nodules in a rock cement. Ascend, with a choice of boiler-plated outcrops and grassy passages, to reach the subsidiary summit with its two cairns, then bear NW to reach the tall summit edifice.

ASCENT FROM GRANGE-IN-BORROWDALE (30)

Via Nitting Haws direct   625m/2050ft   4km/2½ miles

6 Follow the Hollows Farm access road leading S from the middle of the community. Where the metalled road swings right, veer left with the track, which provides access to two camping fields. Turn right through the first recessed parking area and follow the path, passing close by the site toilet block to reach a hand-gate in the bounding wall. The steep fellside beckons. Follow the obvious path leading uphill. This ascends the bracken slope towards the rock headland, not towards the tumbling gill. Upon reaching a shelf of ice-smoothed rock, the path is lost as boulders deny scope for a tangible way. Keep up left close by the juniper shrubbery on the large boulder scree – avoid the small scree, which has been made loose by hasty scree-running descending walkers. Keep up by the rock-wall and short shallow gully, with loose

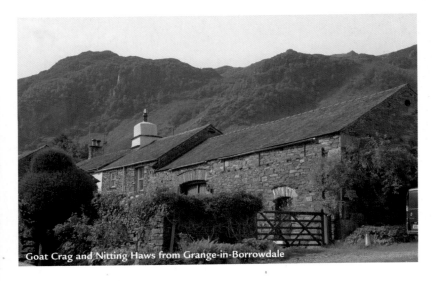

Goat Crag and Nitting Haws from Grange-in-Borrowdale

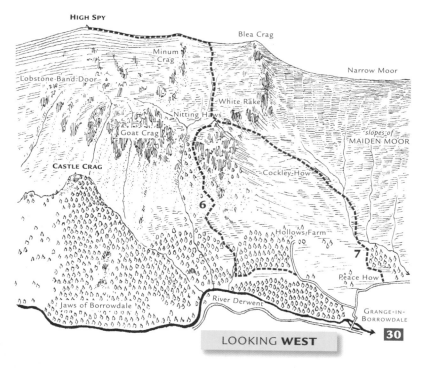

HIGH SPY

Blea Crag

Minum Crag

Narrow Moor

Lobstone Band Door

White Rake

Nitting Haws

slopes of MAIDEN MOOR

Goat Crag

Cockley How

CASTLE CRAG

6

Hollows Farm

7

Peace How

River Derwent

Jaws of Borrowdale

GRANGE-IN-BORROWDALE

LOOKING **WEST**

30

footing, to arrive at the side of Nitting Haws where a simple stroll right brings the rock headland underfoot. The peak is the regular perch of many a resident raven, and a wonderful spot from which the flightless fell-wanderer can survey the setting of Grange and wooded magic of the Jaws of Borrowdale. Wander back from the headland to join the regular path emerging from the undercliff of White Rake (Route 7), and follow this to the summit.

Via Cockley How 595m/1950ft 3.2km/2 miles

7 This canny route that breaks through the rocky armoury of the fell owes its origins to shepherds gathering their flocks from the dale-hidden and remote higher pastures. Follow the road N from the village to find a footpath signed left, just short of Borrowdale Gates Hotel. From the hand-gate a path leads through the scrub and tree-dotted Peace How pasture to a gate, where a path continues by the walled woodland to pass to the left of a wall-reservoir building. Go through the kissing-gate in the fence and embark on the ascending path. This follows up a ridge to ford the gill where it converges, then aims on steeply up the grass slope to crest Cockley How. The top features a split block, an obvious foreground subject for the camera. The path rises and slants half-left, passing beneath the crags of White Rake to come easily onto the higher pasture close behind the Nitting Haws headland. The path curves right and ascends with a gill up the dale-hidden amphitheatre, a great unknown pasture that provides an easy line to the skyline and the regular ridge path, which turns left to the summit.

THE SUMMIT

A stouter, if tumbling version of the Dale Head summit cairn stands impressively back from the scarp edge. At your feet are flakes of splintered rock. The situation is every bit as grand and exciting as Dale Head, with that fell itself and Hindscarth greatly in evidence. Indeed, with high ground sustained for a considerable distance to the north, there are many fine situations to encourage a prolonged admiration of this fell

High Spy summit cairn

North-west from the High Spy summit

Nitting Haws draped in juniper

theatre. To get the best view of Derwent Water, continue N for a little under 1km to the crest of Blea Crag and gaze in wonder.

SAFE DESCENTS

The ridge path can be relied on N for Hause Gate, the depression beyond Maiden Moor, where paths leads left to Little Town and right to Manesty for Grange. A further chink in the armour of the fell lies 400m along this path where, at a cairn, amid a wide grassy space, is the start of a path which leads down to the E. This comes into the secretive amphitheatre behind Nitting Haws, a little peaked spur, and the path bears left short of the peak and follows a shepherds' drove under White Rake Crag and down by the split boulder on Cockley How, direct to Grange.

RIDGE ROUTES

DALE HEAD	↓168m/550ft	↑268m/880ft	2.4km/1½ miles

The well-marked ridge path leads S, well back from the edge, down to a ford of the outflow beck from Dalehead Tarn. The path curves right, left of a large outcrop sheltering an old fold and length of walling, to pass by the tarn's northern shore and embark on the long climb. Modern path-pitching has secured the trail on the tedious plod W to the skyline. Once gained, the slope eases a trifle as you turn SW to reach the stone summit totem.

MAIDEN MOOR	↓86m/280ft	↑9m/30ft	2.4km/1½ miles

The almost level ridge heading N encourages a confident stride, with the scarp-edge views across the gulf of the upper Newlands valley to the fine fells at the heart of the north-western group putting an extra skip in your step. En route make a point of visiting the cairn on the peak of Blea Crag for its exceptional view over the great basin of Derwent Water. This cairn is set to the right of the main thoroughfare, just where it begins a more consistent descent. Come down to an obvious fork, where you take the left-hand path to keep along the western edge to reach the contiguous summit.

PANORAMA

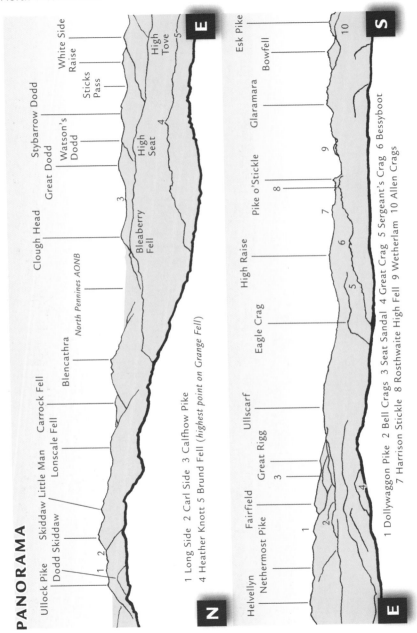

Ullock Pike · Dodd Skiddaw · Skiddaw · Little Man · Lonscale Fell · Carrock Fell · Blencathra · Clough Head · Great Dodd · Stybarrow Dodd · Watson's Dodd · Sticks Pass · White Side · Raise

North Pennines AONB

1 Long Side 2 Carl Side 3 Calfhow Pike
4 Heather Knott 5 Brund Fell (*highest point on Grange Fell*)

Helvellyn · Nethermost Pike · Fairfield · Great Rigg · Ullscarf · Eagle Crag · High Raise · Pike o'Stickle · Glaramara · Bowfell · Esk Pike

1 Dollywaggon Pike 2 Bell Crags 3 Seat Sandal 4 Great Crag 5 Sergeant's Crag 6 Bessyboot
7 Harrison Stickle 8 Rosthwaite High Fell 9 Wetherlam 10 Allen Crags

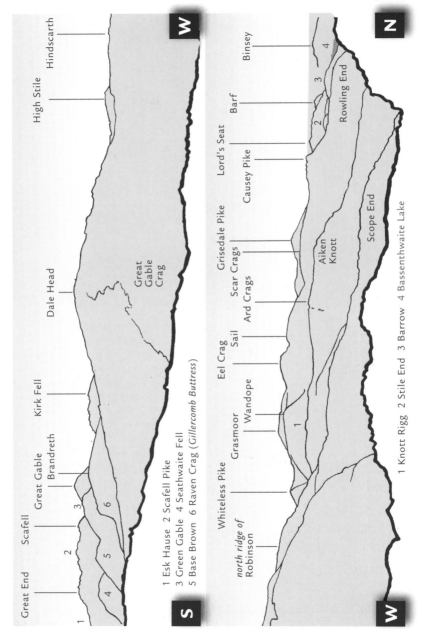

N

Binsey

Barf

Lord's Seat

Causey Pike

Griesdale Pike

Scar Crags

Ard Crags

Eel Crag

Sail

Wandope

Grasmoor

Whiteless Pike

north ridge of
Robinson

4

3

2

Rowling End

Aiken
Knott

Scope End

1

W

1 Knott Rigg 2 Stile End 3 Barrow 4 Bassenthwaite Lake

W

Hindscarth

High Stile

Dale Head

Great
Gable
Crag

Kirk Fell

Brandreth

Great Gable

Scafell

Great End

6

3

5

2

4

1

S

1 Esk Hause 2 Scafell Pike
3 Green Gable 4 Seathwaite Fell
5 Base Brown 6 Raven Crag (*Gillercomb Buttress*)

14 HINDSCARTH *(727m/2385ft)*

I n some respects Hindscarth is a brother to neighbouring Robinson, but nature's sculptor created an altogether different mountain from similar raw materials. A real individualist, this is a fell you will never tire of climbing. Ridge walkers travelling between Dale Head and Robinson often pass by without visiting Hindscarth, oblivious of their inadvertent forfeit. The same cannot be said for walkers viewing the fell from Newlands, from where they are enticed to climb a handsome stand-alone fell.

There is great pleasure to be taken from Hindscarth's lower extended ridge to the north, terminating in Scope End. Heather clad, sharply chiselled, fun in both ascent and descent, here walkers are treated to constant changes in outlook as they trip between one mini-top and the next. The fell-name is a reminder of the former breeding ground of red deer, translating as 'the deer's passage'.

The principal fascination of the fell is the Goldscope Mine, which was opened in 1564 and worked by German miners. They were invited by Elizabeth I to exploit the mineral riches of the Cumberland mountains, winning considerable quantities of copper and lead (no gold) to underpin her personal treasury. All activity ceased at the end of the 19th century because of flooding, and the site is now protected by English Heritage, with no casual underground access.

The fell offers one obvious ridge approach (Route 1), with a roving scrambling alternative high up. To this find a side-door line out of Little Dale (Routes 2 and 3) and a two-pronged climb out of Gatesgarthdale – one a plod (Route 4), the other an engrossing engagement with a heathery gill (Route 5).

146   ↑ Hindscarth and High Crags from Scope End

ASCENT FROM LITTLE TOWN (25)

Via Scope End   610m/2000ft   4km/2½ miles

1 Follow the road to Newlands Church and bear left onto the facing track (private road – permissive path). This duly leads to, and through, the gated yard of Low Snab Farm – an authentic Cumbrian fell farm, alive with hens, where you may partake of a pot of tea, welcome as a late afternoon treat.

Pass through the end-gate and bear up right

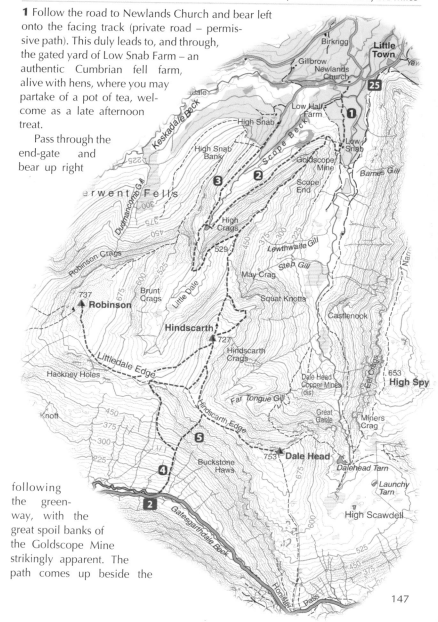

following the greenway, with the great spoil banks of the Goldscope Mine strikingly apparent. The path comes up beside the

Hindscarth and Scope End from Little Town

intake wall. Take a clear path that breaks left, climbing step by step onto the heather ridge of Scope End and passing the upper rift of Pan Holes. The wear of the trail is proof of the understandable popularity of this wonderful ridge. A favourite of many fellwalkers, the route has timeless appeal in its beauty and pedestrian interest. The ridge path keeps below the crest of High Crags, although some walkers may take it in their stride. The main path keeps a bias to the east until the considerable final climb is met and completed without obstacle.

As an intriguing variation you might consider traversing the head of Step Gill to follow the knife edge above Squat Knotts. This has some tempting airy situations, but nothing daunting, the views are excellent and the lack of a path suggests that you will have the fell to yourself, at this point at least.

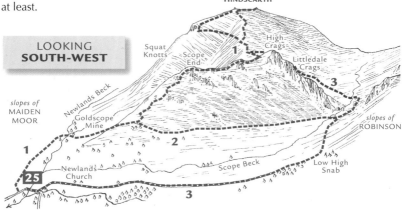

Via the old aqueduct

630m/2065ft   5.2km/3¼ miles

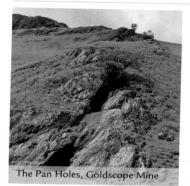

The Pan Holes, Goldscope Mine

2 The green-way (see Route 1) rounds the end of Scope End above the intake wall and runs on to come upon spoil debris, associated with a level and quarried portion of the Goldscope Mine. Make sure you step up here to join the old aqueduct, which contours along the fell-side. Now only a path remains where once there was a wooden trough conveying the water to the mine. As you come close to the reservoir bear up left over the boulders to cross the footbridge and the walled dam, clambering up the bank to join the valley drove to link with Route 3.

Via Little Dale and High Crags

630m/2065ft   5.2km/3¼ miles

3 Follow the no-through road passing Newlands Church. This is a heavenly spot indeed, and the trim little white-washed chapel and old school-room deserve a moment's contemplative admiration. Continue with the tarmac road rising up to High Snab Cottage, passing through the charming environs by gates. The green lane opens at a gate. Keep its company as it gradually becomes more of a drove path and leads above the reservoir. The pool is still deep close to the stepped-wall dam, although the inflowing beck has brought much stony debris. The drove-way mounts

Newlands Church

the bouldery ground, passing below an old holding fold to come above the turbulent ravine. The quartz-streaked boulders are an attractive feature hereabouts.

While you may continue up Little Dale, avoiding the marshy ground to the right, in order to gain Littledale Edge and the ridge path, left, onto the summit, the more pleasing route lies acutely left and leads onto the crest of High Crags. At your convenience ford Littledale Beck and swing up the rising pasture shelf. This area is frequented by contented sheep, but only rarely do they see walkers – hence their somewhat bemused expressions! The top of High Crags can be attained, although you can as easily drift onto the ridge path and take the stern task of climbing the regular way due S to the skyline cairn, and so to the summit.

ASCENT FROM GATESGARTHDALE (2)

Via Littledale Edge   680m/2230ft   2.4km/1½ miles

Any ascent that gets the work done early has to have some merit, and these two variant climbs, directly out of Gatesgarthdale, are no-nonsense routes to the top. **4** Park on the west side of the bridge midway up the dale. Cross the road bridge and ascend left from the solitary boulder. Follow the gill flowing directly into the valley beck at the bridge. A line avoiding the bracken is easy to achieve. Follow the tongue, and two-thirds of the way to the heather slopes find a sheep trod veering left through the bracken to join and accompany the wall/fence. Clamber onto Littledale Edge, bear right with the ridge path and then turn north to make your goal. **5** For greater fun, keep faith with the gill as it tumbles through the steeper heather-clad ground, where the rocks are well broken and encourage a steady climb. The outward scenery is superb towards Fleetwith Pike and the high fells beyond – this is a walk for August when the heather is in full bloom. On reaching the skyline, turn left and follow the ridge path N to the summit.

LOOKING **NORTH**

HINDSCARTH

Littledale Edge

Hindscarth Edge

5

4

Honister Pass >

Gatesgarthdale Beck

2

< BUTTERMERE   slopes of
FLEETWITH PIKE

Summit wind-shelter

THE SUMMIT

The all-important cairn marks a brilliant outlook, although the slightly domed top may tempt the occasional visitor to wander east for a better sense of the upper Newlands valley, taking in the craggy façade of High Spy and Dale Head to best effect. The large cairn situated some 150m north, where the north ridge meets the plateau, transcends the summit as a viewpoint for the Keswick and Skiddaw's company of fells.

SAFE DESCENTS

In poor weather stick resolutely to the north-bound path for Newlands. The quick descent from the north cairn is not fraught with problems. Equally, you can continue along the summit ridge S, finding a short-cutting path curving round from S to SE on the east side of the ridge. The route leads along Hindscarth Edge, continuing via modest outcropping to the tall cairn on Dale Head, from where it heads S for the security of Honister Pass.

RIDGE ROUTE

DALE HEAD	↓70m/230ft	↑96m/315ft	2km/1¼ miles

Begin by following the summit ridge S, finding a short-cutting path on the right-hand side of the ridge that curves round from S to SE along Hindscarth Edge. Rise by modest outcropping (keep an eye open to avoid stumbling on the remnant metal fence posts underfoot) and continue to the reach the unmistakable summit cairn.

ROBINSON	↓155m/510ft	↑165m/540ft	2.4km/1½ miles

Head S, but after some 50m find a path breaking half-right SW off the ridge down the grass slope. This is a short-cut to the head of Little Dale, otherwise known as Littledale Edge. Follow the obvious ridge path by the fence, and on the final rise veer away from the fence NW to the summit.

PANORAMA

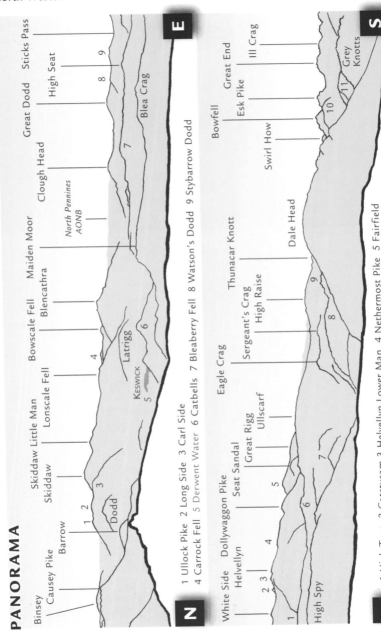

N

Binsey
Causey Pike
Barrow
Skiddaw Little Man
Lonscale Fell
Skiddaw
Bowscale Fell
Blencathra
Maiden Moor
Clough Head
Great Dodd
High Seat
Sticks Pass
Dodd
Latrigg
North Pennines AONB
Blea Crag
KESWICK

E

1 Ullock Pike 2 Long Side 3 Carl Side
4 Carrock Fell 5 Derwent Water 6 Catbells 7 Bleaberry Fell 8 Watson's Dodd 9 Stybarrow Dodd

E

White Side
Helvellyn
Dollywaggon Pike
Seat Sandal
Great Rigg
Ullscarf
Eagle Crag
Sergeant's Crag
High Raise
Thunacar Knott
Dale Head
Bowfell
Esk Pike
Great End
Ill Crag
Swirl How
Grey Knotts
High Spy

S

1 High Tove 2 Catstycam 3 Helvellyn Lower Man 4 Nethermost Pike 5 Fairfield
6 Bell Crags 7 High Crag 8 Bessyboot 9 Rosthwaite High Fell 10 Allen Crags 11 Base Brown

152

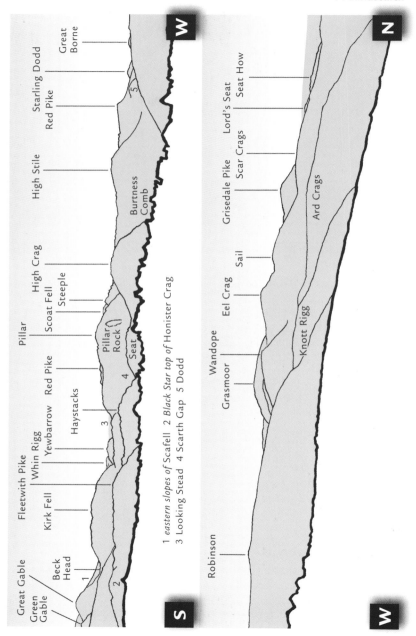

S · **W**

Great Gable · Green Gable · Beck Head · Kirk Fell · Fleetwith Pike · Whin Rigg · Yewbarrow · Red Pike · Haystacks · Pillar · Scoat Fell · Steeple · High Crag · High Stile · Red Pike · Starling Dodd · Great Borne

Pillar Rock · Seat · Burtness Comb

1 · 2 · 3 · 4 · 5

1 *eastern slopes* of Scafell 2 *Black Star* top of Honister Crag
3 Looking Stead 4 Scarth Gap 5 Dodd

N · **W**

Robinson · Grasmoor · Wandope · Eel Crag · Sail · Grisedale Pike · Scar Crags · Lord's Seat · Seat How

Knott Rigg · Ard Crags

15 HOPEGILL HEAD *(770m/2526ft)*

A high-running ridge leads east from Whiteside and angles up after 1.6km (1 mile) to form the shapely peak of Hopegill Head. Thereafter, this high divide curves around the head of the great U-shaped glacial hollow of Hobcarton to peak again, after a similar distance, on Grisedale Pike, from where the main ridge steps down, reaching out towards Braithwaite. Two long deep valleys mirror the ridge to the south, Gasgale Gill and Coledale, giving one high col connection with the main mass of the group on Coledale Hause. Either side of the considerable trench of Hobcarton Gill both major fells have steep valleys splaying to the north-east and north-west. The latter, the dominion of Hopegill Head, is the Hope Gill valley.

For all Grisedale Pike's dominance from Keswick perspectives, Hopegill Head equals it as a classy accomplice, beloved of Cockermouth folk. Two elements mark the fell out – a most stupendous crag, Hobcarton, where rare alpine plant species survive beyond the nibbling teeth of Herdwick and careless tread of walkers, and the northern approach over Ladyside Pike, an airy fellwalking adventure via the notch and slabs at the brink of the great crag.

Routes to the top include the 'peak at the head of the valley' Hope Gill approach itself (Route 2) and the thoroughly rewarding Ladyside Pike ridge, which offers three lines (Routes 3–5) onto the heather-clad Swinside ridge. There are two further natural valley routes up Liza Beck (Gasgale Gill) (Route 1) and Coledale Beck (Route 6), with both routes coming together on the broad saddle of Coledale Hause to head north over Sand Hill.

↑ Hopegill Head from Grisedale Pike

ASCENT FROM LANTHWAITE GREEN (6)

Via Gasgale Gill 722m/2370ft 4.8km/3 miles

1 An engaging walk, although invariably used as a descent from the Whiteside climb and connecting ridge walk. Intriguingly, while the valley is known as Gasgale Gill, the watercourse bears the name Liza Beck.

Traverse the common in an easterly direction to cross the footbridge over Liza Beck. You may turn immediately upstream, although on rounding the corner there is an awkward rock-step beside a waterfall. To avoid this, climb the bank to follow an obvious lateral path right above the lower rock mass. This negotiates a stepped rock-corner too, but of minor significance under normal conditions. The

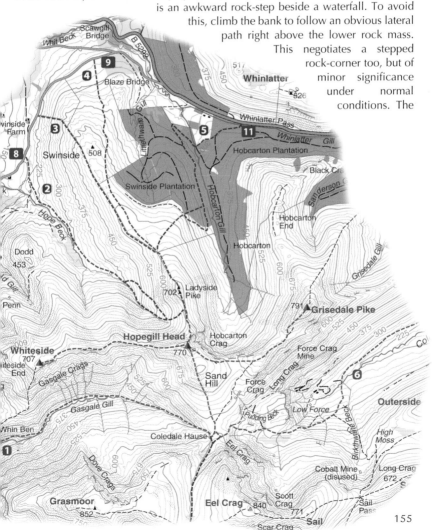

Ladyside Pike and the Hope Gill Valley

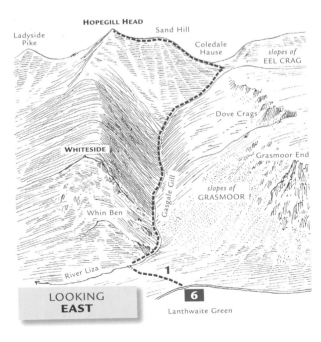

HOPEGILL HEAD

Ladyside
Pike

Sand Hill

Coledale
Hause

slopes of
EEL CRAG

Dove Crags

WHITESIDE

Grasmoor End

Gasgale Gill

slopes of
GRASMOOR

Whin Ben

River Liza

1

LOOKING
EAST

6

Lanthwaite Green

two paths come together and head easily upstream, with views of at least two considerable slumped sections of bank across the beck. Overhead the walker is drawn to gaze at the series of irregular gullies spilling from the Whiteside ridge. As height is gained, with evidence of flood damage to the path, enjoy the succession of small waterslides en route to the dale-head level pasture of Coledale Hause. At which point join the obvious path which leads half-left to join the main spinal ridge path leading N, climbing the loose slope of Sand Hill. From the bare top the going eases to the summit – although be watchful of the profound edge of Hobcarton Crag.

ASCENT FROM HOPEBECK (8) AND SWINSIDE (9)

Three northern approaches can be entertained (Routes 2–4). Commonly ascents begin from the parking space on the fell-road linking Hopebeck with Blaze Bridge GR169242. However, a start can be made from the village of High Lorton by following the narrow lane signed 'Boonbeck and Scales' and either keeping to the road or (best of all) following the footpath running between Scales and High Swinside Farms. Throughout its course the gated path runs as a beautiful green lane to join the open section of the fell-road.

Via Hope Gill   712m/2335ft   4km/2½ miles

2 First in line, and probably least considered, is the Hope Gill valley itself, from which the fell derives its name. A green drove-way leads up the valley keeping to the northern bank of the beck. After the second sheepfold there are two options. You can keep company with the tumbling gill – although the scope for a path diminishes, especially at a rocky nook as height is gained – and shortly after bear away from

Summit of Hopegill Head

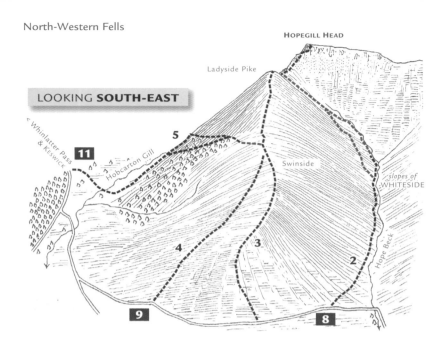

LOOKING **SOUTH-EAST**

HOPEGILL HEAD

Ladyside Pike

< Whinlatter Pass & Keswick

11

Hobcarton Gill

Swinside

slopes of WHITESIDE

Hope Beck

5

4

3

2

9

8

the progressively stony and dry gill, as the heather is lost, to gain the ridge at the dip between Ladyside Pike and the pointed ridge-top outcrop. Alternatively (and the author must confess this a path discovered in descent) some 30m after a land-slipped

Hobcarton Crag rising to the summit from The Notch

Slabs of Skiddaw slate on the north ridge adjacent to The Notch

patch, upstream of the sheepfold, step up onto the heather and find a path that angles up and across the dense heather, becoming more apparent with each stride. Climb out of the heather and make up the pathless slope – in harmony with the equally pathless gill-side variant – to reach the skyline left of the peaked outcrop. The route ultimately crosses over the broken ridge wall and turns right following the ridge path. Skirt round to the west side of the sharp knuckle of rock to come up to the most exciting part of the climb, the slabs and notch, from where there is the most amazing view down Hobcarton Crag. A rock groove provides the obvious and secure scramble to the top.

Via Swinside   715m/2345ft   4.4km/2¾ miles

3 The route of highest elation follows the road N to the road-gate and smartly steps up the bank, right, climbing beside the rising wall onto the ridge top of Swinside. Advance beside the wall upon grass a pace or two from the fringing heather. Follow the ridge wall, with the lure of Ladyside Pike dead ahead. After a rise the wall is defended by fencing, and where the dilapidated wall falters, at a fence junction (and hand-gate on the far side), begin the ascent proper of Ladyside Pike – an elegant name for an elegant little peak. Follow the broken wall up to the twin-cairned summit. The broken wall continues, with the path holding a left-hand bias, through the narrow saddle leading to an awkward arête. Keep to the right, advancing over the rock-steps to mount to the notch at the brink of Hobcarton Crag. Be watchful, but do make the effort to peer over the edge to the extent you feel able – it's a brilliant spot. Follow the groove in the slabs slanting half-right direct to the summit.

Direct   690m/2270ft   4km/2½ miles

4 The most comfortable approach to the Swinside ridge. This begins from the grassy verges on the enclosed section of road between High Swinside and Blaze Bridge at GR176253. Find a suitable area to park your car, east of the new Cartner memorial seat. Go through the gate and follow the open track up to a gate and through the sheep-handling pens onto an obvious green track which continues due S, climbing into the heather banks. The track continues consistently to a hand-gate, after which it dwindles to a conventional path. This leads on to the ridge and arrives at the gate, uniting with Route 3 where the broken wall and fence converge. (This spot can also be attained by following Route 5.) Follow Route 3 to the summit.

ASCENT FROM WHINLATTER GILL (11)

Via Swinside Plantation   716m/2350ft   4km/2½ miles

5 Follow the forest track W, keeping right at the first open track junction. Descend to cross the broad Hobcarton Bridge. The track swings right, then makes a sharp hairpin left at the forest edge, heading S. Land-slip threatens the track at one point. Advance unwavering to a gate at the end of Swinside Plantation. Keep forward through the rushy pasture on a green-way to cross a stile beside a gate in a downward-trending fence. Pass the old sheepfold filled with rushes and bear up smartly right to join a nar-row path that runs up the steep slope in harmony with the fence to cross the hurdle at the top. The adjacent stile at the top edge of the plantation can also be reached by a more direct, and therefore steeper, route off the forest track just before the gate at the edge of the conifers. The continuing path progressively dissolves in the moor grass and rises onto the ridge slanting south-west to reach the hand-gate in the fence-corner where Routes 3 and 4 coincide.

ASCENT FROM BRAITHWAITE (22 – off map NE)

Via Coledale Hause   730m/2395ft   6.8km/4¼ miles

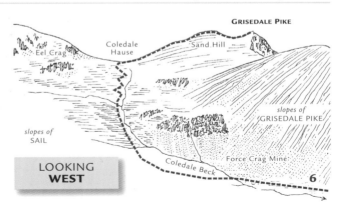

6 Follow the old mine track up Coledale. Where the track forks, short of the derelict buildings associated with the old Force Crag Mine, veer down left to ford Coledale Beck. Stick firmly to the rough trail, leading W and climbing above the side-ravine with a fine view of the impressive Low Force. Higher up, the Fix the Fells team have secured the path with a tidy serpentine section up the steeper slope that comes under Eel Crag to reach Coledale Hause. Bear right (N), following the strong path up the scree bank onto and over Sand Hill, and climb irresistibly to the summit.

THE SUMMIT

Rarely does a cairn survive on this raw rock top, and the splintered nature of the available stones precludes such manifestations of man's passing whim. The summit is sufficient exultation in itself. It is the ultimate point of both the Hopegill valley and Hobcarton Crag – a quite thrilling place to stand, if the breeze allows. To the west lies the inviting ridge to Whiteside, and to the east Grisedale Pike stands aloof beyond a craggy curved cirque edge.

SAFE DESCENTS

The worst option in poor weather is N. Route 4 over Ladyside Pike is fine as long as you take cautious steps at the outset – the grooved bare rock slope can be dicey when wet. If conditions are dodgy then you are better heading S over Sand Hill and down to Coledale Hause, with secure dale paths leading E to Braithwaite and W to Lanthwaite Green.

Hobcarton Crag

Ladyside Pike

The summit of Hopegill Head looking to Whiteside

RIDGE ROUTES

GRISEDALE PIKE	↓95m/310ft	↑116m/380ft	2km/1¼ miles

Leave the summit moving from SE to E – either hugging the edge or taking the more regular set-back path. Ahead rises a nameless knoll – might it merit the name Hobcarton Head? On the rise, a path from Coledale Hause joins from the right. Cross the top, now with evidence of an remnant ridge wall underfoot – weathering and walkers' boots have dealt it a near mortal blow. The ridge mounts easily NE to the summit.

WHITESIDE	↓108m/355ft	↑45m/150ft	2km/1¼ miles

A consistent pleasure from start to finish. The popular path heads W upon a sharp edge, declining, with some rocky sections, to step onto a long heather crest. En route it strides over the 719m (2359ft) east top of Whiteside (higher ground than the acknowledged summit) to land upon the summit. All the way the views down the serried gullies into the Gasgale Gill ravine and across to Dove Crags on Grasmoor are tremendous.

PANORAMA

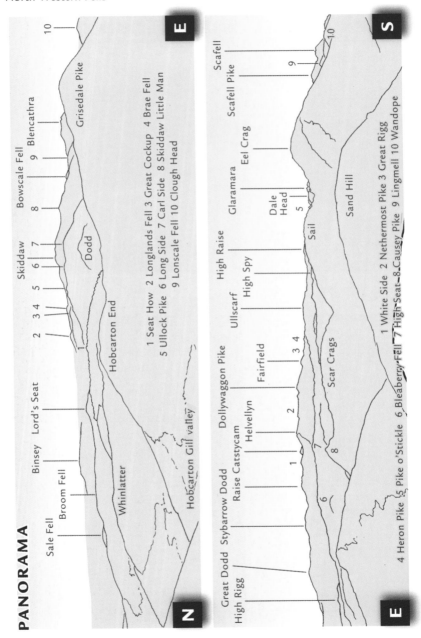

Top panorama (N to E):

Sale Fell — Broom Fell — Binsey — Lord's Seat — Whinlatter — Hobcarton End — Hobcarton Gill valley — Grisedale Pike — Bowscale Fell — Blencathra — Skiddaw — Dodd

1 Seat How 2 Longlands Fell 3 Great Cockup 4 Brae Fell
5 Ullock Pike 6 Long Side 7 Carl Side 8 Skiddaw Little Man
9 Lonscale Fell 10 Clough Head

Bottom panorama (E to S):

High Rigg — Great Dodd — Stybarrow Dodd — Raise — Catstycam — Helvellyn — Dollywaggon Pike — Fairfield — Ullscarf — High Spy — High Raise — Scar Crags — Sail — Dale Head — Glaramara — Eel Crag — Scafell Pike — Scafell — Sand Hill

1 White Side 2 Nethermost Pike 3 Great Rigg
4 Heron Pike 5 Pike o'Stickle 6 Bleaberry Fell 7 High Seat 8 Causey Pike 9 Lingmell 10 Wandope

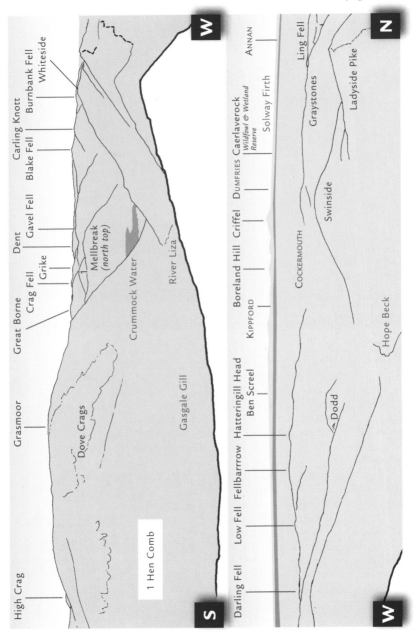

W

Whiteside
Burnbank Fell
Carling Knott
Blake Fell
Gavel Fell
Dent
Grike
Crag Fell
Great Borne
Mellbreak
(north top)
Crummock Water
River Liza
Grasmoor
Dove Crags
Gasgale Gill
High Crag

1 Hen Comb

S

N

Annan
Ling Fell
Caerlaverock
Wildfowl & Wetland Reserve
Solway Firth
Ladyside Pike
Dumfries
Criffel
Boreland Hill
Kippford
Graystones
Swinside
Cockermouth
Hope Beck
Hatteringill Head
Ben Screel
Fellbarrow
Low Fell
Dodd
Darling Fell

W

16 KNOTT RIGG *(556m/1824ft)*

If there can be such a thing, this is the perfect 'nursery' fell (although all fells have the attributes of mountains when it comes to weather, steep slopes and the need for due care and attention). Motorists arrive at Newlands Hause, find ample scope to ease their cars onto the wide verge, and, having gazed amazed at Moss Force, ponder a leg-stretching walk. Knott Rigg beckons to the north, an unthreatening grassy slope rising to a pronounced peak – how can you resist? All-comers, young and old, turn their attention with a skip to the climb, releasing pent-up energies in sampling a real fell walk.

The simplicity of the fell's conformation, akin to the upturned hull of a long ship, combined with its situation, as understudy to greater fells, makes this a worthy objective. Only from Sail Beck valley aspects is it possible to significantly comprehend the knott-and-rigg qualities of the fell, especially during the low-gear grind up the narrow mountain road to the hause from Buttermere. Three lines of ascent are available – from Buttermere (Route 1), the route direct from the hause (Route 2) and, most exciting of all, Keskadale Edge (Route 3), climbing from the farm of that name to the north-east.

ASCENT FROM BUTTERMERE (3)

Via Sail Beck   458m/1500ft   3.6m/2¼ miles

1 For all the fell's convenience from Newlands Hause, many walkers will set their sights on including the fell-top in a greater expedition. The obvious endeavour is to add Ard Crags, before stepping down to the head of Sail Beck and climbing via Sail Pass for a handsome traverse west over Eel Crag. Leave the open road quickly after the last barn, and as the fence bears down find a path, little more than a sheep trod, running just below the road, well above Sail Beck. The path is used by ewes on a regular basis, so the bracken is well pegged back.

After fording Swinside Gill the climb proper begins. Remarkably, the path mounts a broad green carpet, and this time the bracken has been fended off by human not cloven feet. The path is less apparent higher up, but that is not an issue as the way to go is never in doubt as it merges with the direct path from the hause. Follow the ridge, crossing some marshy ground, to claim your mountain.

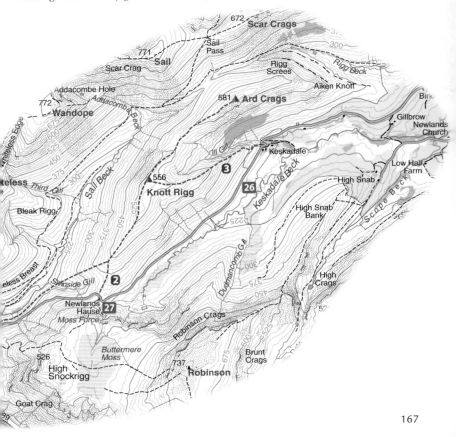

ASCENT FROM NEWLANDS HAUSE (27)

Via the south ridge 230m/755ft 1.6km/1 mile

2 Begin as you will – the several paths that start out come together as the slope steepens. Some

ARD CRAGS

KNOTT RIGG

LOOKING NORTH-EAST

slopes of
WHITELESS
PIKE

3

2 **27**

26

slopes of
ROBINSON

Newlands
Hause

Moss
Force

Keskadale
Beck

BUTTERMERE

3

Knott Rigg from High Snockrigg

pitching and path repair has been necessary (to be respected). Come over the top-knot and shake off the immediate disappointment that this is not the summit. There is further to go and, despite the small area of marsh, it is a good walk to the cairn on the summit.

ASCENT FROM KESKADALE (26)

Via Keskadale Edge 330m/1080ft 2km/1¼ miles

3 There is suitable parking along the verge. Walk NE to Keskadale Farm. Descend the road from the farmhouse down from the first left-hand hairpin. Find traces of a path stepping off the road on the left, clamber up the untidy slope, pass the noisy kennels and cross a fence-stile. The path rises beside a fence to cross a second fence-stile amid bracken.

The path is sufficiently well used to encourage you forward, ascending the steep ridge of Keskadale Edge with a fence near right. There are some splendid views into the secretive depths of Ill Gill, no longer available for casual entry as it is a sanctuary, protected as part of the Keskadale Oakwood National Nature Reserve. The ridge

The summit, looking to Ard Crags

has no physical obstacles. Higher up the scenery is superb, greatly enhanced by the heather upholstery. Pass on by two fenced bogs to reach the summit.

THE SUMMIT

No fanfares or great edifice greet walkers, just a modest pile of stones set on a grassy pillow, befitting a modest fell-top. The view is also modest by comparison with that from its loftier neighbours. But the intimacy of the view into the Newlands valley and east to the Helvellyn range, and the sense of scale engendered by the surround of great fell ridges, is more than ample compensation.

SAFE DESCENTS

As you may surmise, the danger is of a lower order than for many fells in this guide. But in mist you should keep to ridges, rather than slope off aimlessly, avoiding especially a descent to the N or W into the Sail Beck valley, where the declivity is abrupt. The best route is S to Newlands Hause, while E and NE down Keskadale Edge is steep, but the path should never be in doubt.

RIDGE ROUTE

ARD CRAGS	↓50m/165ft	↑75m/245ft	1.6km/1 mile

Head NE, with the ground gently falling to a depression, still on a comparatively narrow ridge. The path is all too apparent on the steady rise to the summit, with heather the attractive accompaniment.

PANORAMA

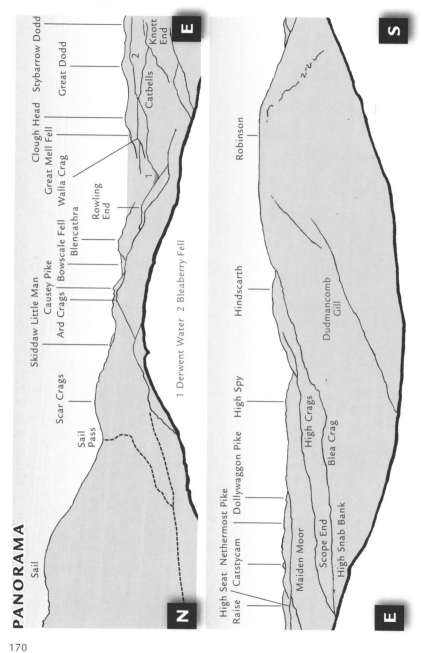

Sail

Scar Crags

Sail Pass

Skiddaw Little Man

Causey Pike

Ard Crags

Bowscale Fell

Blencathra

Rowling End

Clough Head

Great Mell Fell

Walla Crag

Stybarrow Dodd

Great Dodd

Catbells

Knott End

E

N

1 Derwent Water 2 Bleaberry Fell

High Seat

Raise

Catstycam

Nethermost Pike

Dollywaggon Pike

High Spy

Maiden Moor

Scope End

High Snab Bank

High Crags

Blea Crag

Dudmancomb Gill

Robinson

Hindscarth

S

E

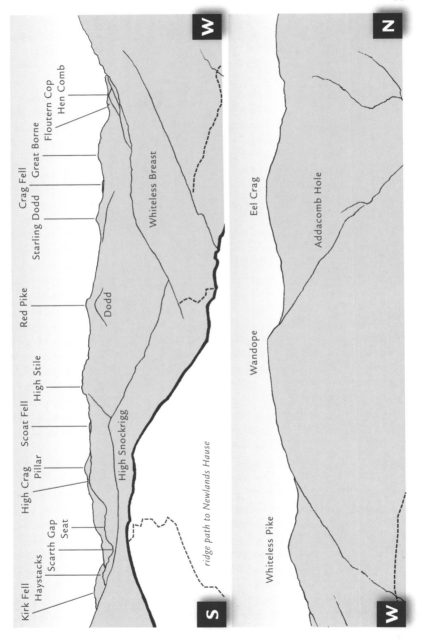

W

Hen Comb
Floutern Cop
Great Borne
Crag Fell
Starling Dodd
Red Pike
High Stile
Scoat Fell
Pillar
High Crag
Scarth Gap
Seat
Haystacks
Kirk Fell

Whiteless Breast

Dodd

High Snockrigg

ridge path to Newlands Hause

S

N

Eel Crag

Wandope

Addacomb Hole

Whiteless Pike

W

171

17 LING FELL *(373m/1224ft)*

T he outlying situation, a little distant from a main road, and apparent lack of features of interest may lead many a walker to turn a blind eye to dear little Ling. However, on a sunny day you will love to be on this fell, which can be climbed or girdled in an almost perfect circle. The heather (the *ling* of the fell-name) shrouds much of this round, contoured, upturned pudding of a hill, and in times past, when the 'glorious twelfth' rolled up, the stock of grouse would have been shocked by the stealthy sportsmen. The tumbled shooting butts remain as a testimony to the sport, but now the guns are silent, and rarely are the birds' startled cries of 'get back' heard, for they can fly wild and free.

ASCENT FROM WYTHOP MILL (15)

Via the Corpse Road   330m/1080ft   2.4km/1½ miles

1 A lovely way that offers a sense of history. The Wythop valley is a world apart, and this walk makes a tentative entry into it to view it from above. Start from the verge before the old school just at the junction above the hamlet of Wythop Mill. Follow the minor road, enjoying the glimpses it gives into the sylvan valley. Watch for the track gate acutely right, short of the Burthwaite access gate. Go through and follow the open track, keeping forward (W) onto the green-way as the more regularly worn track sweeps left.

The green track is known as the Corpse Road, and must formerly have linked the little church in Chapel Wood to the east with the consecrated ground at St Cuthbert's,

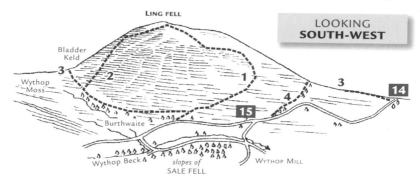

LING FELL

LOOKING **SOUTH-WEST**

Bladder Keld

3

Wythop Moss

2

1

3

14

4

15

Burthwaite

Wythop Beck *slopes of* SALE FELL WYTHOP MILL

Embleton, via Green Lonnen (although the connecting track is lost where the track enters 'improved' pasture, beyond the heathered portion of the fell). Watch to take the left-hand turn uphill from the green-way to the rougher vehicle track in the heather. This climbs easily and quickly becomes in a turf trail. It curves left into a shallow hollow, where there is a line of tumbled stone shooting butts, lurking beneath a northern

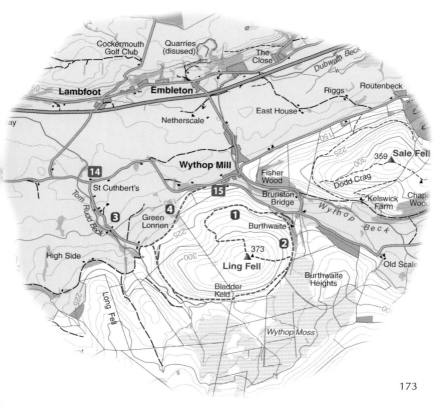

Heather-flanked track leading up by the old grouse butts on the north side of Ling Fell

brow. Coming to a fork bear right, and after 150m step up the path, right, again, thereby venturing to the OS column on the summit.

Via the western fellside   330m/1080ft   2km/1¼ miles

2 A second popularly followed line of ascent can be combined with Route 1 to provide a compact fell-round, suitable to be walked in either direction. From the point of entry onto the fell, stride only to where the tracks fork, and this time swing sharp left with the more evidently worn track, duly heading SE, then S, beside the fell-bounding fence. To the left see the homestead of Burthwaite sheltering in open native woodland. New deciduous plantings show that this wood has a positive future in the dell upstream. Watch for a path leaving the track breaking up the bank to the right – this is some 60m short of a small red wicket-gate in the adjacent fence. This path climbs the western fellside through the bracken, then heather, irresistibly aiming to the summit.

ASCENT FROM EMBLETON (14)

Via Tom Rudd Beck   260m/850ft   3.6km/2¼ miles

3 A pleasing little round-trip can be enjoyed by starting from the lay-by at St Cuthbert's Church. Walk across the road and follow the confined metalled lane due S. This passes some lovely secluded dwellings as it rises beside Tom Rudd Beck. At High Side Farm go through the gate and bear up the lane, Green Lonnen. But at the footpath sign 'Embleton High Common' go through the field-gate and follow the hedge beside burnt gorse to join a track. This leads on by a wall-gate into the Tom Rudd Beck valley. When the track forks, keep left, heading straight on and passing a few large quartz boulders, with quartz evidenced in the small outcrops above. The green track leads to a hurdle-gate. Cross carefully and bear up left, stepping up by several sheep alcoves (scraped into the bank) and adjacent to a little non-event of a spring with the distinctive name, Bladder Keld – meaning 'the gushing bladder'. At this point find a sheep path contouring right through the heather. This leads via a small patch of bracken onto a broad, low-lying grassy plain and joins the track passing the red wicket gate (see Route 2). Walkers can obviously take the opportunity to climb the fell by Route 2 or continue down to the road below Burthwaite. There, turn left to come to the road junction above Wythop Mill and left again, looking for the start of Green Lonnen. **4** A bridleway sign guides onto the quiet byway that rises modestly, providing lovely views over the Embleton valley, before it declines and meets up with the outward leg.

THE SUMMIT

A fine stone-built OS column stands amid a fragmented bed of heather. A small cairn some 30m to the north represents the walkers' contribution to the summit architecture. The best view is of Sale Fell and the Wythop valley backed by the Skiddaw massif. This is found a little way down the grassy slope to the north, just before it falls into the denser heather. Elsewhere from the summit the view is expansive, if not thrilling. The author found the summit animated with flying ants on one of his visits. However, this phenomenon is not exclusive to Ling Fell and should not dissuade you from paying this grand little fell-top an appreciative visit.

OS column on Ling Fell

PANORAMA

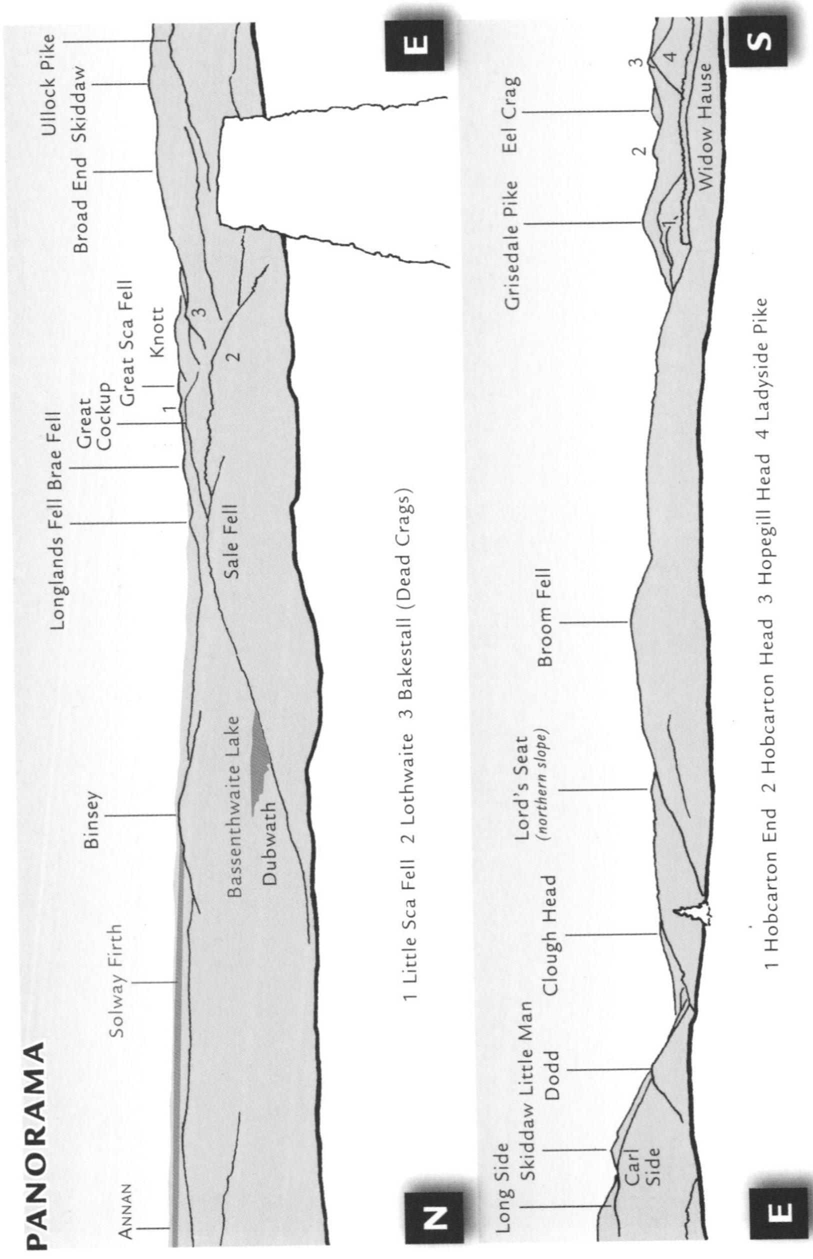

ANNAN
Solway Firth
Binsey
Bassenthwaite Lake
Dubwath
Longlands Fell Brae Fell
Great Cockup
Knott
Great Sca Fell
Sale Fell
Broad End Skiddaw
Ullock Pike

1 Little Sca Fell   2 Lothwaite   3 Bakestall (Dead Crags)

E

N

Long Side
Skiddaw Little Man
Dodd
Carl Side
Clough Head
Lord's Seat
(northern slope)
Broom Fell
Grisedale Pike   Eel Crag
Widow Hause

1 Hobcarton End   2 Hobcarton Head   3 Hopegill Head   4 Ladyside Pike

S

E

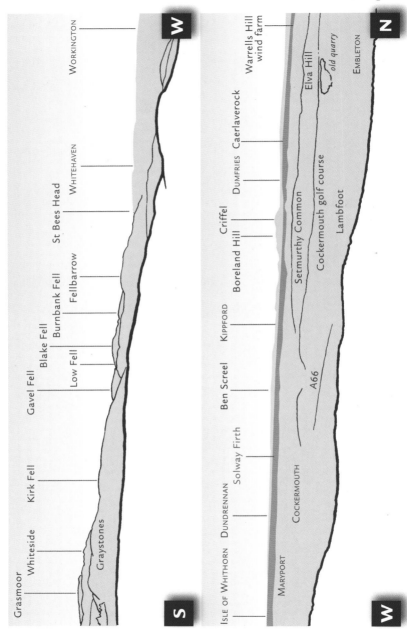

18 LORD'S SEAT (552m/1811ft)

Lord of all it surveys north of the Whinlatter Pass, this fell must always have held an attraction and fully merits its high-ranking name. For all the advance of conifers over the last 80 years the massif, which includes a cluster of five satellite summits, provides a wonderful contrast to the rest of the range.

Felling is slowly opening up grand vistas and made-paths are being created to give leisurely strolls to appeal to the casual visitor, such as that to Seat How (Route 4). The Altura trails (specially constructed mountain-bike routes) have brought life to the sterility of the plantations, and the Go-Ape course is great fun!

Forest ways dominate all ascents – some busy, like the two routes up from Whinlatter Pass (Routes 3 and 4), and some peaceful, such as the pair of routes up the Aiken Beck valley (Routes 1 and 2). Another route is steep, that via Beckstones (Route 5), and the final one, coming in from the north by Beck Wythop (Route 6), manages to retain that precious sense of being a wild and woolly quest.

Grayston

Swire Gill

Scawgill Bridge

Beck

Blaz

ASCENT FROM DARLING HOW (10)

Direct   330m/1080ft   3.6km/2¼ miles

1 Follow the forest track from the barrier and keep to the main track until, with the field-wall coming down to the track (right) and a large larch ahead, find a footpath waymark post on the left, guiding off the track. The path runs beside the right-hand wall, and below and in harmony with the track, until it naturally drifts down to ford Aiken Beck. Follow on upon the ridge to the left of young conifers to meet a wall. Bear left here and ford the gill, continuing with the broken wall (right) until you come to a junction of old walls and here bear right. Ample margin exists between the wall and the young conifers, and you advance in a straight line via one small ford to cross a light fence-stile en route to the upper edge of the plantation. Here cross a more substantial fence-stile beside a gate. A consistent path exists, rising up the rough pasture onto the ridge. Keep left by the fence to join the more regular trail, emerging from Whinlatter Forest, which climbs to the summit.

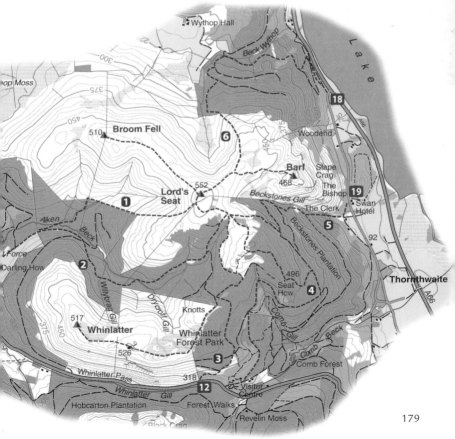

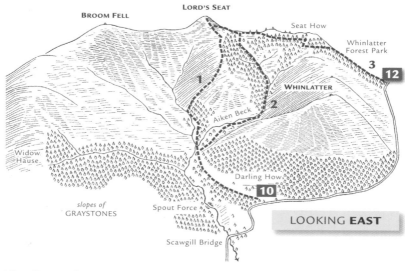

BROOM FELL

LORD'S SEAT

Seat How

Whinlatter
Forest Park

3

12

1

Aiken Beck

2

WHINLATTER

Widow
Hause

Darling How

10

slopes of
GRAYSTONES

Spout Force

LOOKING **EAST**

Scawgill Bridge

Via Aiken Beck 330m/1080ft 4.4km/2¾ miles

2 For a more thorough exploration of the Aiken Beck valley keep company with the main forest track. Follow it until higher in the comb, where the track shapes to swing tight right. Here bear off left at the post with the number 24 affixed. From here a rising

Forest track at the head of the Aiken Beck valley

Whinlatter Forest Park – a place for exciting biking

footpath moves up a conifer-shaded passage to unite with the main graded forest path. Follow this, left, by random conifers to a fence-stile and on up to the summit.

ASCENT FROM WHINLATTER PASS (12)

Direct   235m/770ft   3.2km/2 miles

3 This is the most popular route to the top, which is fine as long as you are content to climb almost entirely among conifers – although it does mean that the summit view takes on a greater than normal significance, a real thrilling moment. The path starts from the road lay-by at the edge of the forest, where you follow the forest track directly up from the barrier. This leads on up by an exaggerated bend up to a wider track junction (forest post number 3), where you keep to the right-hand track (green-topped posts), now almost level, with a slate exposure on the left of the track. Keep left at the next junction (only Altura bikers straight on!) and ignore the next green-topped post. Keep to the level track, which becomes a graded path that leads on, by the convergence of routes, to a fence-stile and completes the ascent of the open fell.

Via Seat How   275m/900ft   4km/2½ miles

4 A route that gives the greatest sense of the drama from the setting of the Forest Park. Pass on through the main car park and below the Whinlatter Forest Park Visitor Centre, incorporating the Siskin Café. Continue by the Cyclewise shop and up the track, bypassing the barrier and the Altura trails trial area. Carry straight on by forest track junction post number 1, rising steadily. Felling on the right side permits long views towards the Helvellyn range as the track curves right, high in the Comb Gill

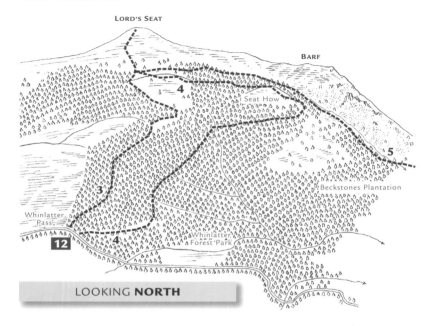

LORD'S SEAT

BARF

4

Seat How

Beckstones Plantation

Whinlatter Pass

4

Whinlatter Forest Park

3

5

12

LOOKING **NORTH**

valley. Having risen, the track now makes a short descent to a track junction. Turn up left, guided by the green-topped post. Watch for the next green-topped post and forest post 54. Here break off the track to the left and follow the graded path winding up into the conifers. This leads steadily up to the bear top of Seat How, described on forest maps as 'Seat Wow' and with good reason. It is a cracker of a viewpoint – particularly eye-catching are the Keswick vale and,

nearer at hand, Grisedale Pike – but there is no seat. The top has the characteristics of Barf. Backtrack from the top and weave through the upper ridge conifers, accompanied by the green-topped posts, on a consistent path. As it comes out of the woods, bear right off the made-path, following a casual path over the open heather ridge top with some marshy ground. Meet up with a made-path merging from the right and, within a few metres, another coming from the left. Here, go right to exit onto the fell-top via the fence-stile.

ASCENT FROM POWTER HOW (19)

Via Beckstones Gill   475m/1560ft   4km/2½ miles

5 Leave the main road upon the byway facing the set-back hamlet of Powter How, with Swan House prominent. A footpath sign on the right directs through a kissing-gate and along a birch woodland way, passing the little white-washed rock known as The Clerk. The path leads over Beckstones Gill to a fence-stile and into the for-estry plantation. Join the ascending path, and avoid being drawn too far right as the steeper woodland is reached. The actual path is probably the less obvious path, going straight up, which comes onto cleared fellside and winds up to meet a forest track. Climb on with this track. You can exit the forestry via the stile and follow up the fence (marshy ground) for a direct ascent. The more appealing route stays within the trees and rises to where the green forest track swings left and contours to find a made-path, acutely right, weaving up to the path junction. Here go right to cross the fence-stile and climb onto the summit.

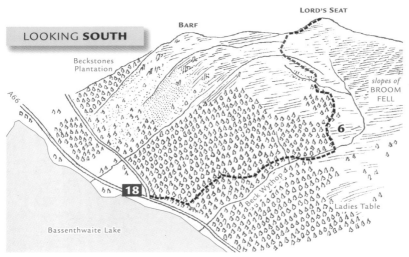

ASCENT FROM WOODEND BROW (18)

Via Wythop Wood   495m/1625ft   3.6km/2¼ miles

6 Head N with the Beck Wythop road (formerly the main road). After 50m find a footpath sign 'Wythop Hall' on the left and follow this, initially parallel to the road-way. The path steps up onto a forest track, but goes straight over (see the footpath waymark opposite), guiding up through the trees with one minor rock-step to reach the same forest track at a higher level. Turn right and follow the track, enjoying a handsome view over Bassenthwaite to Skiddaw at the sharp left-hand bend. Keep to the track and at an open junction swing left. As the track meets a rougher track on the right, branch up this way with felled plantation on the right. Becoming more rutted, this track angles up into the conifers of Hagg and comes alongside the forest fence. Cross over the tall netting fence at this point onto the open fell and naturally follow the rising ridge (pathless). It curves S to join the ridge path from Barf and heads SW to the summit.

THE SUMMIT
Apart from the remnants of an old metal fence, with just one strainer post remaining, the summit is quite bare. The view is anything but barren, with a massive all-round view to keep you counting the tops for several excited minutes.

SAFE DESCENTS
Forest tracks ensure a steady line is always available for Whinlatter Pass, with Route 3 the swiftest descent. Routes 1 and 2 down into the Aiken Beck valley are equally as secure and comfortable in poor conditions.

RIDGE ROUTE

BARF	↓130m/425ft	↑47m/150ft	1.2km/¾ mile

A strong path leads off NE, and during the descent curves E as it moves through marshy hollows to rise, dry again, onto the open summit.

Grisedale Pike from the Lord's Seat summit

184

Ridge path leading north from Ullister Hill

BROOM FELL	↓69m/225ft	↑28m/90ft	1.6km/1 mile

Leave the summit in a NW direction. After the initial bank the ridge is quite level, with two cross-ridge fences to negotiate via stiles in order to reach the tall summit currick.

WHINLATTER	↓90m/295ft	↑55m/180ft	3.6km/2¼ miles

A little bit more of an expedition. Follow the main path S and cross the fence-stile into the open woodland, randomly dotted with self-sown conifers. Follow the made-path, keeping S at the path junction. This path becomes a track and, after swinging right, comes to an unusually wide junction. Keep right only for a few paces, and where the Altura trail slips into the forest, left, find a path immediately to its left. This leads through and over a section of the trail (be watchful for careering bikers) and rises to a hand-gate in a fence-corner. Go through and, keeping the fence close left, follow on SW, with some wet patches, to join the ridge. Bear W to cross Whinlatter Top (the true summit) and continue via a wall-gap to the accepted summit, with its wind-shelter.

PANORAMA

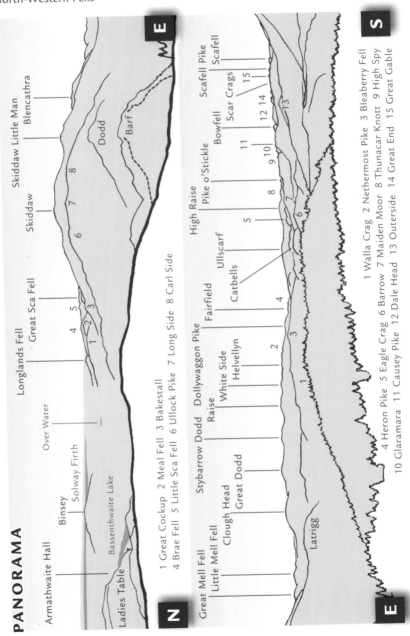

E

Skiddaw Little Man
Blencathra
Skiddaw
Great Sca Fell
Longlands Fell
Dodd
Barf

Armathwaite Hall
Binsey
Over Water
Solway Firth
Bassenthwaite Lake
Ladies Table

1 Great Cockup 2 Meal Fell 3 Bakestall
4 Brae Fell 5 Little Sca Fell 6 Ullock Pike 7 Long Side 8 Carl Side

N

S

Scafell Pike Scafell
Scar Crags
Bowfell
Pike o'Stickle
High Raise
Ullscarf
Catbells
Fairfield
Dollywaggon Pike
White Side
Helvellyn
Raise
Stybarrow Dodd
Clough Head
Great Dodd
Great Mell Fell
Little Mell Fell
Latrigg

1 Walla Crag 2 Nethermost Pike 3 Bleaberry Fell
4 Heron Pike 5 Eagle Crag 6 Barrow 7 Maiden Moor 8 Thunacar Knott 9 High Spy
10 Glaramara 11 Causey Pike 12 Dale Head 13 Outerside 14 Great End 15 Great Gable

E

186

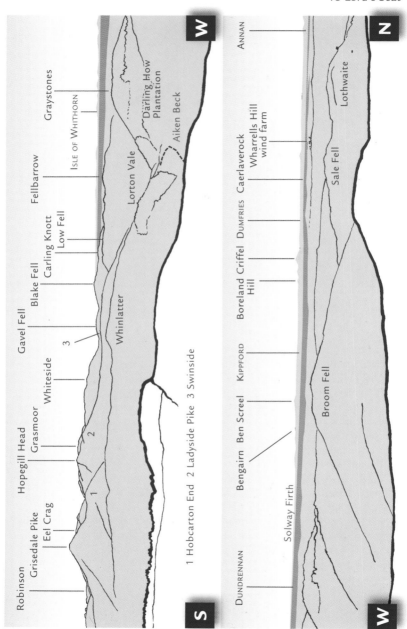

S

Robinson
Grisedale Pike
Eel Crag
Hopegill Head
Grasmoor
Whiteside
Gavel Fell
Blake Fell
Carling Knott
Low Fell
Fellbarrow
Isle of Whithorn
Graystones

Whinlatter
Lorton Vale
Darling How Plantation
Aiken Beck

1 Hobcarton End 2 Ladyside Pike 3 Swinside

W

W

Dundrennan
Solway Firth
Bengairn Ben Screel Kippford
Boreland Criffel Dumfries Caerlaverock
Hill
Wharrells Hill wind farm
Annan

Broom Fell
Sale Fell
Lothwaite

N

19 MAIDEN MOOR *(576m/1890ft)*

Standing back from the plaudits of Catbells, the next step up the growing ridge, Maiden Moor, may lack a great lake view and is often by-passed by ridge walkers intent on the Newlands Horseshoe, yet fell-wanderers will love its summit as the most intimate and telling viewpoint for the Newlands fell scene. The eastern slopes sweep down upon Grange, in contrast to the western declivity, which is steeper and mightily buttressed. The ridge tightens, running south from the summit as the descriptive Narrow Moor to its union with High Spy on Blea Crag.

The enigmatic fell-name could suggest 'unconquered', 'maidens' playground', or even a fell owned by a girl. Take your pick... The fell shares with Catbells custody of Yewthwaite Comb, scene of considerable lead-mining activity, as the bare debris attests. For real insight into this and all other Lakeland mining localities visit the Keswick Mining Museum.

Of the routes to the top all attention is directed at two northern lines – the connecting ridge with Catbells (Route 1) and, for a spot of spicy adventure, the stepped Knott End ridge (Route 2), above Little Town. The popular lines from the east embark from Manesty (Route 3) and High Brandelhow Jetty (Route 4) to join the ridge at Hause Gate.

ASCENT FROM LITTLE TOWN (25)

There are two inviting routes – one commonly followed in shepherding and mining days and reassuringly simple, the other gifted to enthral the seasoned fell explorer.

Via Yewthwaite Comb   380m/1250ft   3.2km/2 miles

1 You may leave the road at the gate in the hamlet or, if parked up at Chapel Bridge, ascend the road and skip over the fence-stile where the wall ends and step up to the track. Go right, and switch left with the higher green track to meet up with the way from the Little Town gate at the first hairpin.

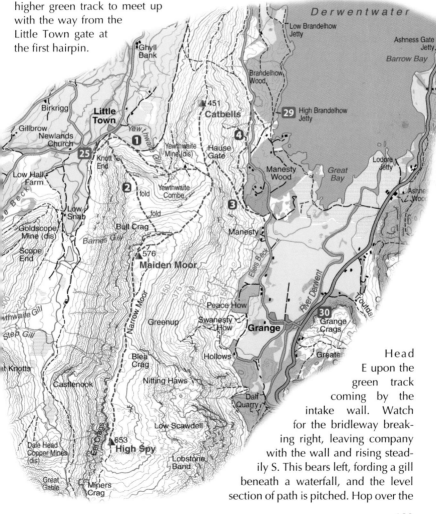

Head E upon the green track coming by the intake wall. Watch for the bridleway breaking right, leaving company with the wall and rising steadily S. This bears left, fording a gill beneath a waterfall, and the level section of path is pitched. Hop over the

189

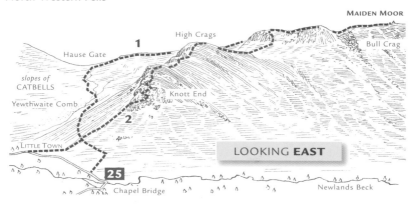

MAIDEN MOOR

Bull Crag

High Crags

1

Hause Gate

slopes of CATBELLS

Knott End

Yewthwaite Comb

2

LITTLE TOWN

LOOKING **EAST**

25

Chapel Bridge

Newlands Beck

second ford to embark on a broad rough path rising to a sheepfold at the upper workings of the old Yewthwaite Mine. The path now comes onto grass and angles easily half-right to the saddle in the ridge, where you turn right and follow the trail of the multitude. Early on there are fine views steeply down upon Derwent Water. Typical of many another, the popular path sweeps onto the ridge oblivious of the actual

Catbells from the northern edge overlooking Yewthwaite Comb

Skiddaw and Catbells from Maiden Moor

summit, so as the ground eases look to take one of two clear optional paths breaking half-right. Either will take you to the summit at the brink of the impressive scarp.

Via Knott End   380m/1250ft   2.4km/1½ miles

2 From the hairpin (see Route 1) leave the regular path and aim for the solitary tree in a low crag directly above, with bracken an issue in summer. Pass to the right of the tree, then angle up to the crag above, aiming to the immediate left of the holly tree on Knott End. You may scramble onto the ridge here or drift a further 50m left to angle onto the ridge on slightly easier ground. Either way, tussle with the heather and simple rock ridge with happy abandon – there are no difficulties if you stick to the ridge. There is no evidence of a path – in fact, the only imprints are those made by resident Herdwick sheep. There are two distinct steps to the rising ridge, and the second clambers over the ambitiously termed High Crags. The view of Catbells is superb from this next top. Decline to pass a small tarn, and above this locate a small sheepfold. Continue on a rising line to a second larger fold on the slope ahead, from where you either clamber straight up or slant left – in either case coming into union with the regular skyline path. Bear right to follow the edge onto the impressive viewpoint of Bull Crag, and the next easy rise brings the summit underfoot.

ASCENT FROM GRANGE-IN-BORROWDALE (30)

Via Manesty   496m/1630ft   2.4km/1½ miles

3 Follow the road north from Grange – this is a popular stroll in spite of the passage of cars and Honister Rambler buses! After Manesty House find a signposted

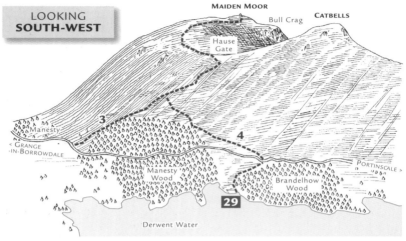

LOOKING
SOUTH-WEST

MAIDEN MOOR

Bull Crag

CATBELLS

Hause
Gate

3

Manesty

< GRANGE
-IN-BORROWDALE

4

PORTINSCALE >

Manesty
Wood

Brandelhow
Wood

29

Derwent Water

path stepping off the road on the left. This rises by a gate and climbs steadily to the Hause Gate saddle, with lovely views back to give you plenty of cause to take it easy from time to time. Follow the ridge path S – a heavy flow of walkers has ensured a torn trail. Higher up, watch to keep right along the brow in order to reach the summit along the scarp edge over Bull Crag, rather than be lured by hasty Newlands Horseshoe walkers who race past this first major step more intent on High Spy.

POTS OF TEA   Bull Crag from Low Snab

ASCENT FROM HIGH BRANDELHOW JETTY (29)

Via Hause Gate   500m/1640ft   3.2km/2 miles

4 While there are numerous suitable verge spaces along the road above Brandelhow Wood, there is no denying the immense pleasure of approaching the adventure from the Keswick launch. Step off the jetty and bear left on a woodland track to a hand-gate, from where a path leads forward before bearing uphill alongside the old Brandelhow lead mine to step onto the open road. Cross and join the graded path leading left from the old quarry. This leads by a seat and plaque to the writer Sir Hugh Walpole, who lived in the house below, Brackenburn. The plaque, set on an outcrop, was installed by his good friend and chauffeur, Harold Cheevers. The path comes to a wall above woodland and forks. Take the rising line to join the Manesty path (Route 3) climbing to the saddle of Hause Gate and to the summit.

THE SUMMIT

This is not a summit for walkers who love peaks, as the sense of being at the highest point on the fell is less convincing than on many other occasions. Yet with a small cairn resting innocently on a flat mat of grass a few paces from the brink, there are sufficient makings of a summit to satisfy. From the near edge revel in a bird's-eye view into the exciting

Summit cairn looking to the cloud-shaded Catbells

upper Newlands Beck valley. Peer down upon the spoil of Goldscope Mine and across the greater gulf to an array of ridges from Dale Head round to Causey Pike, with special attention warranted by the stately presence of Hindscarth.

SAFE DESCENTS

Aim NE to join the main pedestrian thoroughfare to Hause Gate, and here either turn right for Manesty or left for Little Town – both paths are reliable.

RIDGE ROUTE

CATBELLS	↓217m/710ft	↑92m/300ft	2.4km/1½ miles

Head NE, the route quickly merging with the short-cut ridge path from Narrow Moor, which draws down to the grassy depression of Hause Gate and continues easily N via a minor rock slab onto the bare rock summit. To be alone here is unusual.

HIGH SPY	↓9m/30ft	↑86m/280ft	2.4km/1½ miles

A clear path leads S, with the constant pleasure of the profound escarpment always close to the right. There is but one slight rise, passing to the right of the crest of Blea Crag, a top that should be visited for the commanding view it offers over Derwent Water.

Narrow Moor

PANORAMA

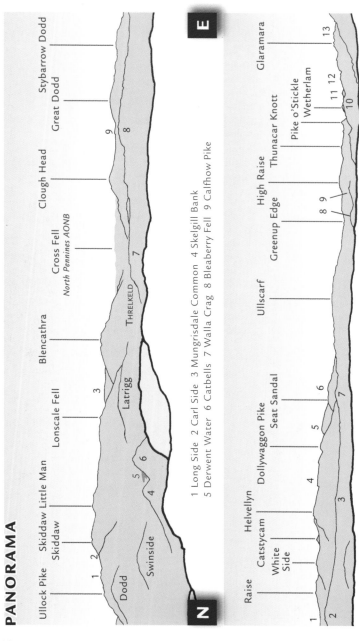

N

Ullock Pike Skiddaw Little Man Cross Fell Clough Head Great Dodd Stybarrow Dodd
Skiddaw Lonscale Fell Blencathra *North Pennines AONB*

Dodd Swinside Latrigg THRELKELD

1 Long Side 2 Carl Side 3 Mungrisdale Common 4 Skelgill Bank
5 Derwent Water 6 Catbells 7 Walla Crag 8 Bleaberry Fell 9 Calfhow Pike

E

S

Raise Helvellyn Ullscarf High Raise Glaramara
White Catstycam Dollywaggon Pike Greenup Edge Thunacar Knott
Side Seat Sandal Pike o'Stickle
Wetherlam

1 Sticks Pass 2 High Seat 3 High Tove 4 Nethermost Pike 5 Fairfield 6 Great Rigg 7 Bell Crags
8 Eagle Crag 9 Sergeant's Crag 10 Bessyboot 11 Swirl How 12 Rosthwaite High Fell 13 Bowfell

E

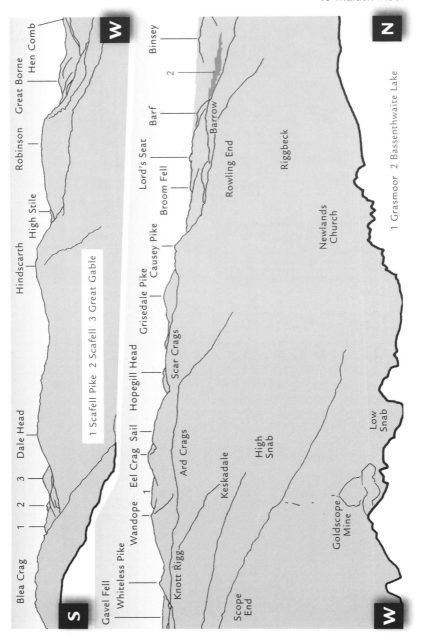

1 Scafell Pike   2 Scafell   3 Great Gable

1 Grasmoor   2 Bassenthwaite Lake

20 OUTERSIDE (568m/1863ft)

The fell's descriptive name refers to the outer edge of the Stonycroft valley. Viewed from Coledale, Outerside rises like the inverted fin of a yacht. It belongs to a sub-group of lesser heights north of Causey Pike, including Stile End and Barrow, that are often drawn together to create the basis of a mini-Coledale round. Walkers could consider climbing Outerside from off the Force Crag Mine approach track via Birkthwaite Beck (Route 1). Alternatively, and again from Braithwaite, trek up to Barrow Door, over Stile End or direct to Low Moss (Route 2), or, in context with its 'outer side' setting, ascend the Stonycroft Gill valley itself to High Moss (Route 3). All these excellent walks give a sense of the fell's enviable situation among lofty mountains.

Coledale aspect of Outerside

Eel Cra

↑ Outerside from the old mine track-bed at High Moss

ASCENT FROM BRAITHWAITE (22)

Via Coledale Beck 500m/1640ft 4.8km/3 miles

1 The ideal approach for anyone wishing to make a round-trip. From the recessed car park simply follow the Coledale track beyond the barrier, and in so doing enjoy the grand views towards the dale head, with the tapered Outerside claiming its own attention. As the mine buildings draw close, fork down left with the track to ford Coledale Beck. Continue beyond, ascending to where, at a cairn, a path veers acutely left. This fords Birkthwaite Beck and sweeps up to join the regular path south of High Moss. Turn N on what quickly becomes a track coming onto the plain, and veer half-left to traverse the marshy hollow of High Moss. Resuming dry ground on the simple climb, curve from N to NE to reach the summit.

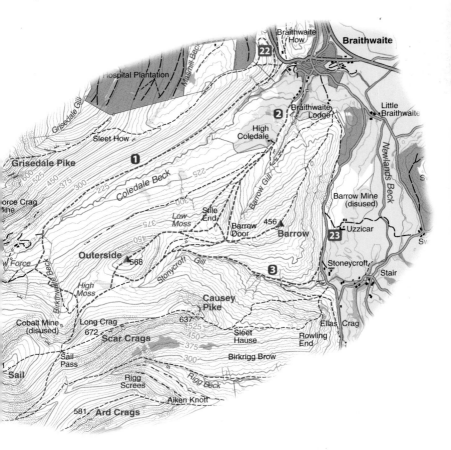

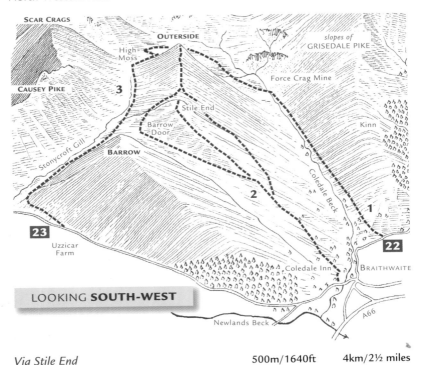

LOOKING **SOUTH-WEST**

Via Stile End   500m/1640ft   4km/2½ miles

2 From the bridge and village shop at the heart of the community follow the street S, rising by Moss Garth and winding up the succeeding track to meet the road, with the Coledale Inn 100m to the right. Turn left and follow this road up to a kissing-gate, where the open track leads on, passing the copse sheltering the ruined High Coledale. At this point the track reverts to a turf path leading through bracken, which opens up as the ridge of Stile End approaches. You may either keep to the path slanting up the northern flank to Barrow Door and ascend the inviting ridge onto Stile End, or hold to the more regular course on the eastern side to meet the ridge top at the pool on Low Moss. By all routes, upon gaining the ridge top bear right (W) and pass over the marshy Low Moss to embark on the north-east ridge amid heather. The path is deeply eroded in parts.

ASCENT FROM UZZICAR (23)

Via Stonycroft Gill   475m//1560ft   3.6km/2¼ miles

3 The old miners' track leads off from opposite the broad verge parking at a gentle gradient, and heads up the Stonycroft Gill valley. As the track eases towards the saddle veer right to contour, initially with a dyke feature, in order to avoid the marsh in

Causey Pike from Stile End

the hollow of High Moss. The ridge path is soon located leading up the west ridge to the summit.

THE SUMMIT

A few stones occasionally survive on the rock-bed of this little peak. Even if Grisedale Pike is 10,000ft higher (metaphorically), this is no reason to diminish the achievement of your ascent.

Outerside summit looking to Skiddaw

Outerside has its pride, and a handsome mid-height view of Coledale is your reward.

SAFE DESCENTS

The easiest walking is found off the east ridge, curving S onto High Moss, from where all ports are accessible. Immediately the Stonycroft mine track gives security either directly E down towards Stair or via Barrow Door N to Braithwaite.

RIDGE ROUTE

BARROW	↓244m/800ft	↑131m/430ft	2km/1¼ miles

The natural ridge NE is fine, but water and walker erosion have made some deep grooves in the path through the rank heather. Descend to the low ridge, passing the shy reedy pool in Low Moss to either skirt along the southern flanks of Stile End or make a positive left turn to include this lovely little top. By either course come down by Barrow Door and march on upon the rising ridge way to Barrow's ultimate ground.

PANORAMA

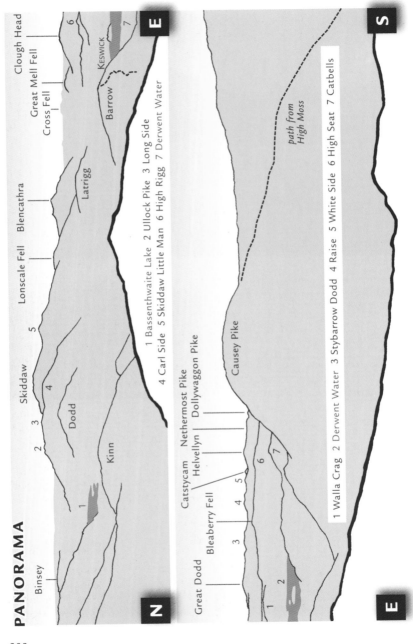

N

Binsey

Skiddaw

2 3 4 5 Kinn Dodd Latrigg

1

Lonscale Fell

Blencathra

Cross Fell
Great Mell Fell

6 Clough Head

KESWICK

Barrow

7

E

1 Bassenthwaite Lake 2 Ullock Pike 3 Long Side
4 Carl Side 5 Skiddaw Little Man 6 High Rigg 7 Derwent Water

S

path from
High Moss

Catstycam Nethermost Pike
Helvellyn Dollywaggon Pike

Causey Pike

Bleaberry Fell

4 5 6 7

3

Great Dodd

1 2

E

1 Walla Crag 2 Derwent Water 3 Stybarrow Dodd 4 Raise 5 White Side 6 High Seat 7 Catbells

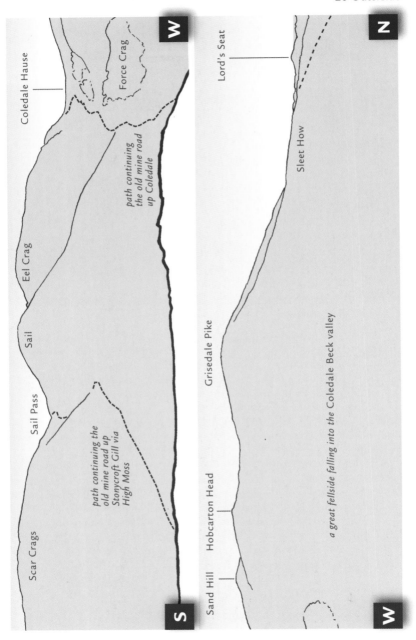

Coledale Hause

Force Crag

Eel Crag

Sail

Sail Pass

Scar Crags

path continuing the old mine road up Coledale

path continuing the old mine road up Stonycroft Gill via High Moss

Lord's Seat

Sleet How

Grisedale Pike

Hobcarton Head

Sand Hill

a great fellside falling into the Coledale Beck valley

21 RANNERDALE KNOTTS *(355m/1165ft)*

Since the Romantic period Rannerdale Knotts has contributed to the dreamlike vision created of the surrounding fells, as it provides the perfect scene-setting foreground on many a canvas portraying the drama and beauty of these majestic mountains. What it lacks in inches it more than compensates for in form, structure and rugged appeal. For one so small it certainly packs a punch.

The fell forms a low connection with Whiteless Breast at the head of Rannerdale at some 290m (950ft). The valley, drained by Squat and Rannerdale Becks, has evidence of Viking settlement close to where these becks meet. The Norse term *ranner* meant 'the shieling frequented by raven', an apt name for this homestead. Rannerdale Beck flows on into Crummock Water, flanked to the left by the sweet pastures of Rannerdale Farm and to the right by the mighty slopes of Grasmoor. For all visitors the greatest pleasure of this vicinity is the open Rannerdale Wood, where in spring you'll find a 'heaven scent' carpet of bluebells to rival the best in the land.

There are three basic lines of ascent and five routes described here, all ideal for the construction of circular walks. Routes 1 and 5 combine to parade along the spine of the ridge, while Routes 2 and 3 come together on the steep western edge above Hause Point, and Route 4 climbs off-beat out of Rannerdale.

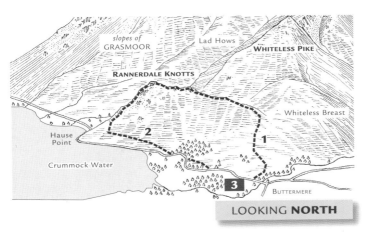

LOOKING **NORTH**

ASCENT FROM BUTTERMERE (3)

Via Low Bank   260m/850ft   2.4km/1½ miles

1 The best of fellwalking is frequently found along high connecting ridges, and this route provides all the ingredients of a classic ridge walk without the horror of the normal ascent and descent! If you start from the National Trust car park, then exit and walk right to find a double footpath sign directing left alongside cottages to a handgate. Continue with the fence close right until you get a first glimpse of Whiteless Pike and a path breaks left. Here there are two inviting path options, and both achieve the same result in climbing Low Bank towards the head of

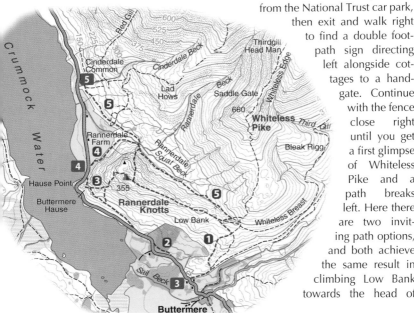

203

Newly pitched
path above
Buttermere
Hause

Fleetwith Pike from the old road on Route 2

Rannerdale. The turf carpets that wind up the bracken slopes are a sheer joy, and the views back give ample encouragement for frequent pauses to admire nature's scenic excellence. Veer left onto the emergent ridge that roller-coasters NW, rounding rocky knotts at the far end, to reach the ultimate rocky top. In this instance route-finding is not rocket science, it is the purest pleasure.

Via the old road terrace   270m/885ft   2.4km/1½ miles

2 This might well appeal as a return route for Route 1, or vice versa. Exit the car park left and follow the road as it dips and metal railing replaces stone walls. Go right and follow the parallel lane in the conifers, re-emerging onto the road opposite the entrance to the exquisitely located guest house Wood House. Keep with the road after the woodland ends to find a green path stepping off from a small lay-by on the right. This is the old road to Buttermere Hause. In the days of horse travel this terrace was the valley thoroughfare – that the present road keeps low and swings round the headland of Hause Point is a comparatively modern development. The views out over Crummock Water are spell-binding. Watch for the path-fork and take the rising path. This meets up with a path from the left to continue onto a pitched section hugging the right-hand outcrop. The path is very evident, and in its later part bears right to come up to the final short climb. Just before this, you may choose to venture left to the isolated cairn at the top of the main craggy headland – it overlooks Rannerdale Farm and the lower dale, with peerless views of Grasmoor and Whiteless Pike.

ASCENT FROM HAUSE POINT (4)

Via Buttermere Hause   256m/840ft   0.8km/½ mile

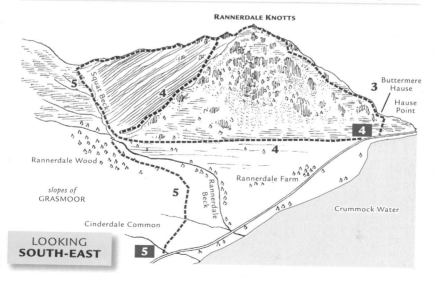

3 Head SW along the road from the recessed parking area. Turn off the road at the footpath/bridleway sign (curiously the latter points as with the road, perhaps a historic inference to the way to Buttermere Hause). The pitched footpath climbs and duly comes to the said Buttermere Hause, where low rock-cut grooves mark the course of wagons of old. Bear up left, with the path irresistibly climbing to a flight of pitching that hugs an outcrop with scree spilling left. The path comes up to bear right and climb on to the highest ground, with its characterful outcropping.

Via the north ridge	256m/840ft	1.2km/¾ mile

4 Follow the path beside the wall, leading NE from the recessed parking. This leads, via a kissing-gate, past the remains of the Viking homesteads of Rannerdale, and passes by the back and under an overbearing outcrop to reach the footbridge. Do not cross, but instead bear right to go through the kissing-gate and walk on, passing under the outcropping to switch up right on the steep grass bank. Take your time – there's no hurry, and no path either! This line brings you to the wall-end at the abrupt lip of outcropping. Bear half-left and keep just above the scree. This southerly line has sheep trods but no hint of boot trods. Press on up to make the ridge simply enough, avoiding all hint of rock obstacle, and come back right to reach the summit.

ASCENT FROM CINDERDALE COMMON (5)

Via Rannerdale Wood	270m/885ft	3.6km/2¼ miles

5 From the large bayed parking area follow the signposted turf track heading SE, fording Cinderdale Beck and advancing to a gate where you enter Rannerdale Wood,

Rannerdale Wood bluebells, a heaven-scent scenic aroma

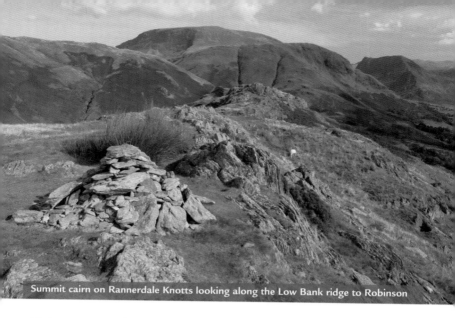

Summit cairn on Rannerdale Knotts looking along the Low Bank ridge to Robinson

with the great mass of Rannerdale Knotts a major focus of attention ahead. The greenway leads on into Rannerdale Wood – in May a joyous tramp through a floral paradise of bluebells, the air filled with the most gorgeous pungencies. The track comes down to a footbridge. Cross it and bear left, going through the gate and following the ensuing path as it winds up the dale in harmony with Squat Beck to reach the saddle at the dale head. Switch right and follow the undulating skyline, a merry rollercoaster ride leading on to the summit.

THE SUMMIT

A neat cairn rests on a rock stand with plenty of other outcropping at hand to lend foreground fodder to your pictures. The view is out of this world and certainly belies the modest effort in ascent. Mellbreak lies to the west, the High Stile range and Haystacks to the south and south-east, and the great partnership of Grasmoor and Whiteless Pike fill the eastern view, with High Snockrigg and Robinson to the south-west.

SAFE DESCENTS

The best descent is along the ridge SE. At the end turn left for Rannerdale or right for Buttermere. Otherwise go W and SW down the pitched path to Buttermere Hause, switching right down further pitching to the road.

PANORAMA

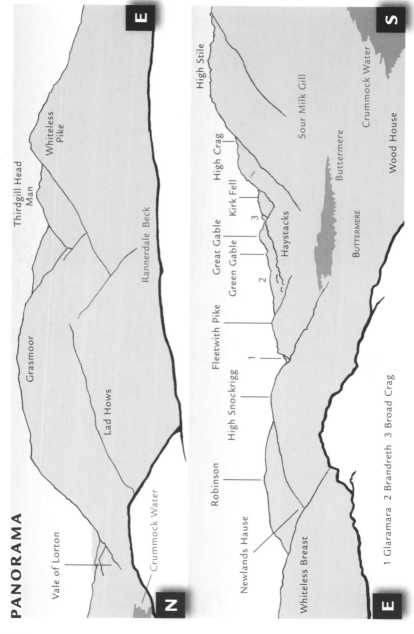

E

Thirdgill Head Man

Whiteless Pike

Grasmoor

Lad Hows

Rannerdale Beck

Vale of Lorton

Crummock Water

N

High Stile

High Crag

Great Gable

Green Gable

Kirk Fell

3

2

Haystacks

Sour Milk Gill

Buttermere

BUTTERMERE

Crummock Water

Wood House

S

Fleetwith Pike

High Snockrigg

1

Robinson

Newlands Hause

Whiteless Breast

E

1 Glaramara 2 Brandreth 3 Broad Crag

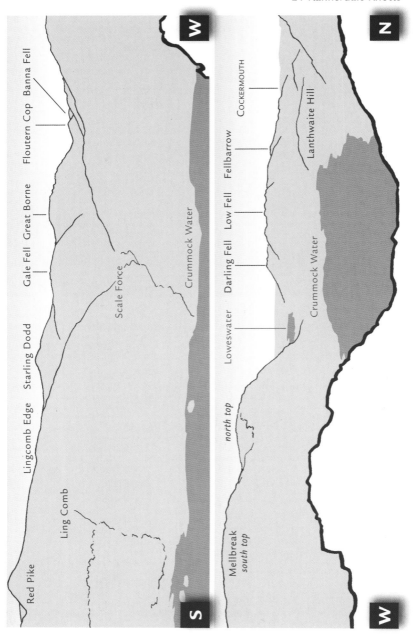

22 ROBINSON *(737m/2418ft)*

Unusually, the name of this fell reflects historical land ownership, being held in the 16th-century by the family of Richard Robinson. The fell has a commanding presence in two revered walking arenas, Buttermere and Newlands, although only from within the latter does the fell deliver strong lines and a striking visual impact. For those driving updale from Braithwaite, Robinson becomes a star attraction – on a par, if not twinned, with Hindscarth. Passing on from Keskadale Farm the sheer scale becomes almost overpowering, and, on reaching Newlands Hause, the walker looks back from Moss Force to comprehend a mountain of real stature. As the objective for a fellwalking day this is a splendid fell, with eight excellent routes to suit all levels of fellwalking ambition.

The leg-up provided by Newlands Hause will tempt many to entertain a there-and-back expedition (Route 6), although the dampness of Buttermere Moss takes something of the gloss off the apparent quick climb. From Newlands valley itself there are four route options, of which the High Snab Bank route (Route 1) is rightly the most popular, but three other inventive routes give variety for the inquisitive walker (Routes 2–4). Higher up Keskadale find a rarely climbed ridge bounding the steep Dudmancomb

↑ Robinson from Ard Crags

(Route 5) – not for novices, this is a classic adventurer's route. From Buttermere village the steep drove-way onto High Snockrigg – which means 'the elevated headland ridge' – provides a sure, uncomplicated line (Route 7). Last but by no means least, the Hassness and Goat Gills route (Route 8), which combines the pleasure of the lakeshore with a stiff pull in an amazing situation, well merits appreciation, although the path is becoming worn higher up overlooking the impressive Goat Gills ravine.

ASCENT FROM LITTLE TOWN (25)

Via High Snab Bank   625m/2050ft   4.8km/3 miles

1 Follow the no-through road signed to Newlands Church. This is a heavenly spot indeed, and the trim little white-washed chapel and old school-room deserve a moment's contemplative admiration. Continue with the tarmac road rising up to High Snab Cottage, and pass through the charming environs by gates. The green lane opens at a gate, after some 120m, and as the wall on the right veers uphill,

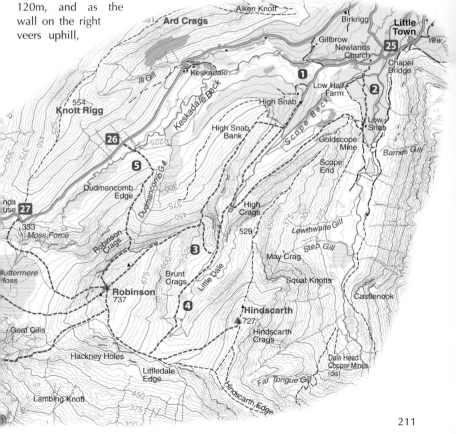

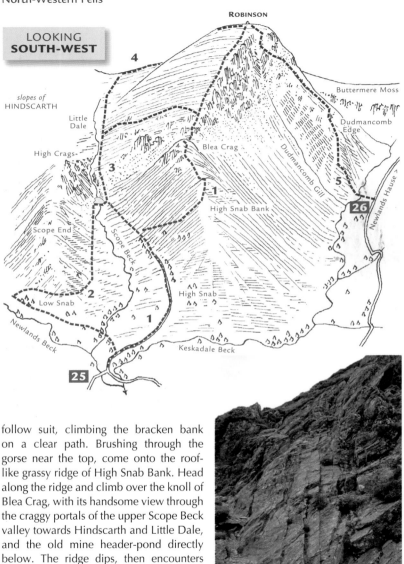

LOOKING
SOUTH-WEST

ROBINSON

4

slopes of
HINDSCARTH

Little
Dale

High Crags

3

Scope End

2

Low Snab

Newlands Beck

25

1

Blea Crag

High Snab Bank

Scope Beck

High Snab

Keskadale Beck

Buttermere Moss

Dudmancomb
Edge

Dudmancomb Gill

5

Newlands Hause

26

Rock-step on the north-east ridge

follow suit, climbing the bracken bank on a clear path. Brushing through the gorse near the top, come onto the roof-like grassy ridge of High Snab Bank. Head along the ridge and climb over the knoll of Blea Crag, with its handsome view through the craggy portals of the upper Scope Beck valley towards Hindscarth and Little Dale, and the old mine header-pond directly below. The ridge dips, then encounters two definite rock-steps (a little tricky in descent). Thereafter the ridge mounts impressively, but without hazard, to the summit plateau.

Blea Crag from the rock-step

Via the old aqueduct   625m/2050ft   6.4km/4 miles

2 Turn left in front of Newlands Church following the open track (private road/permissive footpath) bound for Low Snab Farm. Pass through the charming farmyard inhabited by chickens, and perhaps consider the lovely offer of a pot of tea! At the far end go through the gate and bear up right, following the green track which rounds the end of Scope End above the intake wall. The path runs on to come upon spoil debris associated with a level and quarried portion of the Goldscope Mine. Make sure you step up here to join the old aqueduct which now contours along the fellside – only a path remains here, where once there was a wooden trough conveying the water to the mine. Come close to the reservoir and bear up left over the boulders to cross the footbridge and the walled dam, then clamber up the bank to join the valley drove to link with Route 3.

Via Little Dale   625m/2050ft   6.4km/4 miles

High Snab Cottage

3 Follow the valley track as it opens at a gate beyond High Snab Cottage, and continue with it as, in its later stages, it becomes more of a drove path. Above the reservoir the drove-way mounts the bouldery ground and passes below an old holding fold to come above the ravine. The quartz-streaked boulders are an attractive feature hereabouts. There are two options once in the upper valley of Little Dale. Advance towards a sheepfold and bear up right, a rock band up to the right acting as a shield to the craggy ground. Climb above this onto the shoulder and join the north ridge path (Route 1) above the early rock-steps. **4** Alternatively, follow

Fleetwith Pike from
the top of Hackney Holes

on with the valley path to the sheepfold where, amid a great mass of rushes, the path disappears. Skirt the worst of the damp ground to the right, advancing up Little Dale's peaceful pasture and mounting the dale-head slopes, in the later stages following a strong sheep path, to the skyline. Here join the popular ridge path beside the fence. Higher up you may be tempted to cross the fence and inspect Hackney Holes, an irregular fault fracture. Gain the highest ground and bear up right to reach the summit.

ASCENT FROM KESKADALE (26)

Via Dudmancomb Edge   500m/1640ft   2km/1¼ miles

5 Travellers heading up Keskadale bound for Newlands Hause will casually eye a prominent ridge climbing abruptly to the rock band shielding the northern face of Robinson. Determined and experienced fellwalkers, who understand fell terrain, will, in their small number, relish the ascent it suggests. This is Dudmancomb Edge, simple to unlock in fair weather, but ill suited for descent.

As the road opens beyond Keskadale Farm find a lay-by space on the left. Descend directly, fording the sinuous marshy beck. Set to work clambering up the predominant grassy slope, and find the skyline edge that peers into Dudman Comb (the name suggests 'the hollow where a dead man was discovered' – many moons ago!). There is no trace of a path save the occasional sheep trod. The grass ridge ultimately merges with the scree apron of the upper fell, above which the ground is slightly steeper, with simple rock-steps akin a broad stair. Easing up among the outcropping, climb until the rock band looms. Now veer left to round a corner where the upper gully of Red Gill opens onto a green ramp leading easily onto the domed plateau. The most entertaining route choice is to keep along the brink to the right, with some really breathtaking views down into High Hole.

ASCENT FROM NEWLANDS HAUSE (27)

Direct   430m/1410ft   2km/1¼ miles

6 The tempting height-saving provided by Newlands Hause has made this a regular start point for many over the years. Be mindful that the path leading towards Moss Force is only to assist observation of the crashing waters

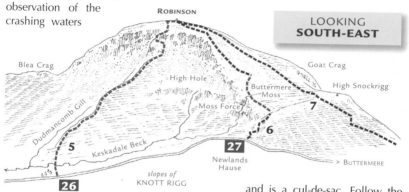

ROBINSON

LOOKING **SOUTH-EAST**

Blea Crag

Goat Crag

High Hole

Buttermere Moss

High Snockrigg

Dudmancomb Gill

Moss Force

7

5

Keskadale Beck

27

Newlands Hause

26

slopes of KNOTT RIGG

> BUTTERMERE

and is a cul-de-sac. Follow the clear trail mounting the leading edge SW from the pass. As the fell-slope eases leave the ridge path, which is bound for High Snockrigg, slanting left onto pathless terrain to ford the outflow of Buttermere Moss. The shallow catchment hollow above is crossed by regular paths from High Snockrigg, but even in dry conditions this is an unpleasant morass. Hence the virtue of this off-beat route, which enables the walker to connect with the regular path (traversing the midst of the morass) on the rising slope of Robinson, keeping to firm turf all the way. The final pull up to the skyline, while in no way problematic, is certainly better done in ascent.

ASCENT FROM BUTTERMERE (3)

Via High Snockrigg   655m/2150ft   4km/2½ miles

7 Buttermere-based walkers will value the old shepherd's drove onto High Snockrigg, a name that meant 'the prominent headland'. This leaves the open road at a small lay-by on a left-hand rising curve and is indicated by a footpath sign. The turf path winds up and has the odd delicate moment, especially where it comes above a steep

Pool (bottom left) and the Goat Gills ravine

ravine. Come up the groove to cross the skyline edge. However, there is every good reason to visit the summit of High Snockrigg up to the right, a fabulous viewpoint both for the High Stile range and the deeply entrenched Buttermere/Crummock vale, with the bird's-eye view of the village particularly impressive. The continuing route heads SE to traverse the upper edge of Buttermere Moss, although it is difficult to avoid wet feet on the peaty sponge. With firm ground restored on the eastern side, climb the steady slope on a strong path to the brink cairn, en route the summit.

Via Goat Gills   670m/2200ft   4.4km/2¾ miles

8 The Goat Gills route is a stiff climb, but in an attractive setting, and it is useful as the 'out route' for an entertaining circuit returning by High Snockrigg. Join the merry band of casual walkers, many engaged in walking around the lake. Leave Buttermere village through the yard of Syke Farm (with its tearoom and tempting home-made ice

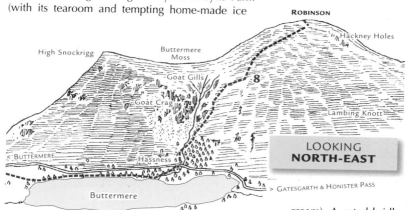

cream). A gated bridle-way leads on along the initial lane to become an open pasture-way and comes to a hand-gate with 'shoreline path' notice. The confined path leads down via a further hand-gate to steps beside a big glaciated slab. Ushered on by a light fence, the path continues via further hand- and kissing-gates to revel in the tree-shaded shore of Buttermere. The shoreline walk provides lovely glimpses of the inspiring fells rising from the far shore, with, from here, diminutive Haystacks a popular subject of attention. The short pedestrian tunnel is a curious attraction – it is not part of a mine, but rather the result of a project by the original owner of Hassness to keep a workforce busy.

On emerging, clamber over the root-covered rock-step and come down to the shore. Ignore the kissing-gate, and instead veer away from the shore, left, beside the wall and come by a small footbridge to a hand-gate onto the road. Cross straight over to go through the facing hand-gate, with a footpath sign to 'Robinson'. Follow up by the wall in woodland to a fence-stile and continue to where the gill constrict. Here step up to the fence-stile in the wall. The path ascends the obvious ridge, with a fine view of the little dam created to capture water for Hassness – a picturesque setting below the great ravine of Goat Gills and Goat Crag. Climbing higher, the path negotiates a flight of steps to a wall-stile. The views back are constantly uplifting across Buttermere to the High Stile range. The steep path, now lined with bilberry and heather, works up to accompany the light fence. The one really steep section is tight between the fence and some outcropping and is uncomfortable underfoot. But this soon relents, and the path climbs on to reach a fence-stile. Cross and ascend the open pasture, with the fence to the right, to gain the ridge top and summit.

THE SUMMIT

A conspicuous cairn rests on a low outcrop, with a parallel outcrop a carriage-way distant. The view is wide and comprehensive, although for the best aspect on the Grasmoor/Eel Crag group you should wander down the slope a little way N, as the plateau takes away all depth from the panorama.

SAFE DESCENTS

If heading for Newlands, you should consider descending Little Dale rather than the north ridge, which has some awkward rock-steps in its latter stages. In which case, head S to accompany the ridge fence SE down to Littledale Edge, where you turn into the pastoral bowl of Little Dale itself and exit into the Scope Beck valley leading down by High Snab. For Buttermere trend SW, descend to cross Buttermere Moss, which can be very spongy, rise over High Snockrigg and follow the drove path steeply direct to the village – you can also veer right down the ridge of High Snockrigg to reach Newlands Hause as the quickest route to a motor road.

The Scafells from the summit of Robinson

Buttermere village from High Snockrigg

RIDGE ROUTE

HINDSCARTH	↓165m/540ft	↑155m/510ft	2.4km/1½ miles

Walk S to come by the ridge fence and follow this SSE, entirely upon a well-worn ridge path. This leads along Littledale Edge, where you take the branch-path half-left and climb diagonally across the west slope of Hindscarth to gain the summit ridge some 100m south of the cairn.

PANORAMA

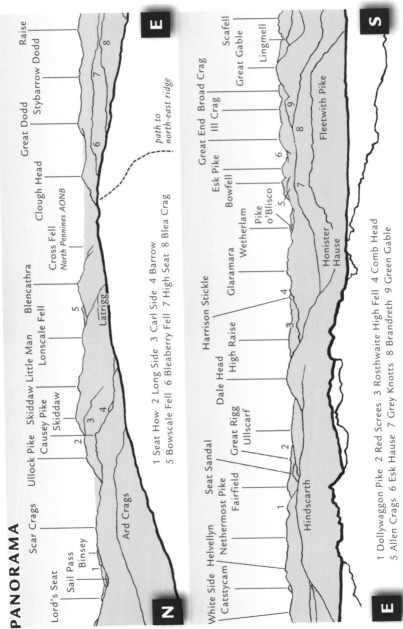

N

Lord's Seat · Sail Pass · Binsey · Scar Crags · Ullock Pike · Skiddaw Little Man · Blencathra · Clough Head · Great Dodd · Raise

Causey Pike · Skiddaw · Lonscale Fell · Cross Fell · Stybarrow Dodd

North Pennines AONB

Latrigg

Ard Crags

E

path to north-east ridge

1 Seat How 2 Long Side 3 Carl Side 4 Barrow
5 Bowscale Fell 6 Bleaberry Fell 7 High Seat 8 Blea Crag

E

White Side · Helvellyn · Nethermost Pike · Seat Sandal · Great Rigg · Dale Head · Harrison Stickle · Glaramara · Esk Pike · Great End · Broad Crag · Scafell

Catstycam · Fairfield · Ullscarf · High Raise · Wetherlam · Bowfell · Ill Crag · Great Gable · Lingmell

Pike o'Blisco

Hindscarth · Honister Hause · Fleetwith Pike

S

1 Dollywaggon Pike 2 Red Screes 3 Rosthwaite High Fell 4 Comb Head
5 Allen Crags 6 Esk Hause 7 Grey Knotts 8 Brandreth 9 Green Gable

220

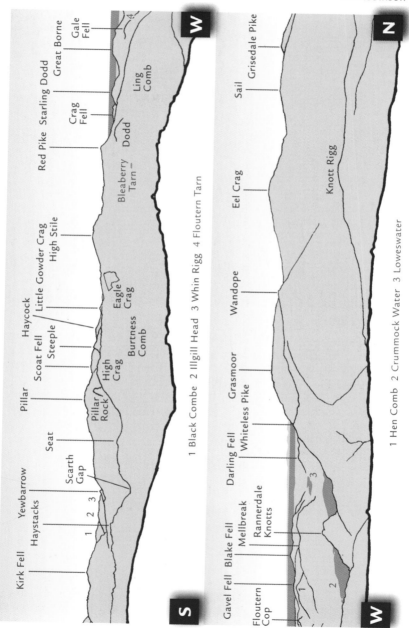

W (top panel)

Gale Fell
Great Borne
Starling Dodd
Red Pike
Crag Fell
Ling Comb
Dodd
Bleaberry Tarn
Little Gowder Crag
High Stile
Haycock
Scoat Fell
Steeple
Eagle Crag
Burtness Comb
Pillar
Pillar Rock
High Crag
Seat
Scarth Gap
Yewbarrow
Haystacks
Kirk Fell

2 3
1

S

1 Black Combe 2 Illgill Head 3 Whin Rigg 4 Floutern Tarn

N (bottom panel)

Griesdale Pike
Sail
Knott Rigg
Eel Crag
Wandope
Grasmoor
Whiteless Pike
Darling Fell
Mellbreak
Rannerdale Knots
Blake Fell
Gavel Fell
Floutern Cop

3
1
2

W

1 Hen Comb 2 Crummock Water 3 Loweswater

23 SAIL *(771m/2529ft)*

By dint of its situation the rounded dome of Sail might be considered a companion fell, performing a supporting role in the greater scheme of things. It is a lovely stepping-stone along the handsome rising ridge from Causey Pike and Scar Crags bound for Eel Crag, and in a breeze walkers may fair sail up it. But why has the name been applied here? In normal circumstances Sail would mean 'where willows grow', something of an impossible scenario in this high and exposed situation. Perhaps it is a transferred name, from the beck below, where the water-loving tree may once have flourished and been coppiced.

The fell is seldom climbed alone. Most particularly it is an integral part of the marvellous skyline-round known as the Coledale Horseshoe. Yet the three routes described emphasise that it is far from one dimensional. Routes 1 and 3 serve to get you onto the fell to customise your own fell-round. Route 2 is for the explorer, whom this landscape richly rewards.

Sail from Outerside

↑ Sail from Knott Rigg

ASCENT FROM BRAITHWAITE (22 – **off map NE**)

Via the north ridge 675m/2215ft 5.6km/3½ miles

1 Ascend the Whinlatter road out of the village and, rounding the right-hand corner, find a footpath signposted left for Coledale Hause. Follow this path through the birch, then gorse, via a hand-gate to join and follow the Force Crag Mine access track into Coledale. Short of the secured mine buildings the track forks. Bear down left to ford Coledale Beck. Keep with the popular, if rough trail and come up above the cascades to the south of Force Crag. As the metal

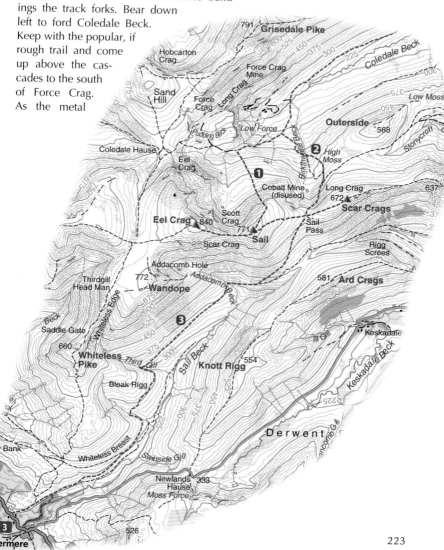

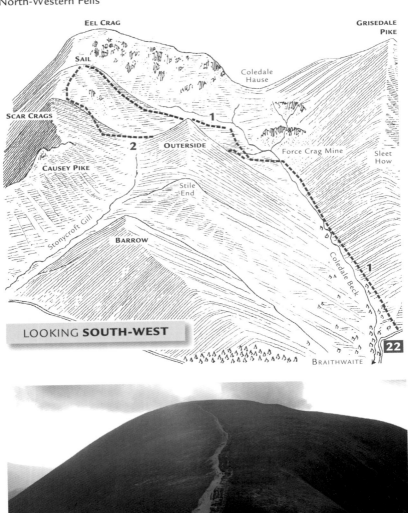

EEL CRAG

GRISEDALE PIKE

SAIL

Coledale Hause

SCAR CRAGS

1

OUTERSIDE

Force Crag Mine

Sleet How

2

CAUSEY PIKE

Stile End

Stonycroft Gill

BARROW

Coledale Beck

LOOKING **SOUTH-WEST**

1

22

BRAITHWAITE

Badly worn ridge path climbing from Sail Pass

culvert pipe is reached bear off left onto pathless fell. Climb the easy mossy bank to confront the steeper north slope, locate the one green strip between scree fans and ascend to the NE shoulder of the fell, all with no hint of a predecessor's footsteps. From here the ridge eases to a gentle swell that rises to the summit.

Via Sail Pass   715m/2345ft   5.6km/3½ miles

2 From the Coledale Beck ford below Force Crag Mine follow the trail up to an early cairn, where a clear path breaks left heading S towards Long Comb. Fording Birkthwaite Beck, the path climbs the pasture and curves right to unite with the regular path from High Moss as the outcropping begins on the north-eastern flank of Scar Crags. Follow this regular path, approaching the top (secured by new pitching) to reach Sail Pass. Ascend W with the worn ridge trail to reach the fell-top.

ASCENT FROM BUTTERMERE (3)

Via Sail Beck   780m/2560ft   6.4km/4 miles

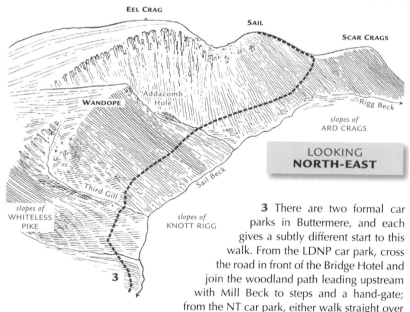

EEL CRAG

SAIL

SCAR CRAGS

WANDOPE

Addacomb Hole

Rigg Beck

slopes of ARD CRAGS

LOOKING **NORTH-EAST**

Sail Beck

Third Gill

slopes of WHITELESS PIKE

slopes of KNOTT RIGG

3 There are two formal car parks in Buttermere, and each gives a subtly different start to this walk. From the LDNP car park, cross the road in front of the Bridge Hotel and join the woodland path leading upstream with Mill Beck to steps and a hand-gate; from the NT car park, either walk straight over the road and from the stile cross the High House Crag brow, or go right with the road and bear off left, guided by the footpath sign, by the cottages to a gate, and follow the field boundary to meet up with the path from the wooded dell. Again, at this point there are two routes up the Sail Beck valley. The more common path, a shepherds' drove, makes a conscious break up left, just where the fence ends and before the

Scar Crags from high on the ascent from Sail Pass

final length of wall. This path moves comfortably through the bracken on Whiteless Breast. It swings into the re-entrant valley, then up and across Bleak Rigg bank to enter, and ascend from, the Third Gill valley before it embarks on a long traverse across the slopes of Wandope. This leads over Addacomb Beck and across a gullied section of path, and climbs with heather to an obvious cairn and path-fork. Bear up left with this path, climbing handsomely to Sail Pass, the saddle with Scar Crags, and bear up left on the sorely worn ridge trail to the summit.

THE SUMMIT

Only a tiny proportion of those who traverse the fell-top actually trouble to visit the summit – an excuse for a cairn beside a summer-dry puddle is no reason to break from the normal course of the ridge route, especially when the best of the view would seem to be from the southern edge. However, many a sandwich has been partaken on the northern edge, away from the general flow of walkers, a quiet situation looking across the nameless comb to the craggy face of Eel Crag.

SAFE DESCENTS

The southern slopes, decorated with heather and scree, are excessively steep, and the

Sail's modest summit cairn and winter pool suitably subdued by low cloud

226

northern slopes fall away quite smartly too, with outcropping on the north-east flank. If you stick carefully to worn trails you will have no difficulty, the most discomfort being the skiddy trail down to Sail Pass. Perhaps one day the Fix the Fells project will find an answer – although they have pitched the descent NE from Sail Pass to good effect.

RIDGE ROUTES

EEL CRAG	↓30m/100ft	↑99m/325ft	0.8km/½ mile

The ridge path leading W is straightforward in mist, but has a few rocky moments that may cause you to watch your footing in wet or icy conditions. The short descent along a narrow ridge is followed by an exciting climb onto the crowning plateau – great fun.

SCAR CRAGS	↓149m/490ft	↑50m/165ft	1.2km/¾ mile

The long loose gravel travail E down to Sail Pass is followed by a soothing rise onto the plateau, which leads to the summit cairn on the scarp brink.

Sail from the top of Tower Ridge on Eel Crag

PANORAMA

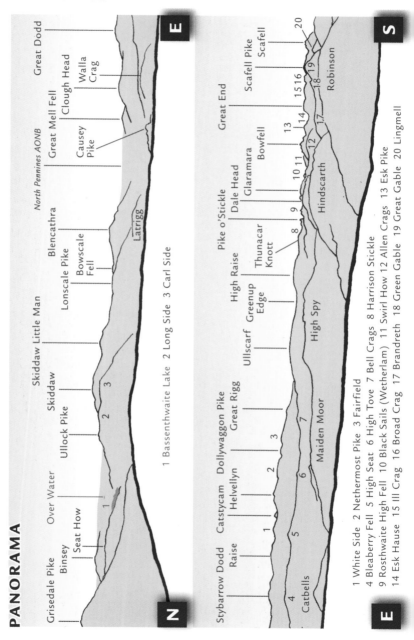

N

Grisedale Pike · Binsey · Seat How · Over Water · Ullock Pike · Skiddaw · Skiddaw Little Man · Lonscale Pike · Bowscale Fell · Blencathra · North Pennines AONB · Great Mell Fell · Clough Head · Walla Crag · Great Dodd

Causey Pike

Latrigg

E

1 Bassenthwaite Lake 2 Long Side 3 Carl Side

E

Stybarrow Dodd · Raise · Catstycam · Helvellyn · Dollywaggon Pike · Great Rigg · Ullscarf · Greenup Edge · High Raise · Pike o'Stickle · Thunacar Knott · Glaramara · Dale Head · Bowfell · Great End · Scafell Pike · Scafell

Catbells · Maiden Moor · High Spy · Hindscarth · Robinson

S

1 White Side 2 Nethermost Pike 3 Fairfield
4 Bleaberry Fell 5 High Seat 6 High Tove 7 Bell Crags 8 Harrison Stickle
9 Rosthwaite High Fell 10 Black Sails (Wetherlam) 11 Swirl How 12 Allen Crags 13 Esk Pike
14 Esk Hause 15 Ill Crag 16 Broad Crag 17 Brandreth 18 Green Gable 19 Great Gable 20 Lingmell

228

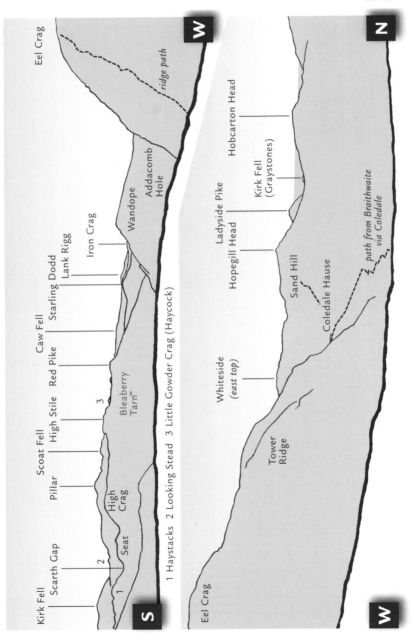

S

Kirk Fell Scarth Gap Pillar Scoat Fell High Stile Red Pike Caw Fell Starling Dodd Lank Rigg Iron Crag Wandope Eel Crag

ridge path

W

Seat High Crag Bleaberry Tarn Addacomb Hole

1 Haystacks 2 Looking Stead 3 Little Gowder Crag (Haycock)

N

Whiteside (east top) Hopegill Head Ladyside Pike Kirk Fell (Graystones) Hobcarton Head

Tower Ridge Sand Hill Coledale Hause

path from Braithwaite via Coledale

Eel Crag

W

24 SALE FELL *(359m/1178ft)*

I t is hard to tire of Sale Fell, with its very own self-contained high-ground circuit and fine view over Bassenthwaite Lake from Lothwaite. It affords shelter to the pastoral valley of Wythop, a task it performs in tandem with Ling Fell. Intriguingly, both the names 'Sale' and 'Wythop' refer to the same natural feature, the willow tree, but in different languages. The fell is bounded by Bassenthwaite Lake, the Embleton vale and Wythop, with the two Wythop streams – Wythop Beck and Beck Wythop – effectively dividing the fell from the Lord's Seat massif. Churches and woodland old and new, on opposing flanks, offer wonderful scope for a delightful variety afternoon strolls.

Opposite the Pheasant Hotel, Dubwath, a low-set wooded mound is crowned by the Iron Age hill fort Castle How, its position suggesting that the current A66 lies on an age-old access route along the southern shores of Bassenthwaite. The name of nearby Piel Wyke, meaning 'the stronghold bay', derives from this hill-fort site. Piel Wyke was also the scene of the very first sailing regatta in the Lake District, established in the 1780s by Joseph Pocklington, who built the house on Derwent Island in Derwent Water.

Turning back to the Wythop valley, as you would always wish, there is something enduring and relaxing about the setting, with native oak wood lending so much to that charm, and Skiddaw, as a backdrop, providing a wonderful sense of drama and scale. As to choice of routes to the top, walkers may sample the forest scarp by following any of the first three routes, or engage with its more open aspects with the subsequent five routes.

ASCENT FROM WOODEND (18)

Via Lothwaite   350m/1150ft   4km/2½ miles

These routes best convey the relationship of the fell to Thornthwaite Forest and Bassenthwaite Lake. A handy car park lies at the western end of the Thornthwaite road where it meets the A66. Follow the almost forgotten old road leading on W, signed as a cycleway, alongside the haste and clamour of the A66.

Here there is a choice of two routes. **1** Keep with the old road to the turning circle and entry off the A66 at Beck Wythop. Pass above the cottages, leaving the truncated road to go up the cycle trail as it rises handsomely through the conifers to cross a forest track. **2** This point can be reached more adventurously by following the footpath signed 'Wythop Hall' off the old road after a matter of 70m. Although well evidenced on the ground, it keeps tight order with the right of way shown on maps and is therefore a more vigorous wild-track. It steps over the forest track at their first encounter and heads up the woodland slope to join the track near a scenic bend. At this point keep to the track, seeking a short flight of steps after some 400m on the right, and follow the path to a footbridge over Wythop Beck. Rise on

Bridle path in Wythop Wood above Beck Wythop

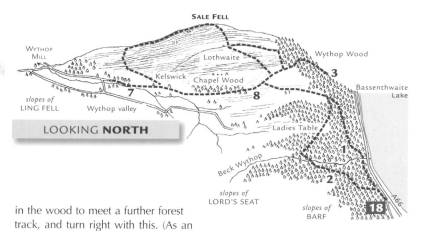

SALE FELL

WYTHOP
MILL

Lothwaite

Wythop Wood

Kelswick

Chapel Wood

Bassenthwaite
Lake

slopes of
LING FELL

Wythop valley

3

7

8

LOOKING **NORTH**

Ladies Table

1

Beck Wythop

slopes of
LORD'S SEAT

2

slopes of
BARF

18

A66

in the wood to meet a further forest track, and turn right with this. (As an aside, watch out for a small cairn on the right indicating the location of the Wilfred Watson memorial seat, a secretive viewpoint over Bassenthwaite Lake towards Dodd and Skiddaw.) Keep to the forest track until, after a slight descent, it encounters a crossing bridleway (Route 1), where you turn left.

The bridle trail winds up on bedrock to reach a gate/stile into pasture. The continuing field-edge track leads on by gates, passing the derelict Lothwaite and a line of gangly thorns, to meet a track at a gate. Go right, rising briefly, then turn left up the bracken-bank path leading over the brow. A cairn on the left might be visited (underfoot see the rigg-and-furrow corrugations – it is unclear whether this is residual 'Dig for

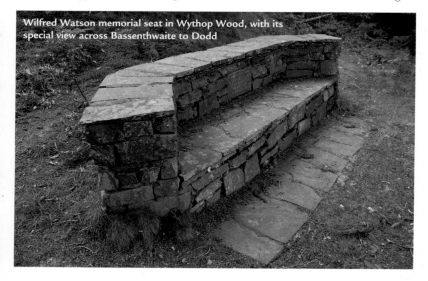

Wilfred Watson memorial seat in Wythop Wood, with its special view across Bassenthwaite to Dodd

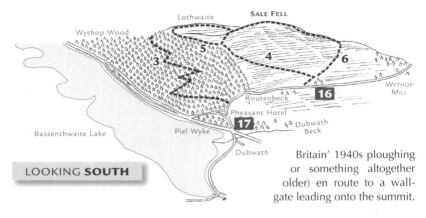

LOOKING **SOUTH**

Britain' 1940s ploughing or something altogether older) en route to a wall-gate leading onto the summit.

ASCENT FROM PHEASANT HOTEL, DUBWATH (17)

Via Wythop Wood   340m/1115ft   3.2km/2 miles

3 Follow the back-road S from the hotel junction. Continue up the hill a little further, and just before the first house in Routenbeck turn left at the signposted footpath (with seat and red squirrel sign). The path gently rises in the mature forest, coming above the timber-built Forestry Commission office buildings and forestry yard. Continue round the hill to take the next acute turn up right. At the top turn acutely left, and then right, and finally take a left turn. When this, too, comes to a junction, continue forward to a gate out of the forestry. (Walkers are at liberty to explore all the woodland tracks in Thornthwaite Forest, but it could be all too easy to keep zig-zag-ging and end up descending

Dodd across Bassenthwaite from the forest track in King's Wood

Dodd Crag and Skiddaw from the old Corpse Road on Ling Fell

and missing the exit onto the fell.) Once out on the drove-way there are two clear-cut options. You can bear up right after 100m on a path that brushes under oak trees to gain the brow and turns left along the scarp top of Lothwaite, an excellent viewpoint for Bassenthwaite and Skiddaw. Alternatively, continue along the green-way to find a path slanting up to the right (in common with Route 1) which joins with the Lothwaite path. It comes past a cairn and over the rigg-and-furrow slope to the wall-gate and the final rise to the summit.

ASCENT FROM ST MARGARET'S CHURCH, WYTHOP (16)

Via Lothwaite   210m/690ft   2.4km/1½ miles

Some 100m E of the Victorian church find a casual lay-by. At this point a gate marks the start of a green-way slanting up above the church through a gateway, from where there are three options (Routes 4–6). **4** Turn left with a well-graded grass track which leads up to a gate. However, instead of marching through, turn right, keeping the wall close left. Come up by a second gate on top of the ridge and bear right with the path onto the summit. **5** To make a sweeping round-trip of the high ground go through the first gate and follow the path running E, parallel to the forest-bounding wall, with some marshy ground, to gain the scarp edge of Lothwaite. Turn right along this crest to unite with Routes 1, 3 and 8.

Fisher Wood and Dodd Crag

Via Dodd Crag   200m/656ft   2km/1¼ miles

6 From the gateway above the church keep right, following the green-way, which eases up to cross the shoulder of the fell beside the wall. Here there is the option of continuing onto the southern flank of the fell to join the lane to Kelswick and link in with the old road to Chapel Wood (Routes 7 and 8). However, the more positive move is to branch up onto the ridge from the wall, following a path that climbs the western ridge above Dodd Crag by quartz boulders to the summit.

ASCENT FROM WYTHOP MILL (15)

Via Kelswick   210m/690ft   1.6km/1 mile

With little scope for parking in Wythop Mill, there is the choice of either using the lay-by near the old school or following the valley road E from the hamlet and parking just beyond Brunston Bridge. **7** Follow the road leading on through by a gate and up to Kelswick Farm. Just short of the buildings a footpath veers left as a terrace path, contouring past a seat to meet the wall on the ridge-end. Here bear up right in common with Route 6.

Via Chapel Wood   210m/690ft   3.2km/2 miles

8 Another much-loved route continues with the road to Kelswick and follows on with the gated track beyond, passing a curious rectangular wall structure. This is the old Wythop Church, built some time in the 14th century and abandoned in the 1860s. Since Victorian times, this has been the scene of an open-air service each August.

Outcrop close to the Sale Fell summit

The situation shows that the Wythop Beck valley once held a strong community identity – see the photo in a case set into the end-wall. This is a place to sit and reflect on times past. Pass on through the base of Chapel Wood, protected by a deer-fence, to unite with Route 1 above Lothwaite Side, pitching up acutely left.

THE SUMMIT

A large convex slate exposure is the only feature of note on a cairnless crest. The view concentrates on Skiddaw and its immediate satellites. Elsewhere, intervening fellsides block out much of stirring merit, although the Helvellyn range forms a considerable eastern horizon.

PANORAMA

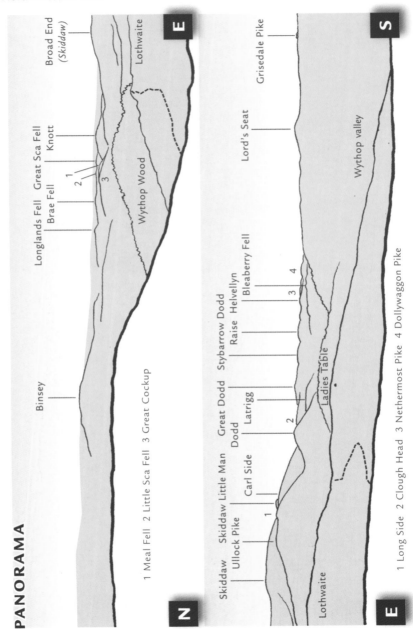

N **E**

Binsey — Longlands Fell — Brae Fell — Great Sca Fell — Knott — Broad End (Skiddaw) — Lothwaite — Wythop Wood

1 Meal Fell 2 Little Sca Fell 3 Great Cockup

E **S**

Skiddaw — Ullock Pike — Skiddaw Little Man — Carl Side — Dodd — Great Dodd — Latrigg — Stybarrow Dodd — Raise — Helvellyn — Bleaberry Fell — Ladies Table — Lord's Seat — Griesdale Pike — Wythop valley — Lothwaite

1 Long Side 2 Clough Head 3 Nethermost Pike 4 Dollywaggon Pike

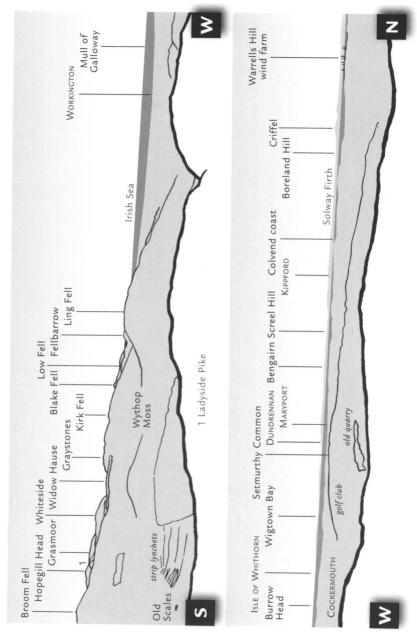

W

Mull of Galloway

WORKINGTON

Irish Sea

Ling Fell

Low Fell
Fellbarrow

Blake Fell

Kirk Fell

Graystones

Widow Hause

Whiteside

Grasmoor

Hopegill Head

Broom Fell

Wythop Moss

1 Ladyside Pike

strip lynchets

Old Scales

S

N

Warrells Hill wind farm

Criffel

Boreland Hill

Colvend coast

KIPPFORD

Solway Firth

Screel Hill

Bengairn

DUNDRENNAN

Setmurthy Common

MARYPORT

Wigtown Bay

ISLE OF WHITHORN

Burrow Head

old quarry

golf club

COCKERMOUTH

W

25 SCAR CRAGS (672m/2205ft)

B ut for the attention-stealing position of Causey Pike, Scar Crags might be more widely known and appreciated. Certainly when viewed close up from the east it is a striking ridge and an inviting climb. When seen from the south, from Ard Crags, the ravaged-by-the-elements southern aspect is broken into an almost regular pattern of arêtes and gullies spilling into the upper Rigg Beck valley. The short western slopes are rocky and included the only cobalt mine in the district, but there is little remaining evidence to the casual eye. The northern slopes are plain, and some walkers might choose to beeline to the summit this way from High Moss, although few would consider this masochistic approach when more civilised options exist.

All routes to the summit are also access points to the greater ridge, of which both Causey Pike and Sail are equal partners. As a novel traverse of the range, it is possible to start from Buttermere, follow Sail Beck and branch up to Sail Pass to claim the summit en route to Braithwaite, but usually expeditions begin from north and east – either Braithwaite (Routes 1 and 2) or the Newlands valley, at the Uzzicar verge (Route 3) or the hairpin at the foot of Rigg Beck (Route 4).

ASCENT FROM BRAITHWAITE (22)

Via Coledale 580m/1900ft 5.6km//3½ miles

1 There are two ways to start the route. You can ascend the Whinlatter road out of the village and, rounding the right-hand corner, find a footpath signposted left for Coledale Hause. Follow this path through the birch then gorse via a hand-gate to join and follow the Force Crag Mine access track into Coledale. Alternatively, start from the recessed car park (22), pass the barrier and follow the mine track direct.

Short of the secured mine buildings the track forks. Bear down left to ford Coledale Beck. Follow the trail up to an early cairn, where a clear path breaks left heading S towards Long Comb. After fording Birkthwaite Beck the path climbs the pasture and curves right to unite with the regular path from High Moss as the outcropping begins on the north-eastern flank of Scar Crags. Follow this regular path and approach the top, secured by new pitching, to reach the ridge saddle of Sail Pass. Bear up left onto the plateau to approach the prominent cairn.

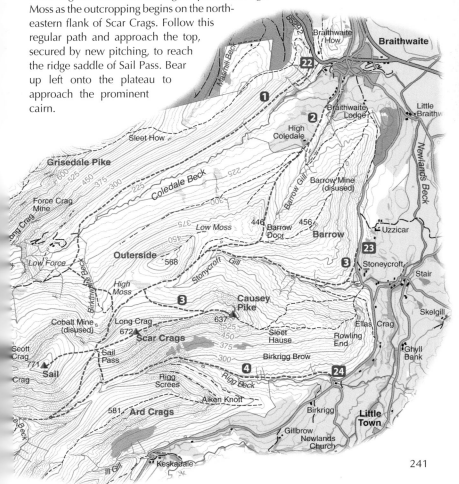

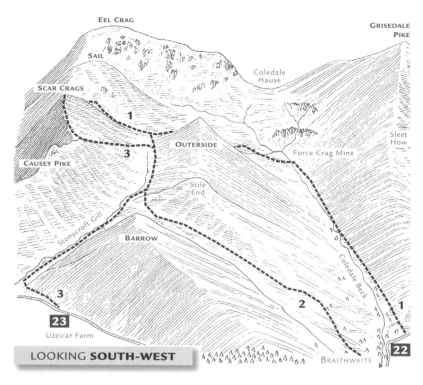

EEL CRAG

GRISEDALE
PIKE

SAIL

Coledale
Hause

SCAR CRAGS

1

Sleet
How

OUTERSIDE

3

Force Crag Mine

CAUSEY PIKE

Stile
End

Stonycroft Gill

BARROW

Coledale Beck

2

1

3

23

Uzzicar Farm

LOOKING **SOUTH-WEST**

22

BRAITHWAITE

Via Barrow Door   585m/1920ft   5.2km/3¼ miles

2 From the bridge and village shop follow the lane S. This leads up to a higher lane by Moss Garth. Veer left short of the Coledale Inn on the metalled lane leading up to a gate. The way proceeds uphill as an open track, passing a reservoir enclosure. As the copse embowering the ruins of High Coledale is passed, head straight on, with the track now a grassy

Scar Crags from Causey Pike

drove. Keep on the main way as it comes under the eastern flank of Stile End to reach Barrow Door. Turn W, contouring under Outerside to join the old mine track up the Stonycroft Gill valley and passing on by High Moss. Either continue as its dwindles to a path that climbs up beneath Long Crag to Sail Pass, or (following Route 3) switch left on the eastward-trending path, climbing to the depression short of Causey Pike then turning back W up the grand edge to the summit.

ASCENT FROM UZZICAR (23)

Via Stonycroft Gill   565m/1855ft   4.8km/3 miles

Route **3** can more naturally start from the broad road verge above Uzzicar Farm and follow the old mine track up Stonycroft Gill, originally constructed as a mineral track-bed to the cobalt mine under Long Crag.

ASCENT FROM RIGG BECK (24)

Via Sail Pass   550m/1800ft   4.8km/3 miles

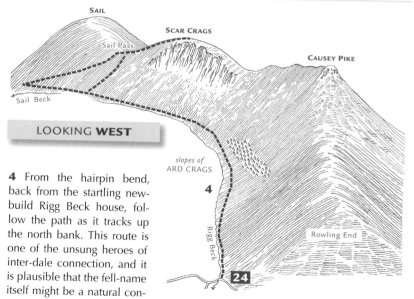

4 From the hairpin bend, back from the startling new-build Rigg Beck house, follow the path as it tracks up the north bank. This route is one of the unsung heroes of inter-dale connection, and it is plausible that the fell-name itself might be a natural contraction of 'scarth' and allude to the passage of this path up the Rigg Beck valley. The scenery is exciting, with the heathery flanks of Causey Pike and Ard Crags glowering over the passage of the path. It is given extra fascination and diversity by the presence of the old coppice oak wood above the line of the path. Walkers can trace sheep trods streaking across the flanks of Aiken Knott as they walk steadily up the narrowing gorge. At the watershed you may break up the heather slope beside a gill to make a direct assault on Sail Pass, or continue down a short way to turn acutely right, at a cairn, on a more measured path that cuts up NE to Sail Pass and continues to the summit.

THE SUMMIT

Walkers plodding up the east ridge will blink to discover a plateau spread before them – their expectation that the ridge would continue to Sail Pass being dramatically overturned. A sizable cairn marks the top spot, with another a little further to the east. The pleasure of sitting at the edge looking down the heather-decked gullies into the Rigg Beck valley is natural and most rewarding. Elsewhere there is much on view, principally on an eastern bias, although the camera will most likely be trained north-west on the striking composition formed by Hopegill Head and Force Crag below.

SAFE DESCENTS

It's all a matter of following paths – ridge paths to be precise. From the western depression, Sail Pass, you can descend the steep heather flanks to the head of Rigg Beck or follow the initially pitched path NE under Long Crag to join the old mine track down to either the Stonycroft valley or, via either Birkthwaite Gill or Barrow

Scar Crags summit cairn looking to Causey Pike

Path leading down from Sail Pass by the old cobalt mine to High Moss

Door, to venture safely to Braithwaite. Most walkers have Causey Pike in their sights, but some might consider the rocky steps off that summit troublesome, in which case the impromptu path that has materialised from the depression due west to High Moss is a handy alternative.

RIDGE ROUTES

CAUSEY PIKE	↓90m/290ft	↑55m/180ft	1.2km/¾ mile

An enjoyable walk that keeps strictly to the ridge descending ENE to lead through the depression, surprisingly adorned with peat groughs, from where the continuing ridge weaves up over the four vertebrae tops to the conclusive final knoll.

SAIL	↓50m/165ft	↑149m/490ft	1.2km/¾ mile

Leave the plateau SW to Sail Pass, from where the worn trail leads on W, drifting SE on the final rise. The path glances to the S of the summit cairn, so watch you don't get caught out and miss it!

PANORAMA

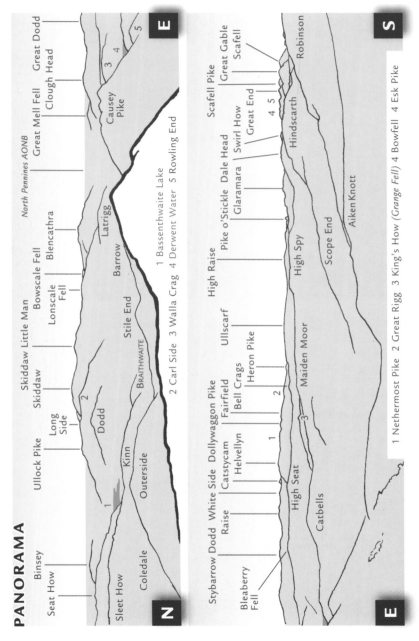

E

Great Dodd
Clough Head
Great Mell Fell
Causey Pike
3 4 5

North Pennines AONB

Blencathra
Bowscale Fell
Skiddaw Little Man
Skiddaw
Long Side
Ullock Pike

Latrigg
Barrow
Lonscale Fell
Dodd
2

Binsey
Seat How

Stile End
BRAITHWAITE
Kinn
Sleet How
Outerside
Coledale

1 Bassenthwaite Lake 2 Carl Side 3 Walla Crag 4 Derwent Water 5 Rowling End

N

S

Great Gable
Scafell
Robinson

Scafell Pike
Swirl How
Great End
4 5
Hindscarth

Great Dodd

High Raise
Pike o'Stickle Dale Head
Glaramara

High Spy
Scope End

Aiken Knott

Ullscarf
Fairfield
Bell Crags
Heron Pike
2

Maiden Moor

Stybarrow Dodd White Side Dollywaggon Pike
Raise Catstycam
Helvellyn
1
3

High Seat

Catbells

Bleaberry
Fell

1 Nethermost Pike 2 Great Rigg 3 King's How *(Grange Fell)* 4 Bowfell 4 Esk Pike

E

246

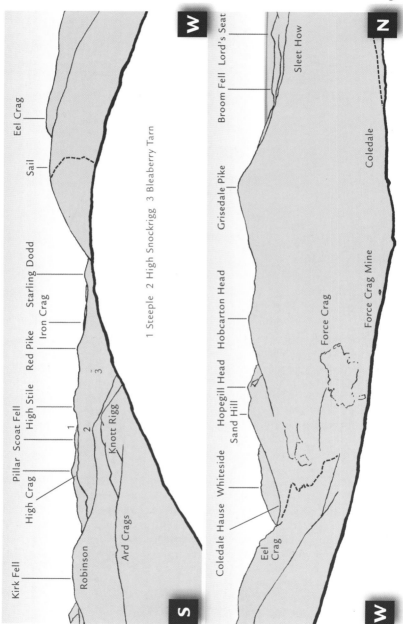

Kirk Fell — Pillar Scoat Fell — High Stile Red Pike Starling Dodd — Sail — Eel Crag

High Crag — Iron Crag

Robinson

Knott Rigg

Ard Crags

1 Steeple 2 High Snockrigg 3 Bleaberry Tarn

W S

Coledale Hause Whiteside Hopegill Head Hobcarton Head Griesdale Pike Broom Fell Lord's Seat

Eel Crag — Sand Hill — Sleet How

Force Crag

Force Crag Mine

Coledale

N W

26 WANDOPE (772m/2533ft)

Wandope is a fell of considerable character, even though it might be considered to languish out on a limb. Whiteless Pike does its level best to outshine it from the south, while Eel Crag lords it to the north. Yet Newlands Hause, and the Knott Rigg–Ard Crags ridge in particular, provide the best perspectives on a bold escarpment peak. It shares with Eel Crag custody of the hanging valley of Addacomb Hole, a wonderful, seldom-visited wild place. The fell is defined to the south by the stony gully and ravine of Third Gill, an unsavoury place for the walker. However, the cairn that stands on the western lip of the fell at Thirdgill Head Man, a place of great scenic merit in its own right, provides a useful guide and focus for walkers seeking to leave the plateau southbound.

The odd fell-name is of uncertain etymology, and the Middle English term *wanhope* ('lack of hope') is one curious attribution. Fellwalkers should know that climbing this proud scarp fulfils quite the contrary emotion. Indeed, the two ascents via Addacomb Beck (Routes 1 and 2) and Thirdgill Edge (Route 3) – the first seldom climbed, and the latter rarely – provide exhilarating experiences worthy of the mountain. Both routes will be remembered long after some of the more popular ridge ascents in the area have merged in your mind. The author witnessed a glider catching the up-draughts along the Eel Crag and Grasmoor scarps from this summit one late summer afternoon, hugging the fellsides apparently precariously – a sight that confirms Wandope as a grandstand summit.

ASCENT FROM BUTTERMERE (3)

The fell is normally included as a variation of the ridge ascent from Whiteless Pike, but more intrepid fell-wanderers, who revel in a spot of off-beat exploration, will delight in the two exclusive climbs of the fell described here. The first, via the edge above Addacomb Beck, has a variant opening stage – hence Routes 1 and 2.

Via Bleak Rigg

690m/2265ft   5.6km/3½ miles

1 There are two car parks in Buttermere village, and each gives a subtly different introduction to this walk up the Sail Beck valley. From the LDNP car park, cross the road in front of the Bridge Hotel and join the woodland path leading upstream with Mill Beck to steps and a hand-gate. From the NT park, either walk straight over the road and from the stile cross the High House Crag brow, or go right with the road and bear off left, guided by the footpath sign, by the cottages to a gate, and follow the field boundary to meet up with the path from the wooded dell.

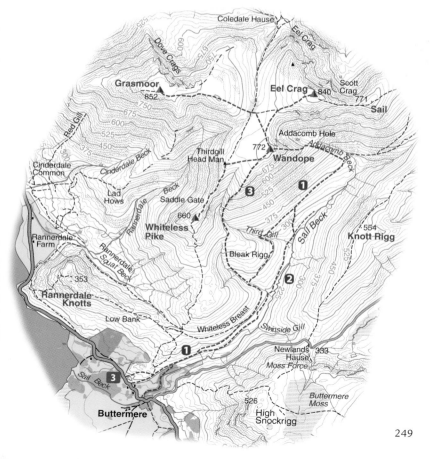

249

Walled bank on Bleak Rigg

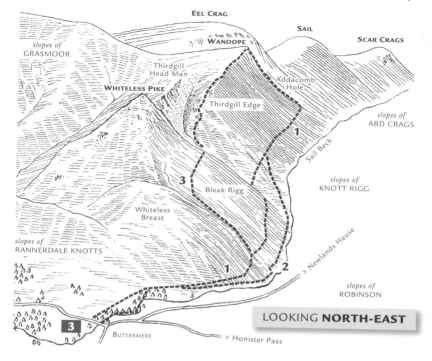

LOOKING **NORTH-EAST**

Again, at this point there are two variant routes up the Sail Beck valley (see also Route 2). The more common path, a shepherds' drove, makes a conscious break up left, just where the fence ends and before the final length of wall. This path moves comfortably through the bracken on Whiteless Breast, swinging into a nameless re-entrant valley then up and across the next Bleak Rigg bank to enter, and ascend from, the Third Gill valley. It then embarks on a long traverse across the slopes of Wandope.

Via Sail Beck

690m/2265ft   5.6km/3½ miles

2 Alternatively, you may keep to the natural line of the path from the wall-end in the lower realms of the valley. After fording Third Gill, above the old fold, the sheep-trod path dwindles and is quickly lost in the rushes. Here, angle up the bank to what appears to be a ruined fold, then slant half-right to avoid the bracken to join the main path high on the slope, which now leads to the ford of Addacomb Beck. Short of the ford bear up the bracken-clad slope, avoiding the uninviting environs of the cascading beck. Walkers may peruse the hanging valley of Addacomb Hole, but the only ascent available is up the east ridge, forming the left-hand edge to the comb. As soon as the ridge begins a narrow trod is found that winds easily and naturally to the summit.

Via Thirdgill Edge   690m/2265ft   4.4km/2¾ miles

3 Of far less appeal to the majority, to judge by the complete lack of a path, is a route directly out of Third Gill. This more exploratory route breaks off the regular drove approach (see Route 1) as it enters the first nameless re-entrant valley. If the bracken is up, then keep to the slightly steeper left-hand grass slope until it is obvious that you can ford the gill and join the old wall-bank climbing up Bleak Rigg. Follow this as it veers sharp right (NE) to partition the better pasture from the headwall of Whiteless Pike. The wall-bank ends as it meets the steep slope falling into Third Gill. Follow the obvious sheep trod, left. The agility and balance of sheep, four feet square to the ground, must be respected as the path takes a delicate line above the steep slope via rock-steps to enter the gorge. Climb straight out and find your feet on the steep path-

less grass bank. Watch your hands on the prostrate gorse as you clamber higher, out-manoeuvring the out-cropping onto the ridge of Thirdgill Edge, with consistently fine views across the ravine to Whiteless Edge. As the slope eases, a path is found, no doubt created by summit visitors walking there and back.

Ascent of Thirdgill Edge

High Snockrigg from Wandope summit

THE SUMMIT

A small cairn occupies a most pleasing perch overlooking the hanging valley of Addacomb Hole and offers a grandstand view of the massive scree-scarred escarpment of Eel Crag. Nonetheless, the greatest excitement lies to the SSE over the shoulder of Robinson and above High Snockrigg, where Great Gable and the Scafells tantalise the eyes, with Haystacks and High Stile completing an amazing mountain collective.

SAFE DESCENTS

The open prairie of grass to the west gives encouragement that an easy way is available. No such luck – steep ground of one sort of another lies in all directions. The popular ridge path heading S from Whiteless Pike is joined from Wandope at Thirdgill Head Man, SW from the summit. The sharp descent from

Thirdgill Head Man

the summit E down the edge by Addacomb Hole is not problematic and gets you onto a good path down the Sail Beck valley to Buttermere quickest of all.

RIDGE ROUTES

EEL CRAG	↓35m/115ft	↑103m/340ft	1.2km/¾ mile

Head NNW, initially guided by the edge, to curve naturally around the comb head and join the main ridge path NE up the plain back of Eel Crag.

GRASMOOR	↓30m/100ft	↑110m/360ft	2km/1¼ miles

Head NNW, guided by the scarp edge, but continue straight to the path cross-ways in the depression. Bear W up the bank on a regular path to a prominent cairn on the brow, from where a terrace path skirts the edge to the summit shelter.

WHITELESS PIKE	↓146m/480ft	↑34m/110ft	1.6km/1 mile

Aim SW to join the regular ridge path at Thirdgill Head Man (cairn), then trend SSW down the narrowing ridge through the dip of Saddle Gate to climb onto the summit.

PANORAMA

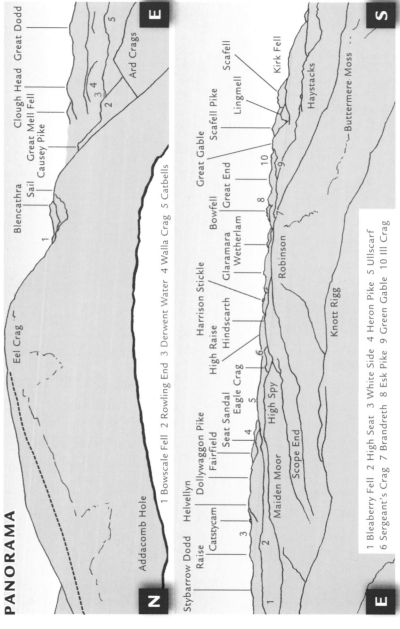

N

E

Addacomb Hole

Eel Crag

Blencathra
Sail
Causey Pike
Great Mell Fell
Clough Head
Great Dodd

Ard Crags

1 Bowscale Fell 2 Rowling End 3 Derwent Water 4 Walla Crag 5 Catbells

E

S

Stybarrow Dodd
Raise
Catstycam
Helvellyn
Dollywaggon Pike
Fairfield
Seat Sandal
Eagle Crag
High Raise
Harrison Stickle
Hindscarth
Glaramara
Wetherlam
Bowfell
Great End
Great Gable
Scafell Pike
Lingmell
Scafell
Kirk Fell
Haystacks
Buttermere Moss

Maiden Moor
High Spy
Scope End
Robinson
Knott Rigg

1 Bleaberry Fell 2 High Seat 3 White Side 4 Heron Pike 5 Ullscarf
6 Sergeant's Crag 7 Brandreth 8 Esk Pike 9 Green Gable 10 Ill Crag

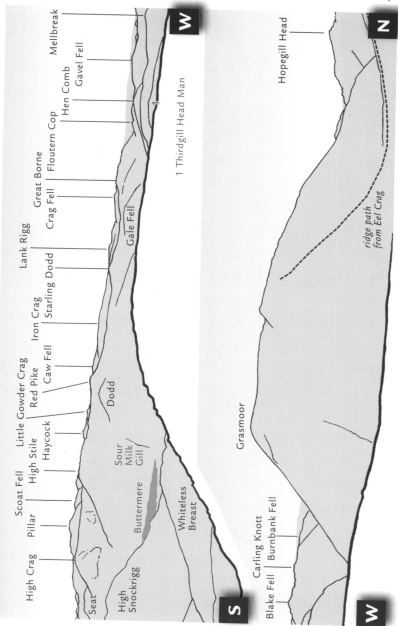

W

Mellbreak
Gavel Fell
Hen Comb
Floutern Cop
Great Borne
Crag Fell
Gale Fell
Lank Rigg
Starling Dodd
Iron Crag
Caw Fell
Red Pike
Little Gowder Crag
Dodd
High Stile
Haycock
Scoat Fell
Pillar
Sour Milk Gill
High Crag
Buttermere
Seat
High Snockrigg
Whiteless Breast

1 Thirdgill Head Man

S

N

Hopegill Head

ridge path from Eel Crag

Grasmoor

Carling Knott
Burnbank Fell
Blake Fell

W

27 WHINLATTER *(517m/1696ft)*

I f the high ground north of Whinlatter Pass were in Scotland, then it would be seen as part of Lord's Seat to the north – a single hill with subservient radial ridges. But as we are in the exquisite confines of Lakeland, and especially since the invasion of conifers, the inclination has been to partition the massif into four separate fells, including Whinlatter. Strangely, the highest point on this section of the fell, known as Whinlatter Top (526m/1726ft), has, by fellwalking convention, been relegated to subsidiary status, while the acknowledged summit is Brown How (517m/1695ft).

No matter by what division or description it is known, for the fellwalker Whinlatter is a most enjoyable westward arm of the massif – a curving ridge of high ground richly endowed in heather. Viewed from deep within the Whinlatter Pass the long scree-streaked slopes look uninviting, yet once on top of the ridge, and this is easily achieved, the views are superb. Most notable are the prospects into the great wild bowl of Hobcarton Gill and back upon Lord's Seat itself. The fell-name is descriptive of 'the steep slope regaled in gorse'.

With the exception of the steep southern slopes, the fell has a thick coat of conifers, although recent felling on the northern slopes is relieving it of some of this ungainly garment. Routes to the top are therefore limited by forest-bounding fences and, of course, the steepness of the southern declivity. Nonetheless, options are not limited to a there-and-back ridge walk from Whinlatter Forest Park – circuits can deftly be crafted using four high keyholes and tracks in valleys of both Whinlatter Gill (Routes 1 and 2) and Aiken Beck (Routes 3 and 4).

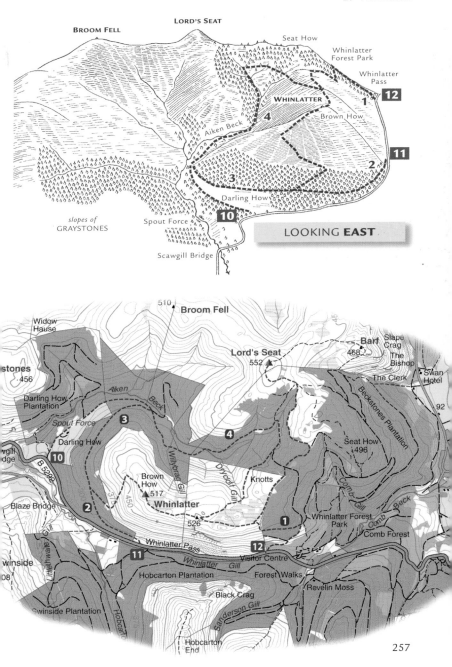

BROOM FELL

LORD'S SEAT

Seat How

Whinlatter
Forest Park

Whinlatter
Pass

WHINLATTER

12

1

4

Brown How

Aiken Beck

11

2

3

Darling How

10

slopes of
GRAYSTONES

Spout Force

LOOKING **EAST**

Scawgill Bridge

510

Broom Fell

Widow
Hause

Lord's Seat
552

Bar

Slape
Crag

468

The
Bishop

stones
.456

The Clerk

Swan
Hotel

Aiken

Darling How
Plantation

Beck

Beckstones Plantation

92

Spout Force

3

4

Willybrag Gill

Dryfoot Gill

Seat How
.496

Darling How

Comb Gill

Comb Beck

vgill
dge

10

B 5292

Brown
How
▲517

Knotts

Comb Forest

2

Whinlatter

Whinlatter Forest
Park

Blaze Bridge

450

526

1

Comb Forest

winside
08

Whinlatter Pass

Littlehwaite Gill

11

12

Visitor Centre

Whinlatter Gill

Forest Walks

Revelin Moss

Hobcarton Plantation

Hobcarton

Black Crag

Swinside Plantation

Sanderson Gill

Hobcarton
End

257

ASCENT FROM WHINLATTER PASS (12)

Via Whinlatter Top   245m/805ft   2.8km/1¾ miles

1 You may choose to begin this route from Whinlatter Forest Park visitor centre and Siskin café. The Honister Rambler bus service pulls in here regularly during the summer season, and you can use the metered car park. The direct start point, however, is the roadside lay-by at the forest edge, to the west of the park entrance. Pass the barrier and ascend the green track. Ignore the first green path left and rise, passing beneath the red squirrel ropeway, to reach the large sweeping bend, with its squirrel habitat panel. Here turn left, off the main track, following the forest track due W. Rise easily to a turning-bay and, beyond this, a hand-gate in the forest boundary fence. Turn abruptly uphill, beside the fence, and climb steeply to arrive quickly on the ridge top. Resume the westward trail coming over the true summit. Duly slip through the cross-ridge wall, advancing into heather and to the west top, Brown How, with its curved wind-shelter.

ASCENT FROM WHINLATTER GILL (11)

Via Brown How   270m/885ft   2.4km/1½ miles

2 Park off the road – a suitable space is available to the left. Step back onto the road and go left, seeking the gateway and barrier on the right. Here embark on a forest track that largely contours at first. This rises, and at its highest point find a ramped green-way that switches acutely back right in the midst of the coniferous tangle. The old drove leads through a wall-gateway in the dark of the forest and comes up to a partial clearing. At this point find a plain fence in the broken wall bounding the maturing plantation. Cross

High-perched sheepfold on the southern flank of Brown How

and bear half-left, with hints of sheep trods and the odd fell-wanderers' path giving encouragement, and avoid the scree and minor outcropping. You may curve up right, although it is better to aim for the skyline on the same trajectory. A strong sheep path is found on the edge, which leads steadily back to the summit, becoming more certain as you travel. The path would seem to have been developed by walkers double-walking – following it NW from the summit on the misapprehension that it is a continuing path, and, finding it to be nothing of the sort, heading back to Brown How. The sheep use it a lot too – well they would; they live here!

ASCENT FROM DARLING HOW (10)

These two routes combine beautifully to make a tidy circuit, exclusive to Whinlatter and best followed anti-clockwise.

Via Brown How   280m/920ft   2.8km/1¾ miles

3 Follow the track leading on beyond the barrier into the Aiken Beck valley. Ignore paths and the one track left. Watch for the acute switchback track taking the route from eastbound to westbound. This rises beside the forest to come into the shadow of the trees above the rising field-wall. Follow this to the highest point, where you come to the part-shrouded drove which bears off up a ramp half-left. Follow this as per Route 2.

Via Whinlatter Top   300m/985ft   4.8km/3 miles

4 Maintain company with the forest track leading up the Aiken Beck valley. Gaining height, this switches S and climbs more into the young forest. Watch for a minor, level, cleared trackway branching half-right, which leads through to a stile in the

Ridge path leading east to Whinlatter Top

Crescent wind-shelter on Whinlatter

bounding fence, where a fence converges on the far side. A regular path ensues, contouring to ford Drycloff Gill before wandering upwards over the rough moor-grass terrain to unite with the main ridge path on the true summit.

THE SUMMIT

As has been mentioned there are two summits, which might be thought a nonsense. Wainwright was aware of the problem, yet stuck to the traditional habit of attributing that status to Brown How. The panorama is given from that point, as any walker coming onto the fell will wish to come all the way to the crescent cairn to experience the ridge in all its glory. However, Whinlatter Top, with its more conventional cairn, is a proper summit right enough. Yet it is the west top that is the better viewing station, and in my book situation and setting are significant factors in identifying a summit. The Hobcarton Gill valley, focused on Ladyside Pike and Hopegill Head, and, nearer left, Hobcarton End, backed by Grisedale Pike, are strong subjects for any camera, and the turf is a fine place to sit and contemplate the larks in the sky.

If you fancy a spot of exploration you might be tempted to pay a visit to an unusually sited sheepfold set on a tiny shelf some 100m down the heather bank, SSE of Brown How, and unseen from the ridge path. What is remarkable is its state of preservation and its position – it seems such an awkward place for a shepherd to operate.

SAFE DESCENTS

Obviously any route S would be a bad move. It is better to head E along the ridge, turning down right at the point the forest fence is met to find a hand-gate and the security of a forest track for Whinlatter Pass. If you follow the same fence NE you can exit the moor at a hand-gate. The path leads through a tunnel of trees to the forest track, where you may turn left and comfortably wander down to Darling How.

RIDGE ROUTE

LORD'S SEAT	↓55m/180ft	↑90m/295ft	3.6km/2¼ miles

Follow the ridge E, coming to the bounding fence. Veer left, dipping to come close to the fence and continuing to a hand-gate in the north-east corner of the open fell enclosure. The path slips through a tunnel, crossing a section of the Altura bikers' trail – watch out for excited sounds and careering wheels! The path emerges onto a fully fledged forest track at an enlarged sweeping junction. Turn right, heading NE, and keep left at the next junction (avoiding the Altura route straight on). The forest track becomes almost level and dwindles to a path, which advances by cross-paths to climb to the prominent summit beyond the forest fence.

Whinlatter Pass

PANORAMA

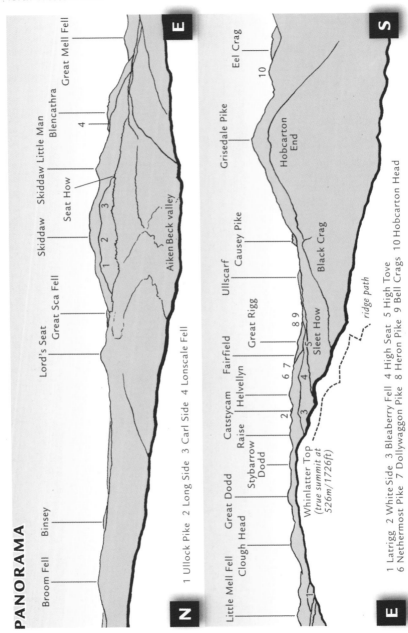

E

Eel Crag

10

Grisedale Pike

Hobcarton End

Causey Pike

Ullscarf

Black Crag

Great Rigg

8 9

Fairfield

Sleet How

5

Catstycam

Helvellyn

6 7

Raise

4

Stybarrow Dodd

2

3

Great Dodd

Whinlatter Top
(true summit at 526m/1726ft)

Little Mell Fell

Clough Head

ridge path

S

E

1 Latrigg 2 White Side 3 Bleaberry Fell 4 High Seat 5 High Tove
6 Nethermost Pike 7 Dollywaggon Pike 8 Heron Pike 9 Bell Crags 10 Hobcarton Head

E

Great Mell Fell

Blencathra

4

Skiddaw Little Man

Seat How

Skiddaw

3

Great Sca Fell

2

Lord's Seat

1

Aiken Beck valley

Binsey

Broom Fell

N

1 Ullock Pike 2 Long Side 3 Carl Side 4 Lonscale Fell

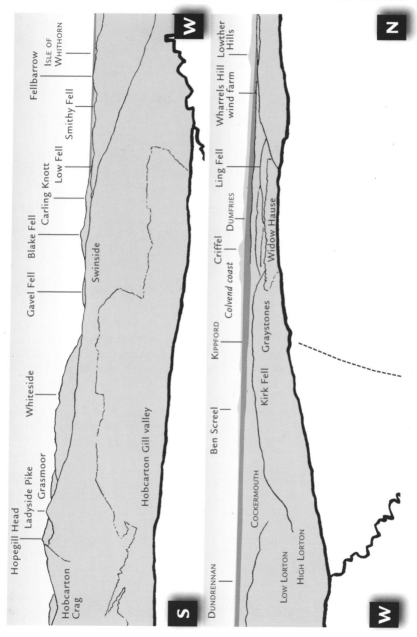

28 WHITELESS PIKE *(660m/2165ft)*

As travellers come along the road by Rannerdale Farm, their eyes are irresistibly drawn to Whiteless Pike. While it is not the biggest mountain in view, for sheer elegance of mountain form this is the peak of perfection. Seemingly standing alone and aloof, it is a glorious gift to the scenic abundance of this much-loved mountain vale, the narrow connecting ridge with the main Grasmoor massif hidden from lowly stations.

The fell is sharply defined to the west by Rannerdale Beck and is connected to Rannerdale Knotts at a low saddle at the head of Squat Beck. Two lower truncated ridges lie to the south and east – Whiteless Breast and Bleak Rigg – divided by gills draining into Sail Beck. The greatest and most deeply cutting of these ravines is Third Gill, which has so incised the northern slopes of the fell as to create a narrow ridge, Whiteless Edge, rising from the Saddle Gate col.

The fell-name is a wonderful enigma, perhaps truncated from 'the pike of Whiteless Breast' – is the 'less' some sort of vernacular corruption, or was it simply considered to be less white than Whiteside? As a ridge-end summit, with difficult slopes on either flank, the options for ascent are limited to the one focal climb. Most ascents begin from Buttermere village, although occasionally walkers begin from Cinderdale Common, wandering into the bluebell-graced Rannerdale and subsequent Squat Beck valley to unite with the primary ascent. Invariably this approach forms the opening gambit on a circuit of the massif. For the majority of fellwalkers, the summit marks the beginning of a great mountain day, bagging fine summits, either as part of a round-trip or with Whiteless Pike as the first stepping-stone in a traverse of the range that ends at Newlands or Braithwaite.

↑ Whiteless Pike and the Rannerdale Wood bluebells

ASCENT FROM BUTTERMERE (3)

Direct   550m/1805ft   2.8km/1¾ miles

An enjoyable climb from start to finish. **1** Three options are available at the start. From
the National Trust car park, pass to the right of the facing quarry, walk up the bank and
from the fence-stile cross the High House Crag brow. Alternatively, start in harmony
with the principal path up the Sail Beck valley, stepping off the village road some 70m
to the right of the car park entrance. Here a double-headed footpath sign points left.
Walk on past the cottage garden to go through a hand-gate, taking the obvious path
that shortly veers half-left up the fell in harmony with the High House Crag path.

As a third option, from the National Park car park in the lower end of the village
beyond the Fish Hotel, walk back up the street and turn left in front of the Bridge Hotel
to join the path on the left bank of Mill Beck (the name of this lower section of Sail
Beck). The path leads upstream in lovely woodland overlooking the dancing beck, and

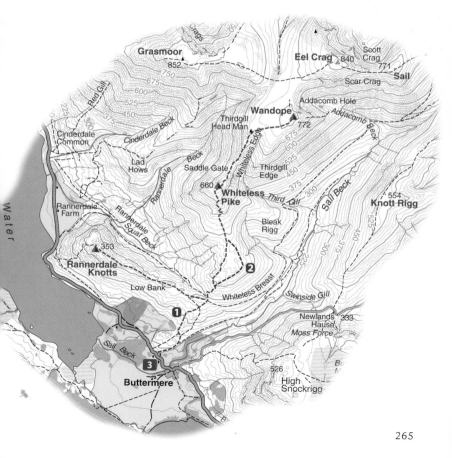

Whiteless Pike from the top of Dale How on Rannerdale Knotts

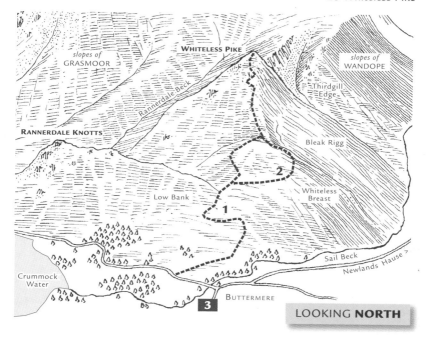

in its later stages climbs a short flight of steps to a hand-gate. Head half-right up the fellside on a path that brushes aside the bracken. This is one of two turf carpet paths clear of bracken that lead naturally up Low Bank to the saddle at the head of Squat Beck. Look out for the winding path climbing N, coming onto the western shoulder on

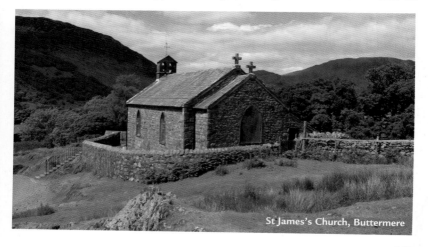

St James's Church, Buttermere

the reverse side of Whiteless Breast. **2** Walkers seldom deviate from the regular path, so sheep have this lower portion of the fell largely to themselves – although a pathless line can be made skirting around the upper eastern slopes for improved views into the Sail Beck valley. Then rejoin the main thoroughfare and set to work on the more earnest part of the climb. Apart from one minor rock-step high up, the climb is obvious, and with modern pitching supporting the heavy use, the way is never in doubt. Your arrival on the summit will be greeted with justified elation.

THE SUMMIT

It is not quite the freestanding peak suggested during the climb, but is sufficient to give a wonderful feeling of achievement. The slight disappointment is assuaged by the magnificent view over the Crummock and Buttermere valley. Grasmoor still looks big, but with the continuing ridge to the north inviting you on to Thirdgill Head Man, the climb no longer looks as daunting. There is minimal hint of a cairn, but the summit has no need of such. If you intend to spend a little time here – and you should – a good place to sit is a short way down the western prow, overlooking Rannerdale, and therefore away from the regular passage of walkers.

SAFE DESCENTS

Just as there is one way up, so there is just the one way down, basically south. Watch for an awkward rock-step quite early on, and as the path gets a real hammering from over-hasty walkers racing off the range loose stones abound, and the ball-bearing effect can be disconcerting.

Whiteless Pike beyond Saddle Gate from Whiteless Edge

Summit cairn looking to
Thirdgill Head and Wandope

RIDGE ROUTES

RANNERDALE KNOTTS	↓370m/1215ft	↑63m/205ft	2.8km/1¾ miles

Take to the regular path that leads off the left edge of the summit southwards. Watch for the rock-step and gully, below which is new pitching to secure the heavily burdened path. The path keeps to the right-hand side of the lower broadened section of the ridge, and angles down to the saddle at the head of the Squat Beck valley – which many incorrectly name as Rannerdale. Move naturally W onto the emerging ridge of Low Bank that leads to the summit – a pleasure every step of the way.

WANDOPE	↓34m/110ft	↑146m/480ft	1.6km/1 mile

Follow the ridge N down through Saddle Gate and up the subsequent Whiteless Edge to Thirdgill Head Man, from where veer ENE over the grass to the cairn.

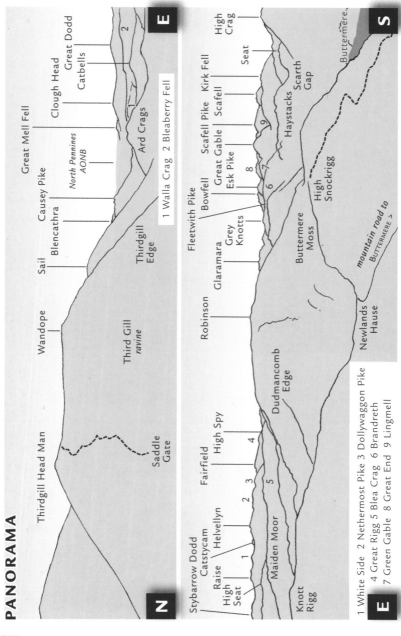

PANORAMA

N

Thirdgill Head Man

Saddle Gate

Stybarrow Dodd
Catstycam
Helvellyn
High Seat
Raise

Fairfield
High Spy

Maiden Moor

Knott Rigg

1 White Side 2 Nethermost Pike 3 Dollywaggon Pike
4 Great Rigg 5 Blea Crag 6 Brandreth
7 Green Gable 8 Great End 9 Lingmell

E

Great Mell Fell

Sail   Causey Pike
Wandope   Blencathra

Clough Head
Great Dodd
Catbells

North Pennines
AONB

Ard Crags

Thirdgill Edge

Third Gill *ravine*

1 Walla Crag 2 Bleaberry Fell

E

Fleetwith Pike   Scafell Pike Kirk Fell
Bowfell   Great Gable Scafell
Glaramara   Esk Pike
Grey Knotts
Robinson

Haystacks
Seat
Scarth Gap

High Crag

Buttermere

Dudmancomb Edge

Buttermere Moss
High Snockrigg

Newlands Hause

mountain road to
BUTTERMERE >

S

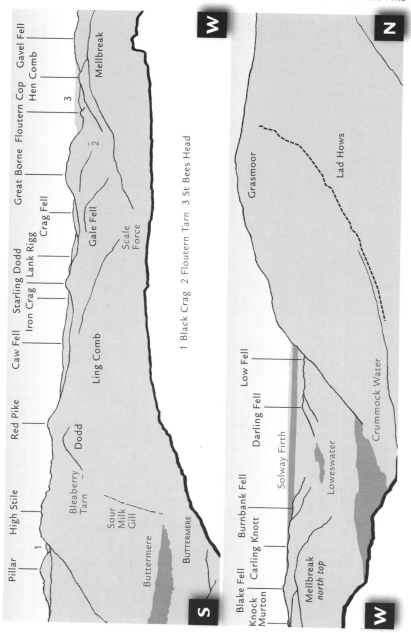

W

N

Grasmoor

Lad Hows

Low Fell

Darling Fell

Solway Firth

Burnbank Fell

Carling Knott

Loweswater

Crummock Water

Blake Fell

Knock Murton

Mellbreak *north top*

W

Gavel Fell
Hen Comb
Floutern Cop
Great Borne
Starling Dodd
Caw Fell
Red Pike
High Stile
Pillar

Mellbreak

Crag Fell

Lank Rigg
Iron Crag

Gale Fell

Scale Force

Ling Comb

Dodd

Bleaberry Tarn

Sour Milk Gill

Buttermere

BUTTERMERE

3

2

1

S

1 Black Crag 2 Floutern Tarn 3 St Bees Head

271

29 WHITESIDE *(707m/2320ft)*

Whiteside is the abrupt western termination of a wonderful ridge, one of the simplest and most enjoyable airy strides in Lakeland. Indeed, many walkers visit the summit on a there-and-back spur indulgence from Hopegill Head, normally while engaged in the Coledale Horseshoe. Yet the fell makes a fine objective, especially when combined with Hopegill Head and Gasgale Gill or the grand footpath running along its base between Hopebeck and Lanthwaite Green.

The fell-name suggests the presence of quartz, but walkers will search in vain for evidence of it, as the gullied east slope falling into the Gasgale Gill valley – no place for the walker – shows no characteristic white streaks. Perhaps there was once a (now lost) prominent pale patch in view from Brackenthwaite. From across the open common at Lanthwaite Green the fell rises handsomely, with Whin Ben the first inviting step.

Conventionally, northern ascents begin from the Hopebeck fell-road. But an enchanting lead-in to the fell-road begins from the village of High Lorton, via Boonbeck Lane, initially upon a field-edge path to Scales and then within a beautiful green lane leading south to High Swinside Farm.

ASCENT FROM LANTHWAITE GREEN (6)

Via Whin Ben   565m/1855ft   2.4km/1½ miles

1 The swiftest and best way to the top. Go over the open road and traverse the common E to cross the Liza Beck footbridge. Embark on the steady upward climb, with heather making the endeavour all the more enjoyable. The pronounced step of Whin Ben provides fine views across the dale gulf, with Grasmoor pre-eminent. The climb is thereafter without incident, although the latter stages provide further cause to linger as you gaze into the Gasgale Gill (Liza Beck) valley and along the ridge, with fine rock architecture in the foreground.

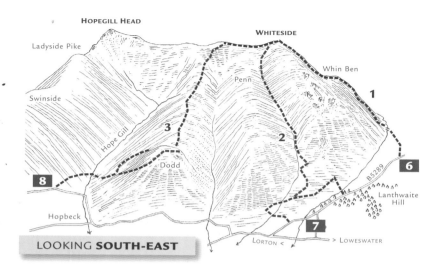

LOOKING **SOUTH-EAST**

Liza Beck tumbling out
of the Gasgale Gill ravine

Low Hollins backed by the Wythe Gill comb

ASCENT FROM HIGH LIZA BRIDGE (7)

Via Wythe Gill   600m/1970ft   2km/1¼ miles

2 A tough but quietly scenic way. Scope for parking is limited (avoid blocking the field-gate). You may consider it better to use Lanthwaite Wood NT car park, and to reach this point via the Pickett Howe footpath. There is an alternative start to this route, described below.

Follow the road N, turning right opposite the 'Give Way 180yds' sign into the bridle lane signed 'Millerplace'. The gravel track leads by Low Hollins, a fascinating vernacular house with the lintel datestone 1687, to a hand-gate entering a confined lane. Coming to a hand-gate, with the handsome pink-toned High Hollins farmhouse and its delightful dripped-moulded windows glimpsed ahead, turn right through the adjacent gate into the field (permissive path notice). The path curves easily up and right onto a green-way by the wall-corner and fords Wythe Gill to reach and go through a hurdle-gate in the intake wall. Quickly step onto the bracken-free footpath, which in its entirety runs from Lanthwaite Green to Hopebeck beside the intake wall.

Alternatively, walk S from High Liza Bridge with the B5289, going through the gate on the left opposite Beck House. At the time of writing, the footbridge was await-ing reinstatement over the Liza (following the floods of November 2009). From the next gate keep close to the wall on the right and advance to the steps and hand-gate in the intake wall. Bear left, rising briefly to join and follow the regular footpath in harmony with the wall. Some 300m beyond the outcropping, join up with the route described above.

Go directly uphill without the aid of a path, coming up by low outcropping and towards the more general bracken slope. Moving up towards the scree, find a sheep

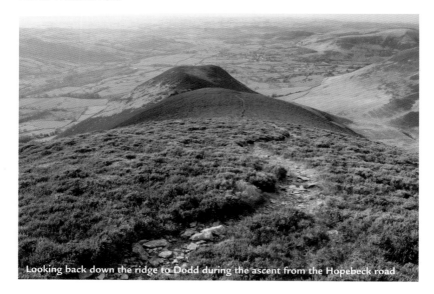

Looking back down the ridge to Dodd during the ascent from the Hopebeck road

path which drifts half-left to reach Wythe Gill, with some outcropping, and continue uphill with the gill. As the watercourse becomes subterranean discover, with some surprise, a path holding to the base of the rising valley. After passing a bield, the path progressively falters, but the way is no less clear straight up the steep bank to the skyline. As the slope eventually eases, the summit comes into view ahead.

ASCENT FROM HIGH SWINSIDE (8)

Via the Dodd ridge   600m/1970ft   3.6km/2¼ miles

3 A characterful climb – particularly to and through the heather. A parking bay close to the road-gate above Hopebeck provides an appropriate launch pad, although a field-path from Boonbeck via Scales and High Swinside serves for walkers starting from High Lorton.

Follow the footpath sign S into the Hope Beck valley. Ford the beck beside the ruined sheep-wash fold and smartly branch half-left via bracken ways. Rise onto a shelf green-way slanting SE along the slope of Dodd. You may consider following the walkers' trod directly up from the bield onto the subsidiary top itself as a stiff start to the overall climb. The more common option curves up into the slate-strewn gap south of Dodd, a wild place fit for an ambush. The path mounts out of the gap S, climbing the heather ridge. Higher up the heather is replaced with grass, and the route becomes less certain underfoot as the ridge opens onto the nameless ridge-top crest. It is sometimes known as the East Top (719m), being a bit higher than the accepted summit, which is reached by following the ridge right (WSW).

THE SUMMIT

A modest cairn sits on top of a rock plinth. It is definitely a summit, but is not **the** summit, in terms of the ridge as a whole. That accolade clearly belongs to the next rise in the ridge, not far short of 1km distant and known as the East Top at 719m (2359ft) (shades of Whinlatter, me thinks, where the conventional top is also lower but accepted by flawed logic). But this is the better spot to stand, with all the fun and excitement concentrated to the south. Standing on the profound craggy escarpment, witness sensational views into the Gasgale Gill valley and across the gulf to Dove Crags, buttressing Grasmoor. To the east the twisting roof of a ridge directs attention tantalisingly towards the peak of Hopegill Head. Camera-toting walkers will relish the view from a little down to the south, which offers the most impressive views along the craggy scarp.

SAFE DESCENTS

The common path leading SSW down the edge to Whin Ben is largely bereft of hazard, although it is quite steep as it makes for the Liza Beck footbridge. But there is a case in harsh conditions for heading NW, going steeply down into the embrace of the Wythe Gill valley to avoid all hint of outcropping and to reach the intake wall. From there a path leads left to Lanthwaite Green and right to the Hopebeck fell-road.

RIDGE ROUTE

HOPEGILL HEAD	↓45m/150ft	↑108m/355ft	2km/1¼ miles

The perennially popular, largely ridge-topping path runs almost due E, with the object peak a wonderful lure. Frequent stops to look over the heathery edge are recommended, and the final third of the journey is perhaps the very best as the crest narrows.

Ridge running west from Hopegill Head, with the deeply set Gasgale Gill down to the left

PANORAMA

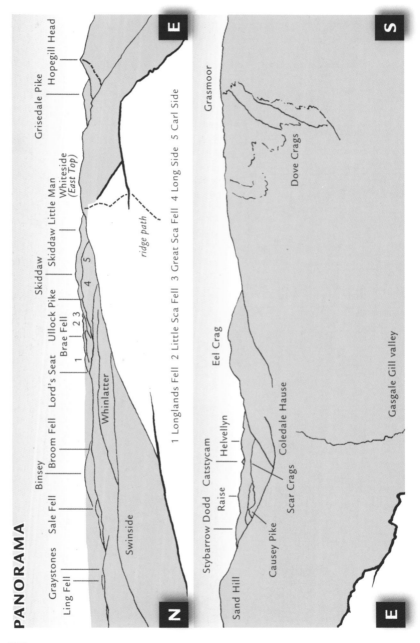

N

E

S

E

1 Longlands Fell 2 Little Sca Fell 3 Great Sca Fell 4 Long Side 5 Carl Side

Ling Fell
Graystones
Sale Fell
Binsey
Broom Fell
Lord's Seat
Brae Fell
Ullock Pike
Skiddaw
Skiddaw Little Man
Whiteside (East Top)
Grisedale Pike
Hopegill Head

Swinside
Whinlatter
ridge path

Grasmoor
Dove Crags
Gasgale Gill valley

Stybarrow Dodd
Catstycam
Helvellyn
Raise
Eel Crag
Coledale Hause
Scar Crags
Causey Pike
Sand Hill

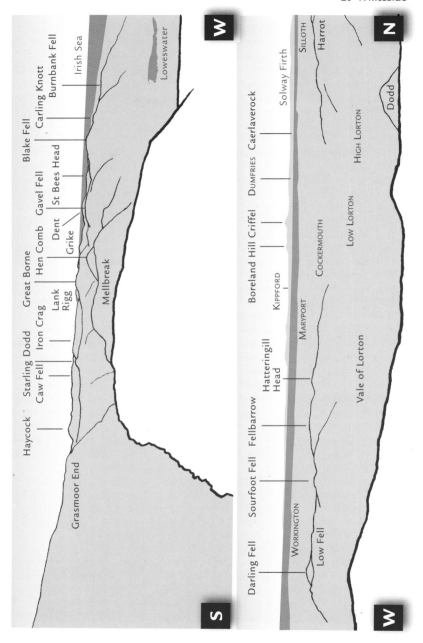

Haycock · Starling Dodd · Great Borne · Blake Fell · Carling Knott
Caw Fell · Iron Crag · Lank Rigg · Hen Comb · Gavel Fell · Burnbank Fell
Dent · St Bees Head
Grike
Mellbreak

Grasmoor End

Lowewater

Irish Sea

W
S

Darling Fell · Sourfoot Fell · Fellbarrow · Hatteringill Head · Boreland Hill Criffel · Dumfries · Caerlaverock · Silloth
Harrot

Low Fell · Vale of Lorton · Cockermouth · Low Lorton · High Lorton
Dodd

WORKINGTON · MARYPORT · KIPPFORD · Solway Firth

W
N

FIXING THE FELLS
FOR THE FUTURE

In preparing this guide I am ever more keenly aware of the work being done to secure the fell paths, making the whole fell environment visually a better place. The National Park Authority in conjunction with the National Trust are playing crucial roles within the structure of the Fix the Fells Project (visit: www.fixthefells.co.uk).

Helicopter delivering path-building rock on the steep slopes of Dollywaggon Pike

A huge amount of work has been devoted to stabilising paths, including intelligent pre-emptive work. Capital projects too, have seen mechanical diggers carried high onto the fells at key points to heal sorely worn paths. Huge quantities of path-pitching stone is carried most economically by helicopter. Sadly worn paths of Wainwright's day have been given a new lease of life. While some walkers may gripe that the hard pitching is tough on the ankles and knees, at least it's not so tough on the mountains themselves. All of which has to be good.

See the difference – 'before and after' on the path above Comb Crags on the upper slopes of Nethermost Pike

In common with so many countryside projects Fix the Fells faces a 'strapped for cash' future, and for its work to continue unabated it looks to The Tourism & Conservation Partnership for assistance. As an associate member of the Partnership I am committed to supporting its work. The charity actively encourages businesses, particularly those that benefit from tourism, to pay into environmental-project funding through 'Payback' schemes that sustain the beautiful landscape so many visitors and locals adore.

Visit: www.ourstolookafter.co.uk.

INDEX

Bold indicates Fell Chapters

LISTING OF CICERONE GUIDES

For full and up-to-date information on our ever-expanding list of guides, visit our website:
www.cicerone.co.uk.

Cicerone's mission is to inform and inspire by providing the best guides to exploring the world

Since its foundation 40 years ago, Cicerone has specialised in publishing guidebooks and has built a reputation for quality and reliability. It now publishes nearly 300 guides to the major destinations for outdoor enthusiasts, including Europe, UK and the rest of the world.

Written by leading and committed specialists, Cicerone guides are recognised as the most authoritative. They are full of information, maps and illustrations so that the user can plan and complete a successful and safe trip or expedition – be it a long face climb, a walk over Lakeland fells, an alpine cycling tour, a Himalayan trek or a ramble in the countryside.

With a thorough introduction to assist planning, clear diagrams, maps and colour photographs to illustrate the terrain and route, and accurate and detailed text, Cicerone guides are designed for ease of use and access to the information.

If the facts on the ground change, or there is any aspect of a guide that you think we can improve, we are always delighted to hear from you.

Cicerone Press
2 Police Square Milnthorpe Cumbria LA7 7PY
Tel: 015395 62069 Fax: 015395 63417
info@cicerone.co.uk www.cicerone.co.uk

CICERONE